DEC   2006

WRESTLING WITH GOD

Patrick M. Garry

WRESTLING WITH GOD

The Courts' Tortuous Treatment

of Religion

The Catholic University of America Press

Washington, D.C.

Portions of this book have appeared previously in the following
journals and are reprinted with permission. Sections of chapter
1 were published in *Wake Forest Law Review,* 39 Wake Forest
L. Rev. 361 (2004); sections of chapter 2 in *Hofstra Law Review*,
33 Hofstra L. Rev. 475 (2005); parts of chapter 4 in *Florida Law
Review,* 57 FLA. L. Rev. 1 (2005); parts of chapters 3, 7, and 8 in
Utah Law Review, 2004 Utah L. Rev. 1155 (2005); and parts of
chapter 5 in *Modern Age* (Summer 2005).

Library of Congress Cataloging-in-Publication Data
Garry, Patrick M.
    Wrestling with God: the courts' tortuous treatment of
religion / Patrick M. Garry.
        p. cm.
    Includes bibliographical references and index.
    ISBN-13: 978-0-8132-1451-1 (cloth : alk. paper)
    ISBN-10: 0-8132-1451-3 (cloth : alk. paper)
    1. Freedom of religion—United States. 2. Religion and
state—United States.   3. Judicial process—United States.
I. Title.
    KF4783.G37 2006
    342.7308'52—dc22
                                            2005021680

For CJS

CONTENTS

INTRODUCTION • A Convoluted Maze of Judicial Doctrines

At a winter holiday party held every year in a New Jersey elementary school, the children often distribute gifts to each other. But when one five-year-old boy started handing out candy canes, he was immediately restrained. Attached to each candy cane was a religious story relating to Christmas. In the subsequent litigation, a court upheld the school's right to restrict the boy from giving those candy canes as presents.[1] The basis for that ruling was the establishment clause of the First Amendment, which states that "Congress shall make no law respecting an establishment of religion."

In a Texas school district, a program called "Clergy in Schools" placed clerical volunteers in the district's primary and secondary schools to provide student counseling and mentoring on secular topics. But when some parents sued, the court ruled that the program violated the establishment clause.[2] Another court used the establishment clause to bar the distribution on school premises of flyers announcing the community activities of local churches.[3] Elsewhere a court held that a school choir's singing of the Lord's Prayer was unconstitutional.[4] And in New Hampshire, a judge ruled that a town's practice of providing free snowplowing for religious organizations amounted to a state establishment of religion.[5]

Religious freedom is the first liberty protected in the Bill of Rights, followed by free speech. Both are fundamental freedoms, and yet the courts seem to treat the two in substantially different ways. The law, for instance, allows regulatory burdens on religious exercise that would not be tolerated in connection with speech. Zoning regulations can restrict the ability of churches and synagogues to accommodate the religious needs of their congregations, even though similar restrictions on the expressive activities of political or cultural groups would not be allowed. Religious speech may be curtailed if found to have an unwelcome effect on nonbelievers, even though profane or indecent speech cannot usually be restricted, no matter how offensive it is to unwilling listeners. Government scholarship programs can refuse to cover a student studying theology, even though such programs could never exclude students wishing to study radical Marxism. And religious proselytizing in public venues can be restricted in ways that raw, violent rap lyrics cannot.

The primary reason why religious expression can be regulated is the establishment clause. As most high school students of American history learn, the constitutional framers intended the establishment clause to prevent the new federal government from setting up and enforcing an exclusive national religion, as the English had done with the Anglican Church. Yet, in the latter half of the twentieth century, American courts began applying the establishment clause not to the big issue of an exclusive, state-mandated religion but to the small issues of candy canes at school and free snowplowing for religious organizations.

In the 1960s and 1970s, nearly two centuries after ratification of the First Amendment, the Supreme Court began using the establishment clause as a trowel in the building of a "wall of separation" between "church and state." But this wall of separation ran counter to America's historical experience. In colonies founded by people wishing to live where they could publicly declare their religious beliefs and use those beliefs to shape their society, a strict wall of separation between church and state was unimaginable. In a young nation that entrusted its educational systems to clergy and religious groups, and in which presidents designated national days of prayer, an impregnable wall of separation between religion and government would have been seen as ludicrous. And in a country whose citizens believed that a necessary ingredient of democracy were the moral values fostered by religious beliefs, a constitutional mandate that pushed religion to the fringes of civil society would have been seen as self-destructive.

For the past two generations, the phrase "wall of separation between church and state" has been a staple of the cultural lexicon. It has been automatically assumed to reflect a basic precept of the American constitutional order. In reality, however, the phrase was practically nonexistent during the constitutional period, as it did not at all reflect the framers' beliefs on the relationship between religion and government. In reality, the phrase "wall of separation" did not enter the nation's constitutional vocabulary until the Supreme Court first employed it nearly a half-century ago. But, despite its historical inaccuracy, the phrase stuck. Undeniably, it carries some instinctive appeal; yet when used to shape constitutional law, the metaphor has produced some perverse and illogical results.

As a way of building a "wall of separation," late twentieth-century judges began reading into the First Amendment an inherent conflict between the establishment clause and the exercise clause, which forbids Congress to make any law restricting the "free exercise" of religion. Courts interpreted the establishment clause as a brake on the exercise clause, aimed at keeping religion from exerting too much influence on America's civil society. Under this view, the exercise and establishment clauses were seen as being "at war with each other,"[6] with the exercise clause conferring benefits on religion and the establishment clause imposing burdens.[7] It was as if the framers had intended the two clauses to cancel each other out, producing a kind of zero-sum result with regard to religion.

Not surprisingly, this conflict-oriented approach has bred increasing litigiousness in every area of interaction between religion and government, leading to a constant battle over the degree of religious presence in public life. Moreover, this litigiousness has produced a legacy of contradiction and inconsistency, resulting in large part from the fact that the courts were taking a view of religion that was sharply antagonistic to the nation's historical experience.[8] Even though the First Amendment obviously embodies a high regard for religious liberty, the "wall of separation" metaphor incorporated a hostility toward religion.

This separationist stance, according to one legal scholar, has "had the profound effect of leading to results which cannot be reconciled with either history or tradition."[9] For example, although the Court has allowed book loans from public to parochial schools, it has prohibited states from providing various instructional materials, such as maps and lab equipment, to religious schools.[10] While permitting states to provide busing for students to and from religious schools, the Court has forbidden states to pay for the busing costs of field trips for those same students.[11] Nativity scenes at city hall are constitutional if surrounded by reindeer and clowns, but not if standing alone.[12] And within the span of one year, a student-led prayer at football games was ruled to be an illegal establishment of religion,[13] but a student-delivered religious message at graduation ceremonies was upheld as constitutional.[14] As one scholar puts it: "The Supreme Court's religious freedom decisions are no thing of beauty."[15]

The conflicted judicial treatment of religion has not only failed to produce clear First Amendment doctrines, it has actually fueled a more intense cultural and legal struggle over the public role and presence of religion. High-profile cases continue to stream into the courts. In 2004 the Supreme Court heard arguments in two different religion cases: *Elk Grove Unified School District v. Newdow*, involving the constitutionality of the words "one nation under God" in the Pledge of Allegiance, and *Locke v. Davey*, involving the state of Washington's withdrawal of a scholarship granted to a student who wanted to study theology. The following year the Court presided over another two religion cases, both of which related to public displays of the Ten Commandments. (While the challengers of these displays called them "enormously divisive," supporters claimed that "the Establishment Clause should not be interpreted to force to state to send a message of hostility toward religion.")[16]

The cultural and political forces pushing for a greater separation between church and state have also grown significantly since the Supreme Court first employed the "wall of separation" metaphor. Following the terrorist attacks of September 11, 2001, apprehension about the dangers of radical religious beliefs intensified, as did cultural opposition to any hint of theocracy in American society. Aside from such reactionary fears, however, there are legitimate arguments in favor of a strict separation of church and state. America has become the most religiously diverse nation in the world, and this diversity only continues to increase; moreover, there is little doubt that religion carries the potential for social divisiveness. Consequently, one way to manage this diversity and maintain cultural tranquility is to lessen the opportunities for public interaction with confrontational religious beliefs or practices. However, this muting of religion can obviously inhibit the vibrancy of religious freedom. Furthermore, the question must be asked as to why cultural tranquility is so desired in connection with religious expression, but not in connection with any other kind of expression. Although cultural order is a much desired and worthy goal, in the American constitutional scheme it is not always the supreme goal. With certain fundamental freedoms like religion, the U.S. Constitution mandates that if a line is to be drawn around the religious presence in public life, it is to be drawn in the way most supportive of religious freedom. Besides, even though it is useful to recognize the potential excesses and abuses of religious fervor, it is also important to note the religious nature of American society. On any given weekend, more Americans attend religious services than watch football on television, and five times more people attend a place of religious worship than go to the movies.[17]

Over the past several decades the establishment clause has been thrust into the center of a wider cultural dispute over the role of religion in contemporary society. This cultural conflict has been going on since the 1960s' social revolt against the influence of traditional religious values. Within this conflict, the establishment clause was employed to help transform the nation's culture into a more secular one. But this use of the establishment clause was possible only because of previous decisions by the Supreme Court, in which the Court had basically used a shotgun to kill a fly.

In drafting the First Amendment, the framers intended to prohibit what in their experience was the most basic cause of religious coercion—a central government's enforcement of a state-dictated religion. The monopoly status and abuses of the Church of England constituted the primary reason for the Pilgrims' settlement in the Massachusetts Bay Colony. A century and a half later, the establishment clause was drafted to prevent a Church-of-England scenario from occurring in America. But throughout the centuries following ratification of the First Amendment, this big threat—a national imposition of a governmentally controlled religion—has never come close to taking place. Instead, the establishment clause has been invoked in cases involving relatively small issues of marginal church-state connections. Many of those issues may have been more appropriately governed by the exercise clause, but the Court nonetheless applied the establishment clause, just because the government was seen to be giving some benefit or concession to some religious group. The Court was so focused on preventing any governmental assistance to religion that it ignored the larger concern of the First Amendment—the preservation of religious liberty. It became so focused on using the establishment clause to build a "wall of separation" between church and state that it lost sight of the actual freedom that the First Amendment accorded to religious expression.

In a case illustrating its overreaching use of the establishment clause, the Supreme Court ruled unconstitutional the inclusion in a public high school graduation ceremony of a prayer said by a local rabbi. Since the prayer was initiated by the school, the Court concluded that it constituted an impermissible establishment of religion.[18] But this case should have been decided under the exercise clause, since the government, according to the Court, was interfering with free-exercise rights by compelling the attendees at a graduation ceremony to participate in a religious ceremony, even if that ceremony lasted only seconds. There was nothing in the school's behavior that amounted to the actual establishment of a particular religion, and yet the Court used a constitutional provision aimed at preventing an American equivalent of the Church of England to sanction religious speech uttered during a public ceremony. Indeed, the whole line of prayer-in-the-schools cases, stretching back more than forty years to *Engel v. Vitale,*[19] should have been decided under the exercise clause, not the establishment clause.

In *Engel,* the parents of ten students filed suit after the New York State Board of Regents composed a prayer to be recited at the start of the public school day. The plaintiffs argued that this prayer violated their religious beliefs.[20] In the first case in which it considered the propriety of prayer in schools, the Supreme Court held that the Regents had violated the establishment clause. But the crucial issue was not whether government allowed a prayer to be recited on public property; it was whether the government actively forced individuals to comply with unwanted religious beliefs.

Despite this issue of individual coercion, courts continued to follow the *Engel* approach in cases involving religious expression in public schools. In *Roberts v. Madigan,* a court held that the establishment clause barred a public school teacher from laying a Bible on his desk during the school day and keeping two Christian religious books on his classroom shelves.[21] And in *Bishop v. Aronov,* a professor at a public university was sanctioned for making various religious remarks to his class and for organizing an after-class meeting on religious topics.[22] Because coercion was at issue, however, these cases should have fallen under the jurisdiction of the exercise clause, not the establishment clause.[23]

By employing the establishment clause in cases where the exercise clause should have applied, the Court vastly overextended the reach of the former. It used a constitutional command focused on preserving the institutional autonomy of religious organizations to govern a single activity involving individual freedom. The Court's remedy was overkill. It used a shotgun to kill a fly, setting a course in which the establishment clause would be applied to every minute instance of religious activity occurring on public property. The result has been a jurisprudence of minutia.

Contrary to the eighteenth-century view of establishment as a government-supported religion whose articles of faith are mandated by the state, the modern notion of establishment often pertains to any point at which religion and state intersect. In Albuquerque, New Mexico, administrators of a city-owned senior center cited the establishment clause when prohibiting a church from showing a film on the Christian faith. In New Jersey, school officials prevented a student from reading to the class his favorite story, which happened to come from the Bible. And in Pennsylvania, a teacher's assistant filed suit after she was suspended for failing to remove a cross she wore on a necklace.[24] The Pennsylvania lawsuit revolved around the claim that the perceived religious actions of any state employee, no matter what position of authority the individual may or may not occupy, can rise to the level of an official state establishment of religion.

None of today's "little establishments" are anything like the creation of a national church, of which Justice Hugo Black warned in one of the first religion cases to be decided by the Supreme Court.[25] Most of them involve governmental actions that are substantially smaller in scope, such as erecting holiday displays, transporting parochial students to extracurricular events, and asking students to engage in a moment of silence for meditation, each of which the Court has found in one form or another to be an impermissible establishment of religion. Yet because of this jurisprudence of minutia, the establishment clause has experienced a kind of creeping evolution, moving from one small issue to another, building a wall of separation between church and state, one brick at a time.

Had the establishment clause not evolved into a jurisprudence of minutia, it might not have been so swept up in the swirling currents of cultural attitudes toward religion. But, instead, it has become trapped in a self-perpetuating cycle: the broader the scope given to the clause, the more it is used as a tool in the secularization of American culture. The establishment clause, for instance, has been employed to try to halt the singing of Christmas carols like "Silent Night" and "Away in a Manger" in public buildings, to deny the tax-exempt status of all churches, to remove the words "In God We Trust" from the national currency, and even to prohibit census questions about religious affiliation.

A teacher at a public elementary school in Cupertino, California, was barred from classroom use of certain documents because of their mention of God or religion—documents such as the Declaration of Independence, the 1682 "Frame of Government of Pennsylvania" by William Penn, excerpts from George Washington's prayer journal, and a handout titled "Fact Sheet; Currency & Coins History of 'In God We Trust.'"[26] When a student in Garwood, New Jersey, wrote a poem about the Pilgrims' practice of thanking God, nervous school administrators removed the word "God" from her piece.[27] In response to an establishment clause lawsuit by the ACLU, the U.S. Defense Department prohibited all military bases from sponsoring any Boy Scout troops or activities, including the famous Boy Scout Jamboree held annually at Fort A. P. Hill. Similar suits have forced the City of Chicago to cease sponsorship of troops in public schools and the State of Connecticut to remove the Scouts from the list of charitable institutions to which public employees may contribute. These lawsuits are based on the Boy Scout oath, which states: "On my honor, I will do my best to do my duty to God and my country."

As the reach of the establishment clause has broadened, with courts taking an expansive view of what constitutes an establishment, certain political and cultural criticisms of religion have increasingly been echoed by judges. In the Cleveland school-voucher case, for instance, Justice Stevens argued that public aid to religion would foster political discord and tear the social fabric of American democracy. Drawing on experiences from the Balkans, Northern Ireland, and the Middle East, Justice Stevens wrote: "Whenever we remove a brick from the wall that was designed to separate religion and government, we increase the risk of religious strife and weaken the foundation of our democracy." Justice Breyer likewise noted that "the Establishment Clause concern for protecting the Nation's social fabric from religious conflict poses an overriding obstacle to the implementation of this well-intentioned school-voucher program."[28]

Ironically, these views prevail amid a heightened multicultural sensitivity in America. Differences in ethnic, racial, and cultural identities are being celebrated and encouraged; tolerance for divergent and opposing attitudes and lifestyles is being valued far more than assimilation of those differences into one uniform culture. Not so with religion, however, which is often seen as a divisive force, with the courts serving as cultural supervisors, quelling any conflicts that might arise from the religious practices of a diverse people. Though tolerance has become the most extolled of public virtues, judges nonetheless wrestle with how much of a religious presence American civil society should have to tolerate.

This judicial suspicion of religion has caused a one-sided focus in establishment clause cases. Courts have been so single-minded in not allowing any government "advancement of religion" that they have permitted governmental discrimination against the public activities of religious organizations. The problem with this one-sided emphasis on "advancement of religion" is that it looks only at whether religion has received a benefit, not at whether the government has somehow restricted religious liberty or whether religious practitioners have seen their opportunities for expression diminished.

Admittedly, over the past decade the constitutional doctrines governing religion have become much more protective against outright discrimination than they were in the 1970s and 1980s. Because of the Supreme Court's adoption of a neutrality approach to religion cases, religious organizations cannot be selectively denied public benefits to which similarly situated nonreligious organizations are given access. Yet this neutrality approach in a sense has only stopped the bleeding; it has not cured the wound inflicted by nearly a half-century of separationist jurisprudence.

Owing to the religious nature and diversity of American society, as well as all the ways in which the government's social welfare programs intersect with the activities of organized religion, the chances for religious disputes and conflict are probably greater than ever before. Consequently, in place of the Court's lurching and often contradictory religion-clause jurisprudence of the past sixty years, a consistent and historically supported model of the establishment clause is needed. Such a model would recognize that the two religion clauses—exercise and establishment—are in fact two aspects of a single, unified religion clause that seeks exclusively to protect religious liberty. When read in this light, the establishment clause is seen not as a check on religion or as the guardian of secular society but as a protection for the institutional integrity of religious organizations (whereas the exercise clause focuses on the protection of individual religious freedom).[29]

This book analyzes how the various establishment clause doctrines have evolved and how the courts have put the establishment clause in conflict with the exercise clause. Reflecting the twisted evolution of the establishment clause, as discussed in Chapter 1, is the disparity in judicial treatment of religious freedoms and speech freedoms. Even though both are fundamental First Amendment liberties, the courts have taken dramatically different approaches to them. Not only do courts scrutinize free-speech claims under a more exacting standard, but they tolerate burdens on religious exercise that are not permitted with respect to speech rights.

One reason for this disparate treatment of speech and religion involves the various judicial interpretations of the establishment clause. Over the latter part of the twentieth century, through an increasingly expansive view of the establishment clause, the courts adopted a somewhat antagonistic or suspicious stance toward religion—a stance based primarily on the "wall of separation" metaphor. Chapter 2 outlines the ways in which this metaphor has influenced the Court's establishment doctrines.

In an attempt to repair some of the damage caused by an overly broad application of the "wall of separation" metaphor, the Supreme Court began using an endorsement test to analyze establishment clause claims. This test, as examined in Chapter 3, tried to move away from a rigid rule of separation by asking in each case whether an observer would perceive a particular government action as endorsing religion. Unfortunately, the endorsement test only burrowed the Court deeper into minutia; outcomes of constitutional challenges became dependent on the psychological perceptions of individuals. Under this approach, even a public school choir's rehearsal of a religious song was held to be an unconstitutional establishment of religion. Even a child's distribution at school of Christmas gifts with brief religious messages attached was seen to be a state endorsement of religion.

The latest judicial effort to combat the discriminatory effects of the "wall of separation" legacy is the neutrality approach. As discussed in Chapter 4, neutrality has become the preferred approach for religion cases, fitting in as it does with the current legal and political prominence of equal protection and antidiscrimination concerns. The neutrality doctrine states that religion must be treated no differently—no worse and no better—than any secular group or individual. The Court has espoused neutrality as a simple solution to all the past inconsistencies in its religion-clause decisions. But, as the doctrine has been applied, it too has become mired in technicalities and formalities. For instance, courts have ruled that neutrality is maintained when religious organizations engaged in secular endeavors receive government funds indirectly, as in a voucher program, but not if the funds go directly to those same religious organizations without technically passing through the hands of private citizens. Such was the ruling involving government aid to the only long-term residential treatment center for drug offenders in Milwaukee, Wisconsin: by channeling the funds directly to the facility without first sifting them through the facility's residents, who were convicted felons, the government did not treat the religious organization with the requisite neutrality and hence violated the establishment clause.

Even though neutrality carries a facial aura of fairness, it may not comport with the framers' constitutional intent regarding religion. The framers did not draft the First Amendment so that religion would be treated like any other social institution. Churches and synagogues are not like convenience stores and meatpacking plants. A zoning law that tells a congregation it cannot expand its church is different from a law that restricts the expansion of a shopping mall. A law that commands all hospitals to provide contraceptive and abortion services affects a Catholic hospital much differently than it does a public hospital. The real problem with neutrality as it pertains to religion cases is that the doctrine only goes halfway: it remedies many of the overt prejudices against religion, but it does not adequately recognize the elevated constitutional status of religious liberty. In a sense, neutrality only pulls religion out of the hole that was dug in the 1970s.

The Supreme Court's religion doctrines have veered away from the constitutional history and intent of the First Amendment. Chapter 5 presents a historical survey of late eighteenth-century America, delving into the meaning of the establishment clause and the framers' intent regarding the public role of religion and the interrelationship between church and state. In particular, this history is examined to determine the legitimacy of the "wall of separation" metaphor that gained prominence in the 1970s. Contrary to the claims of the separationists, there has been a long national experience of intermingling religion and politics. Throughout the eighteenth century and well into the nineteenth, public funds supported religious schools, hospitals, and even churches. Government buildings all across America were inscribed with religious references and phrases. Public expression of religious beliefs was as common as politicians' speeches. George Washington asserted that "it is impossible to rightly govern the world without God and the Bible." Noah Webster, the educator and lexicographer, announced that "the moral principles and precepts contained in the Scriptures form the basis of all our civil constitutions and laws." Abraham Lincoln proclaimed that "it is the duty of nations, as well as of men, to recognize their dependence upon the overruling power of God." President Theodore Roosevelt warned that a churchless community "is a community on the rapid down-grade."[30] And in 1970, during the Apollo 13 crisis, President Nixon issued a national proclamation for prayer.

The historical record also indicates that the framers rejected many of the current arguments being made against both government accommodation of religion and religious expressions in public venues. Chapter 6 examines the motivations and dynamics of contemporary cultural forces hostile to religion, as well as the influence of those forces on the Court's religion-clause cases. Indeed, the way in which establishment clause jurisprudence has evolved has actually opened the door for religious hostility to creep into constitutional doctrines. Even though the First Amendment seeks to protect individual freedoms from the reactions of countervailing social opinion, this has not always happened with the religion clauses. In large part this is because, contrary to the framers' view, contemporary cultural critics see religion as something that threatens civil society. Where religion was once the source of civic morality, now it is seen as the root of irreconcilable division.

Free-speech doctrines, on the other hand, have clearly rejected this socially divisive argument. During the Vietnam War, for instance, the Court upheld the speech rights of protestors to voice their combative antiwar messages to unwilling audiences. Courts have also protected the rights of Nazi groups to march in Jewish neighborhoods, the rights of artists to display in public museums art that denigrates sacred beliefs, and the rights of radio "shock jocks" like Howard Stern to broadcast their sexually explicit programs.

Throughout more than half a century of religion-clause jurisprudence, a comprehensive, enduring model of the establishment clause has eluded the Court. No existing model has created a clear and workable relationship between the establishment and exercise clauses. Nor has there arisen any clear and precise definition of what constitutes an "establishment of religion." Chapter 7 offers an interpretation of the establishment clause that sees it as a complement to the exercise clause in the common pursuit of religious liberty. Under this interpretation, the establishment clause narrowly addresses a specific kind of religious coercion—the kind of coercion that occurs when the government permanently aligns itself with one particular religious sect and then discriminates against all others. This, in the view of the early Puritan settlers, was the worst kind of religious coercion.

Chapter 7 presents a new constitutional model that strives to mend the relationship between the two religion clauses—a relationship that has been strained to the breaking point by nearly four decades of judicial efforts to use the establishment clause as a tool of secularization. According to the model presented in Chapter 7, the establishment clause is not a protection *from* religion, nor is it a protection given *to* a secular society. Rather, like the exercise clause, it is a constitutional guarantee of religious freedom. Whereas the exercise clause insulates individuals from religious coercion by the state, the establishment clause protects religious institutions from unwanted governmental intrusion.

Traditional establishment clause theory has prohibited governmental preference for one religious denomination over another, as well as governmental preference for religion in general. As Chapter 8 demonstrates, however, the constitutional model outlined in Chapter 7 does not, contrary to existing case law, prevent the state from conferring on religion nondiscriminatory benefits not otherwise given to secular groups or institutions. Throughout the eighteenth century an establishment of religion was generally considered to arise only when the state gave preferential treatment to one or more specific religious sects. Public support of all religion, as in nondiscriminatory tax exemptions for religious property, was unquestionably accepted. For without such special treatment, there could be no accommodation of the unique needs of religious exercise, and religion would have to be treated like any secular institution or organization.

The supporters of a wall of separation between church and state claim that such a wall will eliminate a potentially divisive force in society. They argue that society cannot endure the active presence of divergent and passionate religious sects in the nation's public life. France has followed that presumption in its efforts to muzzle the religious exercise of its Muslim immigrants. But, as events have shown, it is the muzzling rather than the religious differences that end up causing the conflict.

There is a tendency to think that all the bizarre legal cases and claims concerning religion are behind us. But without a clearer understanding of the establishment clause, extremist positions will continue to exert themselves. In 1994 historian Leonard Levy, himself a separationist, admitted that certain public references to God or religion are an accepted part of the nation's civic life. One such reference is contained in the Pledge of Allegiance. Not even the most ardent separationist would challenge such a long-standing reference, Levy argued. And yet, just ten years later, such a challenge was heard by the U.S. Supreme Court.

CHAPTER 1 • INEQUALITY AMONG EQUALS

Disparities in the Judicial Treatment of Speech and Religion

The first liberty protected by the Bill of Rights is religious freedom. The next is freedom of speech. Both are fundamental, individual freedoms.[1] The exercise clause, which guarantees religious liberty, "embraces a freedom of conscience and worship that has close parallels" with the free-speech clause.[2] And yet, over the course of the last half-century, courts have taken a very different approach to the two freedoms.

The disparity in treatment can be seen through a comparison of two early cases. In *Minersville School District v. Gobitis,*[3] the Court rejected a free-exercise challenge by Jehovah's Witnesses to compulsory saluting of the American flag. But just three years later, in *West Virginia State Board of Education v. Barnette,*[4] when a free-speech claim was added to the case against a school district rule requiring students to salute the flag, the Court upheld the challenge.

Courts have been consistently protective of free speech, especially since the 1960s. In *Sable Communications v. FCC,*[5] the Supreme Court overturned, on free-speech grounds, a ban on diala-porn telephone messages. Later, in *United States v. Playboy Entertainment Group, Inc.,*[6] the Court struck down regulations confining sexually explicit television programming to the hours of 10:00 P.M. to 6:00 A.M. With respect to religious liberty, however, the courts have been far less protective. In *Roberts v. Madigan,*[7] the Tenth Circuit Court of Appeals upheld a school's order that a teacher keep his personal Bible out of sight and that he remove any religious books from the classroom shelves. In *C.H. v. Oliva,*[8] teachers were able to single out a student drawing of a religious subject, placing that drawing in a deliberately obscured position on a display wall. In *Aguilar v. Felton,*[9] the Supreme Court ruled unconstitutional a special education program that supplied remedial English and mathematics assistance to parochial students who were economically disadvantaged. Likewise, in *Santa Fe Independent School District v. Doe,*[10] the Court struck down a school district's practice of having a student, who was annually elected to the office of student council chaplain, deliver a prayer before each varsity football game.

One reason for the disparity in treatment between the two freedoms (speech and religion) lies in how the courts have applied the establishment clause. Under those applications, the reactions of objecting viewers and listeners are sometimes accorded near veto power in religious-expression cases, whereas viewer or listener sensibilities are rarely considered in free-speech cases, even when the speech is highly offensive. But there are other differences in treatment that cannot be attributed to establishment concerns. For instance, free-speech claims are given a more favorable standard of review: most governmental restrictions on speech are judged under a strict-scrutiny standard, whereas many religious-exercise issues receive a much lower standard of review.

The disparity in judicial treatment of speech and religious liberty cases has produced more than just a constitutional imbalance. It has also created a constitutional distortion, in which plaintiffs seeking religious protection frequently abandon the exercise clause and resort instead to the free-speech clause. Thus, what should otherwise be characterized as religious exercise is labeled free speech. The result is that the free-speech clause is incorporating more than it should, and the exercise clause is becoming increasingly emptied.

Religious Exercise Is Not Diminished by the Establishment Clause

The First Amendment protects both speech and religious freedoms, but only with the latter is there an accompanying establishment clause. The presence of this clause is often used to explain why speech and religion receive such disparate judicial treatment. It is argued that courts must take an adversarial stance toward any governmental accommodation of society's religious beliefs or practices, lest that accommodation somehow rise to the level of a state-established religion. While government can do all it wants to assist and encourage speech, it cannot do so regarding religion; under the First Amendment, there is never a danger of "too much speech."

This argument, however, rests on several misconceptions of the establishment clause that have been reinforced through decades of judicial misinterpretations. The first such misinterpretation involves the scope of application of the establishment clause. In *Everson v. Board of Education,* the Supreme Court ruled that the Fourteenth Amendment's due process clause had incorporated the establishment clause for application to state and local governments.[11] This ruling followed the general trend at the time, in which all the liberties contained in the Bill of Rights were held to be incorporated within the Fourteenth Amendment and hence applicable to the states. But the establishment clause was much different from any of the other provisions that had been incorporated. As numerous scholars have demonstrated, the establishment clause was simply a "means for effecting a policy of federalism on questions of church and state."[12] As such, the framers meant it to apply only to the national government, restraining it from interfering in any matter with individual state policies regarding religion. Thus application of the establishment clause to the states actually contradicted the very essence of the clause, completely inverting its original purpose.[13] Unlike the other provisions in the Bill of Rights that were incorporated into the Fourteenth Amendment, the establishment clause focused not on individual rights but on jurisdiction and governmental structure: it prohibited the national government from interfering with how states handled religion.

Not only did the First Amendment framers not intend the establishment clause to pertain to the states, but the evidence also suggests that the framers of the Fourteenth Amendment did not intend it to apply to any entity except the federal government.[14] Whatever their intentions regarding the Bill of Rights generally, the framers of the Fourteenth Amendment "did not intend to incorporate the Establishment Clause for application to the states."[15] Following the adoption of the Fourteenth Amendment, for instance, Congress specifically rejected in 1875 and 1876 a resolution called the "Blaine Amendment," which was designed to make the establishment clause applicable to the states.[16]

Even if this incorporation error is ignored, and indeed it is unlikely that the Court will reverse itself on this point, the establishment clause still does not justify giving religion less protection than speech. For one thing, there is no constitutional basis for interpreting the establishment clause as contradictory to the exercise clause.

Over the past several decades, courts have tended to see the exercise and establishment clauses as being at odds, with the freedoms of the exercise clause negated by the establishment clause.[17] Proceeding under the assumption that the two clauses embrace contradictory purposes, the exercise clause is viewed as conferring benefits on religion, whereas the establishment clause imposes burdens on religion.[18] But such an approach makes no textual sense, because the exercise clause is essentially being nullified by the establishment clause.[19] Moreover, the establishment clause was never meant to silence or subdue religion, but to "limit the power of the state and thereby afford more breathing room for the church to be the church."[20]

Instead of one being a brake on the other, the two clauses should be seen as protecting a single central liberty—religious liberty—though from two different angles.[21] According to Michael Paulsen, the establishment clause "prohibits the use of the coercive power of the state to *prescribe* religious exercise, while the exercise clause prohibits the use of government compulsion to *proscribe* religious exercise."[22]

On several occasions the Court has expressed the view that the two religion clauses are complementary.[23] In *Wisconsin v. Yoder,* noting that the clauses work together as complementary protections of religious liberty, the majority wrote that "[t]he Religion Clauses had specifically and firmly fixed the right to free exercise of religious beliefs, and buttressing this fundamental right was an equally firm, even if less explicit, prohibition against the establishment of any religion by government."[24] Some scholars argue that the establishment clause is entirely in the service of free exercise,[25] and that forbidding establishment is just one means of achieving complete free exercise for those who "might dissent from whatever religion is established."[26] Thus, taken together, the two clauses prevent two separate threats to religious freedom: on one hand, government action that restricts the religious practices of individuals or minority sects, and on the other, government action that interferes in the institutions freely chosen and shaped by the various religious denominations.[27]

Textually, the Constitution provides greater protection for

religious practices than for any secular-belief-related activities. Not only does the exercise clause protect religious practice and beliefs, but the free-speech clause protects religious expression; and freedom of association, as well as the establishment clause, protects the integrity and autonomy of religious organizations.[28] Therefore, to apply the establishment clause in a way that limits religion makes no sense, just as it makes no sense that secular, nonreligious speech should receive more protection than religious speech. But if the establishment clause is more narrowly interpreted to prevent the threat to religious liberty that exists when government interferes in the institutional autonomy of religious organizations, it then provides no basis for the disparate manner in which courts deal with speech and religion cases.

Speech Claims Are Scrutinized More Carefully Than Religion Claims

Cases involving content regulation of speech trigger a heightened judicial review. Normally, the strict scrutiny test is used.[29] Under this test, laws regulating content are upheld only when they are justified by compelling government interests and employ the least restrictive means to achieve those interests.[30] Such laws cannot be approved simply because there has been no restrictive intent on the part of government.[31]

With respect to speech, even content-neutral laws are closely scrutinized. Because such regulations (e.g., those that may impose a complete ban on the posting of all signs anywhere in the city) could actually stifle more speech than content-discriminatory laws could, courts have stated that content-neutral laws should receive careful scrutiny and not be given a "free pass."[32] Therefore, when reviewing content-neutral laws that have an impact on speech, courts generally employ some variation of intermediate scrutiny.[33]

In the area of religious exercise, however, the standards of review are significantly lower.[34] The Supreme Court's decision in *Employment Division v. Smith* outlines the judicial approach to free-exercise claims. The *Smith* Court upheld a law banning all use of peyote, including the sacramental use of peyote in the religious practices of the Native American Church. In so ruling, the Court employed a two-part inquiry: first, to determine whether a law that burdens religion is neutral, or whether on its face it targets religion; second, to determine whether the law is "generally applicable" or whether it takes aim at religion through its "design, construction, or enforcement." Under *Smith,* a law that is neutral and generally applicable, even if it does burden religion, is presumptively constitutional.[35] In rejecting the compelling-interest test that prevailed in earlier cases when a governmental action incidentally burdened religion,[36] the *Smith* Court ruled that the use of strict scrutiny in free-exercise cases "would open the prospect of constitutionally required religious exemptions from civic obligations of almost every conceivable kind." Thus, under current free-exercise doctrine, a neutral law of general applicability, even if it burdens religious exercise, receives minimal scrutiny and hence will almost always be upheld. Facially neutral laws burdening religious exercise will be unconstitutional only if the imposition of that burden was the intended object of the law.[37]

Even when a law lacks facial neutrality toward religion, some jurisdictions still do not require a strict-scrutiny standard of review. Heightened scrutiny is required only if the law places a "substantial" burden on the exercise of religion,[38] or if the purpose of that law is to suppress religion.[39] In *KDM v. Reedsport School District,* for instance, the court ruled that a state regulation prohibiting religious schools from receiving government-funded special education services did not violate the free exercise of religion.[40] Despite acknowledging that the regulation was not facially neutral (as applied, the rule required those students attending religious schools to travel to religiously neutral settings in order to receive the same government benefits provided to public school students on-site), the court concluded that the purpose of the regulation was not to suppress religion or religious conduct.[41]

Many commentators have looked on *Smith* and its abandonment of strict scrutiny as "the death knell of free exercise."[42] In the wake of *Smith,* even such traditional practices as the use of wine in the Eucharist or Passover seder could be prohibited as long as the prohibition was generally applicable to all persons.[43] Yet the *Smith* approach does make room for certain exceptions where strict scrutiny would apply. Under the "hybrid-rights exception," for instance, strict scrutiny will be given when a free-exercise claim is coupled with another, independent constitutional claim.[44] Consequently, a free-exercise claim needs something else, something more, to qualify for strict scrutiny. Unlike free-speech issues, free-exercise issues cannot by themselves receive heightened judicial scrutiny.[45]

Another illustration of a lower level of scrutiny used with religion cases can be found in *Heffron v. International Society for Krishna Consciousness, Inc.*[46] In that case, followers of the Krishna religion challenged a Minnesota state fair regulation stating that the distribution or sale of printed materials could only occur at special booths reserved for that purpose. To the plaintiffs, the distribution of religious materials constituted a practice of the Sankirtan religion. Nonetheless, the Court used the deferential standard of review applicable to routine time, place, and manner regulations, completely ignoring the plaintiffs' religious-exercise claims.

Aside from differing levels of scrutiny, the two freedoms—speech and religious exercise—also differ in their relative scope. Free-speech doctrines protect not only speech but any conduct "commonly associated" with speech[47] or "normally engaged in for the purpose of communicating an idea."[48] Also falling within the scope of protection is "the location where speech occurs and the means by which speech is communicated."[49] But this is not the case with conduct related to religious exercise, which merely receives the highly deferential rational-basis review outlined in *Smith* (as long, of course, as the laws infringing on that conduct are neutral laws of general applicability). Consequently, under free-speech doctrine, regulations limiting the time, place, and manner of expressive or symbolic speech receive a more rigorous form of scrutiny than do, for instance, land-use laws that effectively prevent a congregation from expanding a church or using it in whatever way its religious beliefs dictate.[50]

Because of the imbalance between the way courts protect speech and religious exercise,[51] current First Amendment doctrines encourage litigants to classify every type of religious activity as speech, in the hope of obtaining a higher scrutiny of governmental activity.[52] But if speech is defined broadly enough to cover all areas of religious exercise, then the exercise clause may become meaningless. Moreover, giving religious exercise less protection than speech may lead to a morass of litigation over whether each particular religious activity constitutes speech. And herein lies yet another difference in the way courts handle speech and religion cases: while just about any form of expressive conduct (including video games) qualifies as constitutionally protected speech, courts are more selective and questioning regarding the beliefs and practices that constitute a religion.[53]

The Differing Placement of Burdens

Another area in which the judicial treatment of free-speech issues differs from that of religious expression issues involves the way in which courts accommodate the interests of the unwilling observer or listener. With speech cases, the objecting audience is given very little consideration. In *Cohen v. California,* where it was held unconstitutional for the state to convict a person for wearing a jacket plainly bearing the phrase "Fuck the Draft" in a public venue, the Court rejected the argument that government could restrict the use of vulgarity because of its offensive impact on observers involuntarily exposed to the message.[54] And in *U.S. v. Playboy Entertainment Group, Inc.,* the Court ruled that confining the Playboy channel's sexually explicit programming to late-night hours posed too great a burden on the speech interests of the programmers, and that it was the duty of those offended by such programming to simply "avert their eyes."[55]

This judicial indifference to the sensibilities of the listener or viewer, however, does not exist when it comes to religious expression. In *Lee v. Weisman,* the Court ruled unconstitutional a prayer given at a graduation ceremony by a rabbi who had been invited to do so by the school principal. Underlying this decision was the Court's finding that the prayer exerted "subtle coercive pressures" on those objecting to the religious message.[56] But this forbidden coercion was primarily the result of nongovernmental social pressure—"peer pressure," in the words of Justice Scalia.[57] Moreover, since social pressure usually consists entirely of other individuals' speech, what the Court in *Lee* referred to as social or peer pressure was probably expression protected under the First Amendment.

Similar social or peer pressure was found in *Santa Fe Independent School District v. Doe,* where the Court ruled that a student-led prayer before varsity football games was offensive and coercive to dissenters.[58] Likewise, in *Lassonde v. Pleasanton Unified School District* the court upheld a school's denial of a student request to include religious comments in his commencement address, finding that such comments would have an impermissible coercive effect on dissenters.[59] Yet even though the Court sees the religious expressions in *Lee* and *Santa Fe* as coercive on those who object to such speech, it does not view the mandated teaching of certain subjects (e.g., evolution) as unconstitutionally coercive on those students whose religious beliefs are offended by such teaching. Under this double standard, courts object to singling out religion for special protection under the exercise clause, but have no qualms about singling out religion for special prohibitions under the establishment clause.

The judicial sensitivity to listeners and viewers of religious expression took a slightly different turn in *Lynch v. Donnelly,* which involved the constitutionality of a holiday display (including a crèche) located on public property. Justice O'Connor's concurring opinion proposed an endorsement test for determining whether an establishment clause violation had occurred. This test reflected a concern that religious expression on public property might send "a message to nonadherents that they are outsiders, not full members of the political community."[60] In other words, the presence of religious symbols might create an environment in which nonbelievers would feel unwelcome. Later, in *Capital Square Review and Advisory Board v. Pinette,* which dealt with the issue of whether a private group could place a cross on public property, Justice O'Connor again used the endorsement test to analyze whether private religious speech had ostracized nonadherents and therefore violated the establishment clause.[61] Thus, under the endorsement test, the courts examine private religious expression on public property from the standpoint of the objecting listener or viewer, to see if as a result of that speech those listeners or viewers might perceive themselves as social outsiders.[62]

This approach—considering the feelings and reactions of objecting listeners and viewers—is not the approach taken in free-speech cases.[63] In those cases, the right of control is given to the speaker, and the burdens of tolerance are placed on the objecting listener. When secular speech is involved, unwilling listeners must opt out of the unwanted-speech environment. In *Cohen v. California,* for instance, the Court held that listeners must avert their eyes and ears from speech they find offensive and move on.[64] Similarly, in *Lamont v. Postmaster General,* the Court ruled that the government may not screen out sexually offensive materials in advance, and hence may not place an opt-in burden on those who wish to receive such materials.[65] And in *Boler v. Youngs Drug Products Corp.,* the federal government was prevented from banning the unsolicited mailing of condom ads—a law that again favored the offended viewer while burdening the speaker.[66]

The opposite result occurs, however, when the speech constitutes religious expression in a public venue. As illustrated by *Lee* and *Santa Fe,* the courts find that the First Amendment has been violated if private religious speech infiltrates a public ceremony in such a way that the religious dissenter must opt out of the ceremony so as to avoid participating in an offensive religious activity. The permissibility of such religious expression depends on whether nonadherents are *not* forced to opt out—or, from the reverse angle, whether the religious expression is offered in a manner in which the only people participating in that expression are those who have specifically *opted into* it. This outcome is reflected in a wide array of cases upholding limits on student distribution at school of religious pamphlets, religious newspapers, and invitations to religious meetings.[67] Thus, whereas in speech cases the burden is on the viewer to avert his eyes and ears from speech he finds offensive, in religion cases the burden is on the speaker to avoid ostracizing the listener.

Still another difference in how courts treat the burdens permitted on speech rights and those on religious-exercise rights lies in the degree of burden allowed. Generally, in speech cases, any burden is sufficient to warrant constitutional scrutiny. The courts do not try to rank or prioritize the particular burden at issue. As one court stated, "the First Amendment does not permit us to tolerate even minimal burdens on protected rights where no legitimate government interest is truly being served."[68] In another case, licensing and disclosure requirements on charitable fundraisers were struck down, even though such requirements were described as imposing a "minimal burden."[69] On the other hand, courts are more tolerant of so-called minimal burdens on religious exercise. In *Thomas v. Anchorage Equal Rights Commission,* the court stated that a governmental regulation that merely "operates so as to make the practice of an individual's religious beliefs more expensive does not impose a sufficiently substantial burden to trigger Free Exercise Clause scrutiny."[70]

Differing Treatments of Offensiveness

The more favorable judicial treatment of free-speech claims (over free-exercise claims) can be seen in the area of school curriculum. Academic freedom, an offshoot of free speech, almost always takes precedence over free-exercise rights. For instance, educators cannot in any way be restrained in their teaching of evolution; yet when students who believe the biblical account of creation are required to treat evolution as true, they are in a sense being compelled to express views hostile to their faith.[71] An even more subtle indoctrination can occur when textbooks and class lectures portray illegitimacy or sexual promiscuity as normal and acceptable, in direct contrast to the religious beliefs of some students.

Parents and students have no free-exercise right that can defeat the academic freedom of a teacher to present viewpoints offensive to religious beliefs.[72] However, when a teacher—an authority figure—endorses an idea (e.g., homosexuality, divorce, moral relativism, or methods of AIDS prevention) that contradicts a student's religious beliefs, that student may feel ostracized and even tormented. These feelings may be further intensified if the student's classmates all appear to accept and affirm the idea. The student may feel like an outsider in the same sense that a religious dissenter might have felt marginalized in *Lee* and *Santa Fe.* Paradoxically, proreligious speech can violate the establishment clause, but speech that denigrates or belittles religious beliefs does not violate the exercise clause. As they have evolved, First Amendment doctrines expect the religious to endure a kind of offensiveness that the nonreligious do not have to tolerate.

Some scholars have argued that the type of coercion found in *Lee* should also support "the right of religious children to seek protection from public school curricula that they, or their parents, believe hostile to faith."[73] Under the reasoning of *Lee,* public school instruction that offends a child's religious beliefs should constitute a violation of the exercise clause. If some nonreligious students are coerced by religious expressions of the type occurring in *Lee* or by the posting of the Ten Commandments, then it seems logical that religious students might be similarly coerced by certain secular values they are taught in school. But in *Mozert v. Hawkins County Board of Education,* where parents sought to have their children excused from using a reading series that promoted values contradictory to the family's religious beliefs, the court decided that state-compelled exposure to ideas (including those hostile to religion) did not constitute a recognizable burden on free exercise. Thus the court expected children to absorb teachings that offended their religion.[74] However, it is difficult to imagine many more direct burdens on free exercise than state-mandated exposure to doctrines contrary to religious faith. A compulsion to read and recite teaching inimical to religious tenets may burden the free exercise of religion just as the forced recitation of religious tracts may violate the rights of the nonbeliever.[75]

Religious objections to curriculum often involve charges that schools are in effect imposing an orthodoxy of secular humanism that undermines and belittles religious beliefs.[76] In *Altman v. Bedford Central School District,* for instance, a group of parents objected to aspects of a New Age curriculum that they claimed was religious in content and offensive to their own beliefs.[77] But instead of being belittled, the expression of religious viewpoints is often simply forbidden. This contradicts traditional free-speech theory, which envisions expression of the widest possible diversity of views and ideas. Truth is seen to emerge from the unfettered exchange of competing views. With respect to religious expression, however, it is automatically assumed that nothing but dangerous results will ensue. The argument is made that religious speech is socially and politically divisive and hence should be discouraged from entering the public sphere.[78] Such a view was first expressed by Justice Frankfurter in a 1948 case in which he portrayed religion as a divisive force, arguing that the Court's role was to quell any separatism that might arise from religious convictions.[79] But perhaps, as in the free-speech realm, an open airing of religious ideas might foster a greater appreciation of religious pluralism. Perhaps, as the free-speech doctrine holds, the fact that some might feel uncomfortable in the presence of religious expression is not sufficient reason to forbid such expression. The Supreme Court, after all, has said that the "nation's future depends upon leaders trained through wide exposure to that robust exchange of ideas which discovers truth out of a multitude of tongues, [rather] than through any kind of authoritarian selection."[80]

Mere Risk versus Likely Probability

In speech cases, the courts do not allow the government to justify content regulation on the basis of assumptions or generalizations. In *United States v. Playboy Entertainment Group,* the Court held that certain regulations pertaining to indecent programming on cable television could not be justified merely because of the assumption that viewers *might* see sexually explicit

images due to signal bleed. Even though the government pos-
sessed statistical evidence of the probability that signal scrambling did not always work and that nonsubscribing viewers could
see the sexually explicit programming, the *Playboy* Court held
that "probability" was not enough.[81] For speech to be regulated, a
close causal nexus must exist between the speech and the harm
sought to be prevented;[82] otherwise, any threat of future harm
would be enough to justify speech regulation. Consequently, the
state may not restrict speech on the grounds that it *might* cause
injury; it may only do so on the grounds that the speech is on the
very verge of causing such injury.[83]

This imminence standard is the crux of the modern free-
speech doctrine set forth in *Brandenburg v. Ohio,*[84] which rejected the mere "bad-tendency" test that formerly prevailed in cases
such as *Gitlow v. New York.*[85] In *Tinker v. Des Moines Independent Community School District,* the Court ruled that content
regulation could not be based on "a mere desire to avoid the discomfort and unpleasantness that always accompany an unpopu-
lar viewpoint."[86] This rule was repeated in *Burch v. Barker,* which
stated that the government had to show much more than mere
discomfort, unpleasantness, undifferentiated fear, or apprehension of disturbance in order to suppress undesired speech.[87]

These requirements of precision and certainty, however, do
not apply in religious-expression cases. In those cases, it is as if
the mere risk of marginalizing or offending religious dissenters
is enough to restrict the expression. As applied in *Allegheny v.
ACLU,* where the Court ruled that a crèche placed on the steps
of a county courthouse was unconstitutional,[88] the endorsement
test holds that the constitutionality of religious expression on
public grounds depends on the perceptions of viewers, which in
turn depends on the context in which the expression or symbol
is presented.[89] But such an approach involves "subjective line-
drawing."[90] Moreover, the subjectivity is not confined simply to

the physical context in which the religious symbol or expression appears;[91] it also involves a consideration of the individual traits of those likely to view the symbol or expression. For instance, the age of the viewer might influence perception, which in turn will determine constitutionality. Courts have allowed restrictions on religious expression in schools on the grounds that schoolchildren are easily impressionable and might feel that their only choice is to either follow the crowd (and join in the religious expression) or be alienated from the school community.[92] Based on these judicial assumptions about students and their perceptions, an elementary school teacher was forbidden to read his Bible silently during noninstructional times.[93] But even in the public university setting, among older and more mature students, the courts have sometimes refused to tolerate religious expression. Despite an instructor's having prefaced certain religious remarks made to his class by labeling them his "personal bias," the court ruled that such comments violated the establishment clause.[94]

In free-speech cases, the courts do not assume that private speech occurring on government property or being supported by public funds will in fact be attributable to the government. The expressions or messages of an artist are not attributable to the government, even though the artistic work has been funded by the National Endowment for the Arts.[95] But such an assumption is often made with respect to religious speech. Therefore, government funding of programs in which money is given to religious organizations to carry out secular purposes must be structured in such a way as to rebut the automatic presumption that the religious organizations are speaking or acting on behalf of the government.[96] Sometimes, even under such a structured program, courts assumed, often without evidence, that observers will attribute to the government the religious expression of private organizations receiving public funds—an assumption that will then warrant the finding of an establishment clause violation.[97]

Thus, in various respects, free-speech rights enjoy a higher degree of protection from the courts than do religious-exercise rights. Indeed, it was not until religious activists adopted a free-speech strategy in their litigation posture that they began receiving more constitutional support for their activities.

The Free-Speech Strategy in Religion Cases

During the 1970s and 1980s, courts used the establishment clause to strike down many instances of religious expression in public venues. When it was the free-exercise claims of religious practitioners versus the establishment clause defenses of separationists, the latter seemed to prevail more often than not. But then religious activists began pursuing a free-speech strategy in their litigation. Under this strategy, they cast their activities not as religious exercise but as free speech—and courts responded favorably.[98]

Prior to this free-speech strategy, religious-expression cases had a tough time in the courts. In a steady stream of cases that arose in the years following *Engel v. Vitale,*[99] the Supreme Court invalidated a state program that allowed public school students to read Bible verses to their fellow students during the school day; a law that set aside a moment of silence for meditation in schools; a statutory prohibition on the teaching of evolution (unless equal time was devoted to instruction on creationism); a law that required the posting of a privately financed Ten Commandments in classrooms; and a school district's practice of inviting clergy to deliver a prayer at commencement ceremonies.[100] When religious activists began bringing their cases under the free-speech clause, however, the tide shifted. Following the precedent set in *Widmar v. Vincent,*[101] courts started relying on free-speech rights, rather than free-exercise rights, to protect religious activities.

In *Widmar,* the Supreme Court held that a state university

policy encouraging the use of its facilities by student organizations but prohibiting any use "for purposes of religious worship or religious teaching" violated the free-speech clause.[102] Later, in a case similarly turning on the speech clause, the Court held that a policy permitting community use of school facilities for "social, civic, or recreational uses" but not for "religious purposes" constituted viewpoint discrimination. As the Court stated, denying access to school facilities solely because the group discussed otherwise permissible subject matter from a religious viewpoint violated the free-speech clause. According to the Court, government cannot "regulate speech in ways that favor some viewpoints or ideas at the expense of others."[103]

Free-speech protections were expanded in *Rosenberger v. Rectors and Visitors of the University of Virginia* to include religious student groups' access to university funds. The Court held that the free-speech clause did not allow the University of Virginia to refuse to pay the printing costs of a student religious organization's publication after the university had paid such costs for all other student publications.[104] Having made the decision to sponsor student publications covering a broad range of subject matter, university officials could not exclude from eligibility one that reflected a religious viewpoint. Again, being decided under a free-speech analysis, *Rosenberger* ruled that the deliberate denial of funding to religious publications amounted to viewpoint discrimination.

Following *Rosenberger,* courts across the country looked increasingly to the free-speech clause to analyze religion cases.[105] In *Clark v. Dallas Independent School District,* a Texas federal court found that a school policy prohibiting student groups from distributing religious materials was an unconstitutional burden on free-speech rights.[106] In *Hsu v. Roslyn Union Free School District,* the Second Circuit Court of Appeals held that a student religious club could limit its officers to those who were "professed Christians," despite a school district policy prohibiting discrimination on the basis of race, sex, or religion. The court concluded that the club's rules requiring officers to be "dedicated Christians" were "cal-culated to make a certain kind of speech possible" at the club's meetings.[107] And in *Chandler v. James,* the Eleventh Circuit Court of Appeals departed from the establishment clause framework set by *Engel v. Vitale* when it analyzed the issue of student-initiated prayer under the free-speech clause, holding that an Alabama statute permitting such prayer during certain school-sponsored events was constitutional.[108] The court ruled that the suppression of those prayers would violate the free-speech clause, and that the "prohibition of all religious speech in our public schools implies . . . an unconstitutional disapproval of religion." Contrary to earlier establishment cases, the court found that the state has a constitutional duty to tolerate religious expression.[109]

The Eleventh Circuit followed up *Chandler* with *Adler v. Duval County School Board,* in which it upheld a school policy permitting high school seniors to vote upon the delivery of a student-chosen religious message as part of graduation ceremonies. Although the facts of the case were similar to those in *Santa Fe,* where the Supreme Court had ruled against such prayers, the Eleventh Circuit rejected the arguments that the school's "role in providing a vehicle for a graduation message by itself transformed the student's private speech into state-sponsored speech," and that "Duval County's policy would have the impermissible effect of coercing unwilling listeners to participate in a state-sponsored religious exercise."[110]

With its decision in *Good News Club v. Milford Central School,* the Supreme Court further bolstered this free-speech approach to religion cases. In *Good News Club,* the Court struck down a provision in an elementary school's community-use policy that prohibited after-hours use of school facilities "by any individual or organization for religious purposes." The Court noted that the policy permitted use for all purposes, including the promotion of "the moral and character development of children."[111] Therefore, it ruled that the school's exclusion of a Bible club, which sought to address from a religious standpoint a subject otherwise permitted under the use policy (the teaching of morals and character), amounted to viewpoint discrimination "in violation of the Free Speech Clause of the First Amendment."[112]

In the wake of *Good News Club,* a host of cases demonstrated how the free-speech strategy has expanded religious liberty beyond what previously existed in the absence of such a strategy. In *Hills v. Scottsdale Unified School District,* for instance, the Ninth Circuit ruled that a school district could not ban the distribution of a brochure advertising a summer camp offering Bible study courses. The court held that the prohibition of such brochures constituted impermissible viewpoint discrimination against speech of a religious nature. It also dismissed concerns that distribution of the brochure might be interpreted as carrying a government endorsement of religion. The court stated that despite the risk of a possible misconception about endorsement, the "school's proper response is to educate the audience rather than squelch the speaker."[113] In *Westfield High School L.I.F.E. Club v. City of Westfield,* a Massachusetts federal court likewise struck down a school's attempt to forbid a Bible club from distributing religious literature during noninstructional time.[114] In *Donovan v. Punxsutawney Area School Board,* the Third Circuit held that the exclusion of a Bible club from school facilities was viewpoint discrimination.[115] And in *Nichol v. ARIN Intermediate Unite 28,* a Pennsylvania federal court ruled that a school's garb statute could not be used to require an elementary school instructional assistant to remove a cross that she regularly wore on a necklace. In holding that the garb statute violated the First Amendment, the court ruled that the wearing of a cross was symbolic speech, against which there could be no viewpoint discrimination.[116]

Consequences of the Free-Speech Strategy

Giving more protection to free speech than to free exercise encourages litigants to define religious exercise as speech, thereby obscuring or even undermining the exercise clause, since religious practice is protected only insofar as it falls under the free-speech clause.[117] Land-use ordinances reflect one way in which free exercise, without the cover of free-speech protections, can be burdened. Zoning laws, which are by nature neutral and of general applicability, can prevent religious sects from expanding their places of worship in large sections of a city.[118] The discretionary nature of zoning decisions, especially those concerning individual-use permit applications, is a "wide-open door to discrimination against religious uses," argues Anthony Picarello, general counsel of the Becket Fund, a public interest law firm dedicated to protecting religious liberty rights.[119] Even though zoning regulations are increasingly being turned against many churches that are trying to offer an array of services, including child and senior day care, religious education courses, and Alcoholics Anonymous meetings, the courts are not intervening. In *Congregation of Jehovah's Witnesses, Inc. v. City of Lakewood,* for instance, the court rejected a congregation's challenge to a zoning ordinance that forbade religious uses of all residential zones, permitting churches in only about 10 percent of the city.[120] Such zoning laws, which restrict places of worship, rarely receive rigorous judicial scrutiny under a free-exercise review.[121] Perhaps this is because courts do not see a close correlation between the construction of a place of worship and the exercise of essential religious beliefs.[122] But in most religions, such a connection does exist.[123]

Other types of cases also show how free-exercise claims, without any accompanying free-speech right, can carry relatively little weight. In *Tenafly Eruv Association, Inc. v. Borough of Tenafly,* a group of Orthodox Jewish residents sought permission to attach *lechis* (thin black strips of plastic) to neighborhood utility poles.

These *lechis* create an *eruv* (a ceremonial demarcation of a particular area) allowing Orthodox Jews, whose religious beliefs forbid them from pushing or carrying objects outside their homes on the Sabbath, to treat the entire space within that *eruv* as their home. Without such an *eruv,* Orthodox Jews who have small children (and must carry them or push them in a stroller) or disabled relatives (who must be pushed in a wheelchair) cannot attend synagogue on the Sabbath. In *Tenafly,* Jewish residents obtained injunctive relief against enforcement of an ordinance forbidding signs to be placed on public property, which on its face prohibited attachment of the *lechis* to the utility poles. Contrary to the city's claim, the court held that the ordinance was not a neutral law of general applicability, since it had never been uniformly applied in the past. The court cited the following exceptions that Tenafly had made to the general enforcement of the ordinance: orange ribbons had been allowed to remain on utility poles during a controversy over school regionalization; lost-animal signs were frequently posted; and each year the Chamber of Commerce attached holiday displays to the poles.[124] But the implication of this decision is that, had the Orthodox Jews lived in a community where such exceptions had not been made, or where people tended to post their lost-pet notices in the local newspaper rather than on utility poles, they would have no right to an *eruv.*

In *Rader v. Johnston,* a first-year student at the University of Nebraska requested an exemption from the university's parietal rule requiring all first-year students to live on campus. Rader, believing that many of the things occurring in the dormitories were immoral and would threaten his spiritual life, wanted to live in a religious fellowship house off campus. Only because the university's policy provided for three exceptions—students nineteen years or older, married students, and students living with their parents—did the court hold that the policy was not generally applicable under *Smith,* hence granting Rader his request.[125] But again, if the university had not provided any specific exceptions, Rader would have had to live in the dorm, contrary to his religious beliefs.

Cases involving religious objections to a state-ordered autopsy provide yet another example of how powerless free-exercise claims can be without the aid of a free-speech issue. In *Montgomery v. County of Clinton, Michigan,* conservative Jewish parents objected on religious grounds to an autopsy being performed on their son, who had died in an automobile crash. They argued that there was no question as to how their son had died, and the investigating police at the scene agreed, having witnessed the "massive head and upper body injuries" of the deceased. The court, however, upheld a state law that required autopsies in such types of death, even though in this case there was no evidence of foul play or use of drugs. And since the state law was one of general applicability that provided for no exceptions, the parents had no effective free-exercise claim.[126]

Even in cases where a free-speech claim is present, that claim is sometimes insufficient to rescue the religious exercise claim. In *Cole v. Oroville Union High School District,* the Ninth Circuit Court of Appeals upheld a school policy allowing the principal to edit or reject student graduation speeches—a policy used to prohibit a student from exhorting the audience to "accept God's love and grace" and "yield to God in our lives."[127]

In *Fleming v. Jefferson County School District,* the court upheld the refusal of officials at Columbine High School to permit tiles painted with religious symbols to be displayed on the walls of the school. As part of a healing process following the fatal shootings at that school, administrators solicited members of the community to paint or decorate individual tiles with messages of hope and healing, but only those tiles containing religious messages were denied display. Reversing the lower court's decision that the school had violated the free-speech rights of those painting the tiles, the Tenth Circuit stated that the speech restrictions only had to be "reasonably related" to the school's concerns that displaying the tiles would make the walls "a situs for religious debate, which would be disruptive to the learning environment."[128] But this approach, unlike the *Tinker* approach used in secular speech cases, presumed without proof that such disruption would occur.[129]

Even though a free-speech strategy does not always protect religious expression, the use of such a strategy threatens the viability of the exercise clause. A focus on free speech may blind the courts to certain accommodations that free exercise might demand. The exercise clause carries an affirmative aspect (a requirement of accommodation) that the free-speech clause does not. Whereas the latter encompasses a negative freedom, a simple prohibition of government infringement, the former requires that government may have to affirmatively require certain accommodations so as to ensure religious liberty. For instance, contrary to current doctrine, the exercise clause may actually mandate a time to be set aside during the school day when prayer is allowed. If students want to pray together, or if their religion demands it, they might ask for a designated time so as to minimize any school disruption. But if the school denies their request, such a denial might well infringe on the associational aspects of free exercise.[130]

By comparing the judicial treatment of speech and religion cases, it becomes apparent that the latter are treated less protectively than the former, and yet both freedom of speech and the free exercise of religion are fundamental rights. Perhaps the disparity arises from the fact that judges are more comfortable with speech cases than with religion cases; indeed, they have demonstrated a willingness to grant greater freedom to religious expression when it is sought under a free-speech claim than when it is pursued under a free-exercise claim. Or maybe the disparity is caused simply by decades of judicial expansion of the establishment clause, in a way that has come to exert a significant restraint on free exercise. And this problem has not been cured by the free-speech strategy that religious practitioners have pursued in the courts. As the framers recognized, religion is not just speech. It is individual beliefs and life practices; it is forms of worship and identity; it is communal association and support.

Justice White was correct in his *Widmar* dissent when he warned that equating religion with speech could empty the religion clauses of their content.[131] As legal scholars have noted, the expansion of constitutional rights that has occurred over the past four decades has "all but escaped the consciousness of the federal judiciary when it came to religion."[132]

CHAPTER 2 • TURNING THE FIRST AMENDMENT AGAINST RELIGION

The courts have often treated the two religion clauses as if they are at odds, with the exercise clause demanding government accommodation of religious expression and the establishment clause attempting to muffle any such expression occurring on public property.[1] Because of this conflict, religious expression can actually end up in an inferior constitutional status.[2] Moreover, if used to prohibit government from even recognizing religious principles, the establishment clause may contribute to a marginalization of religion in society.[3]

Those who see a war between the two clauses generally adhere to the privatization thesis: that religion is a private affair and should not play any role in public life.[4] But following this approach to its logical end would mean that the exercise clause could not really protect religious liberty, since the establishment clause could be used to strike down most instances of religious expression in public venues.[5] Such an approach would also severely block the democratic dynamics of society. Because religious beliefs "embody the most important values a citizen has," it is fundamentally undemocratic to restrict the public expression of those beliefs. Furthermore, owing to the interconnection between religion and democracy, "a radical separation of Church and State is an oxymoron."[6]

Building the Wall of Separation

Under the pattern developed over the past several decades, the establishment clause has come to govern every religious practice, however small, that may take place on public land or that might carry some indirect governmental involvement. The contorted, confusing, historically contradictory course of modern establishment doctrine began with *Everson v. Board of Education,* which marked the Court's entry into what would become a convoluted maze of establishment clause jurisprudence. In ruling on the constitutionality of a program allowing parents to be reimbursed for the costs of transporting their children to and from parochial schools, the *Everson* Court gave its view of the establishment clause:

> Neither a state nor the Federal Government can set up a church. Neither can pass laws which aid one religion, aid all religions, or prefer one religion over another. Neither can force nor influence a person to go to or to remain away from church against his will or force him to profess a belief or disbelief in any religion. No person can be punished for entertaining or professing religious beliefs or disbeliefs, for church attendance or non-attendance. No tax in any amount, large or small, can be levied to support any religious activities or institutions, whatever they may be called, or whatever form they may adopt to teach or practice religion. Neither a state nor the Federal Government can, openly or secretly, participate in the affairs of any religious organizations or groups and vice versa. In the words of Jefferson, the clause against establishment of religion by law was intended to erect a "wall of separation between church and state."[7]

The specific examples given here by the Court—establishing an official church, aiding or giving preference to any one religion, forcing a person to profess a belief in any religion—seem straightforward enough and consistent with history. But it is the last sentence of this passage that has proved to be the curse of establishment clause jurisprudence over the past half-century, for it is anything but indicative of the framers' intentions regarding the constitutional treatment of religion. As discussed in Chapter 5, not only did the framers not believe in a wall of separation between church and state, but they never once used such a phrase during the debates on the First Amendment.

One year after *Everson,* the Court decided *McCollum v. Board of Education,* striking down a public school program that provided for one hour of religious instruction per week by sectarian teachers in public school classrooms. In its decision, the Court maintained that the "wall of separation" articulated in *Everson* "must be kept high and impregnable."[8] This metaphor continued to influence the course of constitutional law throughout the 1960s, as the number of establishment clause cases reaching the courts steadily increased.[9] Then, with the 1971 decision in *Lemon v. Kurtzman,* the "wall of separation" metaphor launched a new phase in establishment clause jurisprudence. In *Lemon,* the Court examined the constitutionality of two state statutes that provided public money to parochial schools. In striking down the statutes, the Court articulated what would be known as the three-part *Lemon* test: "first, the statute must have a secular legislative purpose; second, its principal or primary effect must be one that neither advances nor inhibits religion; finally, the statute must not foster an excessive government entanglement with religion."[10]

Throughout the next decade and a half, the *Lemon* test prevailed as the standard by which courts adjudged establishment clause issues. But the "net effect" of the decisions coming down from the Burger Court during the 1970s was to "raise the wall of separation to a height never before reached."[11] In *Lynch v. Donnelly,* however, the Court began rethinking the separationist view that had been articulated in *Everson* and later incorporated into *Lemon.* In upholding the constitutionality of a Christmas display that included a crèche and that was owned and maintained by the city of Pawtucket, Rhode Island, the *Lynch* Court stated that the wall of separation "is a useful figure of speech" but "not a wholly accurate description of the practical aspects of the relationship that in fact exists between church and state."[12]

Yet even as the Court was starting to reconsider the separationist stance of *Lemon,* its decisions continued to express the kind of religious tension that had become linked with the "wall of separation" metaphor. In *Aguilar v. Felton,* decided a year after *Lynch,* the Court addressed the constitutionality of a special education program first enacted in 1965 as a cornerstone of President Lyndon Johnson's Great Society agenda. The program provided remedial English and mathematics assistance to both public and private school students who were economically disadvantaged.[13] In the nineteen-year history of this special-education program, not a single instance of unconstitutional involvement of agents of one school system in the other was documented by the program's opponents. Nonetheless, the Court invalidated the program on grounds of excessive entanglement, finding that the proponents of the program, not its opponents, had the burden of proving that there would never be a problem in its administration.[14]

Four years later, in *County of Allegheny v. ACLU,* the separationist approach led the Court to strike down a city's practice of allowing a private religious group to place a crèche on public property during the Christmas season. In the very same case, however, the Court upheld another holiday display, also located on public property—a display that combined a forty-five-foot Christmas tree and an eighteen-foot menorah. Distinguishing the unacceptable crèche in *Allegheny* from the permissible one in *Lynch,* the Court examined the setting and found that, unlike the elephants, clowns, and reindeer that surrounded the crèche in *Lynch,* nothing in the *Allegheny* display muted its religious message. The menorah, on the other hand, represented a holiday with both sectarian and secular aspects. Moreover, the placement of the menorah next to the Christmas tree (unlike the display with just the crèche) symbolized two faith traditions—one Jewish and one Christian—conveying the message that the city recognized more than one manner of celebrating the holiday.[15]

By taking a separationist approach, the courts have communicated to the American public a "categorical opposition to the intermixing" of religion and politics.[16] But this approach is appropriate only if one believes that there should be a limit on the public presence of religion, that religion should be primarily a private matter, existing outside the public square. Moreover, the *Everson* legacy has distorted the constitutional meaning of separation. To the extent that the First Amendment requires separation, it does so as a way of preventing government intrusion on individual and institutional religious autonomy. The constitutional intent behind separation was as a means of protecting religion, not the secular state.[17] The framers never intended the notion of separation to justify discrimination against religion's role in the public sphere.[18] As recognized by the Fifth Circuit Court of Appeals, the First Amendment "does not demand that the state be blind to the pervasive presence of strongly held views about religion," or that religion and government "be ruthlessly separated."[19] Likewise, Justice Goldberg has observed that "Neither government nor this Court can or should ignore the significance of the fact that a vast portion of our people believe in and worship God and that many of our legal, political and personal values derive historically from religious teachings. Government must inevitably take cognizance of the existence of religion."[20]

Not only does the "wall of separation" metaphor contradict the spirit of the First Amendment, but it provides a completely inappropriate constitutional doctrine. As Justice Reed pointed out, a rule of law should not be constructed from a figure of speech that was lifted from a letter Thomas Jefferson wrote, years after the First Amendment was ratified, to the Danbury Baptists, who

sought relief from discriminatory treatment by the Congregation-
alist establishment in Connecticut.[21] Furthermore, as historians
have pointed out, the "wall of separation" metaphor does not even
reflect an accurate portrayal of Jefferson's beliefs.

Thomas Jefferson's influence in the area of law and religion
has been immense. But most of this influence has stemmed from
a single phrase (from among his more than sixty volumes of writings) recited by the Court in *Everson:* "In the words of Jefferson,
the clause against establishment of religion by law was intended
to erect 'a wall of separation between Church and State.'"[22] Subsequent to *Everson,* the Supreme Court has constructed three
different establishment tests, all based on Jefferson's metaphor:
the *Lemon* test, the endorsement test,[23] and the coercion test.[24]
Indeed, the vast majority of establishment clause cases have either cited or relied upon Jefferson's metaphor. And yet, according
to numerous historical studies, the Court's reliance on Jefferson
and his metaphor has been misplaced.

Daniel Dreisbach's *Thomas Jefferson and the Wall of Separation between Church and State* addresses the historical origins
of the view that the First Amendment was designed to create a
wall of separation between religion and government. Dreisbach
argues that the traditional interpretation of Jefferson's phrase is
flawed and that Jefferson was merely attempting to convey his
view that there was a wall of separation between the *federal* government and religion, not between the various *state* governments
and religion.[25] Thus Jefferson's idea of separation was based in
part on the principle of federalism, not on a belief that the establishment clause set up a rigid separation between religion and
government.[26]

Even though the Court's reliance on Jefferson's views is so extensive that his pronouncements have become "a virtual rule of
constitutional law," Dreisbach argues that a careful review of Jefferson's actions throughout his public career suggests that he be-

lieved "state governments were authorized to accommodate and even prescribe religious exercises." Dreisbach also argues that Jefferson's wall of separation differs in both "function and location" from the "high and impregnable barrier erected in 1947" by Justice Hugo Black in *Everson v. Board of Education*. As Dreisbach explains, "Whereas Jefferson's wall explicitly separated the institutions of church and state, Black's wall, more expansively, separates religion and all civil government."[27]

Casting doubt on Jefferson's own belief in a strict separation of state and religion, as interpreted by modern courts, are his actions as president. During Jefferson's presidency, for instance, Congress approved the use of the Capitol building as a church building for Christian worship services, which Jefferson attended on Sundays. Jefferson even approved of paid government musicians' assisting the worship at those church services. He also supported similar worship services in his own executive branch, both at the treasury building and at the war office.[28] Later, when Jefferson founded the University of Virginia, he designated space in its rotunda for chapel services and indicated that he expected students to attend religious services there.

Some scholars argue that, even if *Everson*'s use of the "wall of separation" metaphor did reflect Jefferson's view, that view was hardly shared by the individuals actually responsible for drafting and ratifying the First Amendment.[29] (Not only did Thomas Jefferson not participate in the debates on the First Amendment, he was not even in the country at the time.) The essential themes that run through the preenactment debates on the religion clauses were limited to the preservation of individual liberty and institutional autonomy.[30] The historical record demonstrates that, in the years leading up to adoption of the First Amendment, the colonies, states, and Continental Congress frequently enacted legislative accommodations of religions and religious practices. There is "no substantial evidence that anyone at the time of the Framing viewed such accommodations as illegitimate, in principle."[31] Furthermore, during the debates over the First Amendment, not one of the ninety framers ever mentioned the phrase "separation of Church and State."[32] Yet it seems logical that if this had been their objective, at least one would have mentioned the phrase that, through the *Everson* decision, later came to shape the constitutional relationship between church and state.

The modern judicial misreading of Jefferson's metaphor was well documented by Justice Rehnquist in his dissenting opinion in *Wallace v. Jaffree:*

> It is impossible to build sound constitutional doctrine upon a mistaken understanding of constitutional history, but unfortunately the establishment clause has been expressly freighted with Jefferson's misleading metaphor for nearly 40 years. Thomas Jefferson was of course in France at the time the constitutional Amendments known as the Bill of Rights were passed by Congress and ratified by the states. His letter to the Danbury Baptist Association was a short note of courtesy, written 14 years after the Amendments were passed by Congress. He would seem to any detached observer as a less than ideal source of contemporary history as to the meaning of the Religion Clauses of the First Amendment. . . . Whether due to its lack of historical support or its practical unworkability, the *Everson* "wall" has proved all but useless as a guide to sound constitutional adjudication. It illustrates only too well the wisdom of Benjamin Cardozo's observation that "[m]etaphors in law are to be narrowly watched, for starting as devices to liberate thought, they end often by enslaving it."[33]

Because of the misapplication of Jefferson's metaphor, the courts have created a confusing maze of case law restricting public expressions of religious belief and often pushing religion to the fringes of civil society, exactly contrary to the framers' intent. One reason for this, according to Richard John Neuhaus, is that "secularized elites" in academia and the judiciary became embarrassed by the profoundly religious nature of America's founding and historical development. Consequently, they manufactured a revisionist history that tried to explain away the framers' beliefs in the value and role of religion in American democracy. And in the course of this effort, those elites have attempted "to strip the public square of religious opinion that does not accord with their opinion."[34]

As Justice Arthur Goldberg once wrote, the strict separationist approach carries an attitude of "a brooding, and pervasive devotion to the secular and a passive, or even active, hostility, to the religious."[35] By using an inappropriate "wall of separation" metaphor, the establishment doctrines of the past have tried to reduce religion in scope and strip it of any special consideration.[36] But the First Amendment was never intended to create or foster a secular society free of religion, as Chapter 5 will argue in more depth.

The *Lemon* Legacy

Following *Lemon,* the courts began taking a view of religion that was sharply contradictory to the nation's historical experience.[37] The theory arose that the establishment clause existed to create a secular state and that under the First Amendment nonreligion was just as important as religion.

Prior to the 1970s, the courts had repeatedly recognized the religious presence in American public life. In 1931 the Supreme Court declared that Americans were a religious people, and in 1963 the Court held that the First Amendment prohibited judicial "hostility" toward religion.[38] But with *Lemon v. Kurtzman,* the courts turned sharply separationist in their opinions regarding public aid or accommodation of religion, and they have used the establishment clause to enforce "a strict separation of church and state at all levels of American government."[39] As illustrated in *Sloan v. Lemon,* the Court tended to see the slightest benefit derived by a religious institution from a publicly funded program as evidence that such a benefit was the primary motivation of the program in question.[40] Whether the program helped children or parents or society as a whole was treated as irrelevant. The only thing that mattered was that religion not be allowed to receive any publicly funded benefit.

The more religious an organization, the more scrutiny given to it by the courts. In *Bowen v. Kendrick,* for instance, the Supreme Court declared that direct governmental aid violates the establishment clause if it goes to "pervasively sectarian" institutions. A "pervasively sectarian" school was deemed to be one "in which religion is so pervasive that a substantial portion of its functions are subsumed in the religious mission."[41] Earlier, in *Hunt v. McNair,* the Court had ruled that "aid normally may be thought to have a primary effect of advancing religion when it flows to an institution in which religion is so pervasive that a substantial portion of its functions are subsumed in the religious mission or when it funds a specifically religious activity in an otherwise substantially secular setting."[42] This rule incorporated the presumption that secular instructional materials would be impermissibly used for religious indoctrination whenever religious institutions obtained public funds.[43]

The judicial suspicion of religion so characteristic of the *Lemon* legacy continues to assert itself. In *Freedom from Religion Foundation, Inc. v. Bugher,* a federal appeals court addressed an establishment clause challenge to Wisconsin's telecommunications access program that provided grants to both public and private schools for video and data linkups. Even though the grants were accompanied with instructions that the funds were to be used only for educational technology purposes, the statute itself imposed no restrictions on schools' use of the grant money. However, not trusting the religious schools to abide by the nonstatutory instructions, the court overturned the program, emphasizing that the establishment clause permits direct public grants to the secular educational programs of religious schools only when "there is a statutory prohibition against sectarian use and an administrative enforcement of that prohibition." Without statutory prohibitions or administrative enforcements in place, the court speculated that the religious schools might divert the government money "for maintenance of the school chapel or for the religious instruction classrooms or for connection time to view a religious website, instead of payment for the telecommunications links."[44]

Throughout the post-*Lemon* era, conflicts over the public expression or presence of religion have become virtually institutionalized. In Dickson, Tennessee, public school officials refused to let a student submit a paper on the life of Jesus Christ for a ninth-grade English class.[45] Elsewhere, school officials removed a kindergartner's drawing of Jesus Christ from a display of student posters depicting things for which they were grateful.[46] A court ruled that coaches could not participate in their student-players' prayers.[47] School authorities refused to allow the distribution of brochures advertising a summer Bible camp.[48] In Florida, one county even banned Christmas trees from being displayed on public property, after its county attorney decided that they qualified as religious symbols.[49] And the American Civil Liberties Union claimed an establishment clause violation when the Ten Commandments appeared in a public display of such documents as the Mayflower Compact, the Declaration of Independence, the Magna Carter, and the Bill of Rights.[50]

The establishment tests that the Court has articulated have not only failed to provide a consistent guide to the relationships between government, public employees, and the religious practices of society, the tests have almost completely failed to bring about any kind of social harmony or agreement on the issue of religion in the public arena. As one legal scholar has observed, "we are moving less toward any type of consensus on this matter than toward a state of increased polarization and divisiveness."[51] Moreover, according to Carl Esbeck, in the hands of the modern courts the establishment clause "has come to mean much more" than simply prohibiting the creation and maintenance of a national church or religion.[52]

CHAPTER 3 • JUDICIAL EXPERIMENTS IN ESTABLISHMENT DOCTRINES

A Confused Jurisprudence

Over the past several decades, the courts have applied a host of different tests to determine whether a particular governmental action constitutes an establishment of religion. The first and most prominent of these the tests was outlined in *Lemon v. Kurtzman.* But the *Lemon* test and its progeny have failed to provide any consistent basis for evaluating establishment clause cases.[1] As one legal scholar puts it: "There is no underlying theory of religious freedom that has captured a majority of the Court," and every new case "presents the very real possibility that the Court might totally abandon its previous efforts and start over."[2] Another scholar notes that the establishment doctrines being applied by the courts are "in nearly total disarray."[3]

The separationist legacy of *Lemon* was perhaps best revealed in *Committee for Public Education and Religious Liberty v. Nyquist,* which held that aid provided to parents through a tax deduction was legally no different from providing direct aid to religious schools, and hence was a violation of the establishment clause. The Court recognized "the validity of the State's interest in promoting pluralism and diversity among its public and non-public schools," yet found that the tuition relief in question gave parents an incentive to send their children to religious schools and hence to practice religion.[4] The Court also suspected that public funds would be used by the religious schools for improper sectarian purposes.

Because of its hostility to religion, *Lemon* has produced an inconsistent legacy.[5] For instance, although the Court had previously held that states could lend textbooks to religious schools,[6] in *Lemon* it ruled that states could not supplement the salaries of religious school teachers who taught the same subjects offered in public schools.[7] Though it later allowed book loans from public to parochial schools, the Court prohibited states from providing to religious schools various instructional materials, such as maps and lab equipment.[8] In one case, the Court struck down a state's provision of remedial instruction and guidance counseling to parochial school students, only later to uphold another state's provision of speech and hearing services to such students. Whereas some cases have permitted states to furnish religious schools with standardized tests[9] and pay the costs incurred by religious schools to administer such exams,[10] others have prohibited states from helping finance the administration of state-required exams that were prepared by religious school teachers.[11] As some scholars have suggested, "it is plausible to conclude that today's establishment clause doctrine communicates at least one thing very clearly: that the intermingling of political and religious authority is categorically bad."[12]

Establishment clause doctrines became so unpredictable that the Court took the unprecedented step of overruling a decision it had reached under *Lemon*,[13] even though it still adhered to *Lemon* as providing the applicable law. This unpredictability stems from the fact that the second and third prongs of the *Lemon* test often call for distinctions that are too ambiguous to support a consistent constitutional jurisprudence.[14] In one opinion, the Court even recognized that the inconsistencies of *Lemon* would continue until it could find a different, less fact-sensitive test.[15] And some members of the Court have issued sharp criticisms of *Lemon*.[16] Their criticisms revolve around the fact that the secular-purpose prong of the *Lemon* test often creates the assumption that any law motivated by a desire to promote religious freedom or to accommodate religious practice automatically constitutes an establishment.[17]

As *Lemon* began falling into disrepute, the Court experimented with other establishment clause tests. In *County of Allegheny v. American Civil Liberties Union,* involving the constitutionali-ty of holiday displays on public property, the Court employed the endorsement test.[18] Then, in 1992, in a case involving a rabbi-led prayer at a public high school graduation ceremony, the Court tried out the coercion test.[19] Finally, in *Zelman v. Simmons-Harris,*[20] where the constitutionality of Cleveland's school-voucher program was upheld, the Court embraced the neutrality approach, which will be examined further in the next chapter.[21]

Pitfalls of the Endorsement Test

In cases like *Texas Monthly, Inc. v. Bullock* and *Lynch v. Donnelly,*[22] the Court began using the endorsement test to decide establishment clause issues. Subsequently, this test has become the Supreme Court's preeminent means for analyzing the constitutionality of religious symbols and expression on public property, and has to some degree been accepted by every current sitting justice.[23]

The coercion test, used in *Lee v. Weisman,* had a relatively short existence. Under that test, a religious activity is unconstitutionally coercive if the government directs it in such a way as to force objectors to participate. At issue in *Lee* was a prayer offered by a school-invited rabbi at a graduation ceremony. The Court held that because graduation exercises are virtually obligatory, objectors to the prayer were unconstitutionally coerced into participating.[24] A problem with this approach, however, involves the Court's definition of participation. The Court said that "non-governmental social pressure occurring in a government-provided forum could constitute coercion forbidden by the establishment clause." But this finding equates private social pressure occurring in a state-created forum with actual government compulsion.[25]

Since the unconstitutional coercion occurring in *Lee* was a result of peer pressure, the question arises whether a private prayer included in a state-sponsored event taking place at an institution of higher education, where the participants would be older and hence less susceptible to peer pressure, would similarly violate the establishment clause. In *Tanford v. Brand,* the Seventh Circuit Court of Appeals ruled that a religious invocation as part of a graduation ceremony at a state university was not coercive. Finding that students did not feel compelled to participate in the invocation, the court characterized it as "simply a tolerable acknowledgment of beliefs widely held among the people of this country."[26] However, in a later case involving the constitutionality of supper prayer at a state-operated military college, the Fourth Circuit Court of Appeals reached the opposite result.[27] Although recognizing that grade-school children are particularly susceptible to peer pressure and that military cadets are not children, the court nonetheless ruled that the college-age cadets were "plainly coerced" by the supper-prayer policy.

After a relatively brief life in establishment clause jurisprudence, the coercion test gave way to the endorsement test as defined by Justice O'Connor.[28] Under this test, the government unconstitutionally endorses religion whenever it conveys the message that a religion or particular religious belief is favored by the state. In *Allegheny,* the Court decided that the display of a crèche violated the establishment clause but that the display of a menorah next to a Christmas tree did not. The crèche was considered an endorsement of the Christian faith, but the tree and menorah were acceptable, insofar as together they did not give the impression that the state was endorsing any one religion.[29]

A problem with the endorsement test is that it contains a degree of subjectivity regarding a court's conclusions as to what impressions viewers might have of some religious display or speech. Because the test calls for judges to speculate about the impressions that unknown people may have received from various religious speech or symbols, it is incapable of achieving certainty.[30] One judge has written that the endorsement test requires "scrutiny more commonly associated with interior decorators than with the judiciary."[31]

Exemplifying the inherent subjectivity of the endorsement test is *Doe v. County of Montgomery, Illinois,* where the court ruled that a sign that had hung on a courthouse for more than fifty years had to be removed.[32] The sign, which read "The World Needs God," was found to be an endorsement of Christianity, since according to the court the sign praises the redemptive powers of God and sends the message that the world needs to be saved by God. But to reach the conclusion that the "God" referred to in the sign was specifically the Christian God, the court obviously assumed that spectators would draw the same subtle and theological inferences that the court drew.

Justice Kennedy, a critic of the endorsement test, declared it to be "flawed in its fundamentals and unworkable in practice." According to Kennedy, the endorsement test results in a "jurisprudence of minutia" that requires courts to consider every little detail surrounding the religious speech, so as to determine whether an observer might read into the speech an endorsement by the government. In *Allegheny,* this meant that the Court had to examine "whether the city has included Santas, talking wishing wells, reindeer, or other symbols" to draw attention away from the religious symbol in the display.[33]

This warning about a "jurisprudence of minutia" turned out to be well founded. In *Walz v. Egg Harbor Township Board of Education,* for instance, the court ruled that a four-year-old child's passing out of pencils with religious messages attached, during an in-school holiday party, could in fact convey the school's endorsement of that religious message.[34] But in what other circumstances could a four-year-old act as an official agent of the government, and in such an important role as to establish a state religion? And how could little pencils with brief religious messages attached rise to the level of the tax-supported Anglican Church in England?

This context is what produces the subjectivity. Sometimes, however, courts don't even bother with the context of the religious speech or symbol; sometimes they simply pronounce a conclusion as to what is occurring in the mind of the observer. The court took this approach in *Buono v. Norton,* where it ordered that a cross be removed from a federal preserve. The cross was a memorial to veterans who died in World War I; it had been erected by the Veterans of Foreign Wars in 1934, sixty years before the land on which the cross stood was made part of the federal preserve. The preserve comprised approximately 130,000 acres, and the cross, less than eight feet tall, stood on undeveloped land, well off one of the narrow secondary roads winding through the preserve. Almost all the viewers of this cross were automobile travelers who had made a conscious decision to drive on that particular secondary road. But, contrary to free-speech cases, the court did not require offended viewers to take any steps to "avoid the harm," such as taking another road or not looking up at the cross as their car passed by. The court also seemed indifferent to the context of the cross, concluding that "the size of the cross and the number of people who view it are not important for deciding whether a reasonable observer would perceive the cross" as a governmental endorsement of religion.[35] In making this ruling, the court disregarded the plaque displayed at the base of the cross, which specified the purpose for which it had been erected.

Even though the endorsement test requires courts to consider all the circumstances surrounding the religious expression, they often tend to look only at those facts that might suggest government sponsorship of religion. In *Buono,* for instance, the court gave no weight to the fact that the cross had been standing sixty years before any complaint was made. But to another court, in a similar case, such a fact was seen as highly relevant. Ruling that a Ten Commandments monument on the grounds of a state capitol did not violate the establishment clause, the court in *Van Orden v. Perry* noted that the monument had stood for forty-two years without any complaint. "History matters" when considering the message conveyed by a government practice, the court wrote. Thus, a reasonable observer knowing the age and history of the monument "would regard the decision to leave it in place as motivated in significant part by the desire to preserve a longstanding plaque." To rule otherwise, the court stated, would be to replace a "sense of proportion" with an "uncompromising rigidity at a costly price to the values of the First Amendment."[36]

Perception is the key in endorsement cases; but this perception can be a widely fluctuating concept.[37] Public school teachers, for instance, are prohibited from engaging in religious speech while on the job, because no matter how vociferously they disavow official sanction of their views, the courts presume that the students will perceive a link, which in turn will automatically cause an establishment clause violation. A court has held that a school improperly endorsed a religion when a classroom teacher studied his Bible in front of students during a fifteen-minute silent reading period.[38] In another case, even though the students were adults and not children, endorsement occurred when a professor at a public university organized an after-class meeting on religious topics, which was attended by several of his students.[39] And when a high school biology teacher denied the theory of evolution and discussed his religious views with students during the school day, the court held that the government had improperly endorsed a religion.[40]

The courts have been so insistent on avoiding any possible connection between religion and government that they have forced public employees into a Hobbesian choice: if you work for the government, you cannot express your personal religious beliefs for the majority of your waking day. Indeed, courts have tended to view any religious expression by public officials as an automatic equivalent of establishment, no matter how much that single religious expression may be surrounded by secular messages. In *American Civil Liberties Union of Ohio Foundation v. Ashbrook,* the court ruled that a judge had violated the establishment clause by hanging a poster of the Ten Commandments in his courtroom.[41] Yet this poster was surrounded by a replica of the Bill of Rights, the seal and motto of the State of Ohio, and portraits of Thomas Jefferson, James Madison, Alexander Hamilton, and Abraham Lincoln. In addition, the lobby just outside the courtroom contained a display of some thirty-eight different posters, including reproductions of the Mayflower Compact, various presidential inaugural speeches, the Declaration of Independence, the Gettysburg Address, and General McAuliffe's "Christmas Message" of 1944. In contrast to the *Ashbrook* decision, however, the Fifth Circuit in *Van Orden v. Perry* ruled that a Ten Commandments monument surrounded by twenty other historical-type monuments constituted a "museum setting" that negated any endorsement message conveyed by the Ten Commandments display.[42]

The courts have given mixed signals regarding this aspect of "context," namely, the issue of when a religious text or symbol has become sufficiently "diluted" by surrounding secular texts and symbols as to prevent it from becoming an endorsement of religion. One year after *Allegheny* was decided, the Sixth Circuit Court of Appeals in *Doe v. City of Clawson* found no establishment clause violation in the display of a crèche in front of city hall. According to the court, the presence of other "holiday artifacts" and secular symbols had "diluted" the religious message of the crèche.[43] A similar result occurred in *Jocham v. Tuscola County*, where the court held that a crèche located on a courthouse lawn was sufficiently diluted by secular objects like toy soldiers and decorative wreaths, as well as by a sign indicating that the display was privately funded.[44] The presence of such a disclaimer proved to be controlling in *Americans United for Separation of Church and State v. City of Grand Rapids,* in which the court upheld a private group's display of a twenty-foot-tall steel menorah in a downtown public park. Although recognizing that the display sent a religious message and did not include secular symbols, the court gave great weight to the presence of two disclaimers indicating that the display was privately sponsored and did not constitute an endorsement of religion. The court found that these disclaimers allowed a reasonable observer to distinguish "between speech the government supports and speech that it allows."[45]

Under the endorsement test, no concrete boundary exists as to where establishment begins and ends. There is nothing so minute that it cannot rise to the level of an official government endorsement of religion. Leaflets dropped in student mailboxes announcing church social activities have been ruled an unconstitutional establishment. This occurred in an Ohio school district, whose policy permitted nonprofit community groups such as Little League, the Red Cross, and the YMCA to distribute leaflets advertising their activities. Religious groups could also distribute their materials, but only after the principal scrutinized their leaflets, ensuring that they only advertised specific activities and did not engage in proselytizing. Moreover, the leaflets were not even handed out personally to the children; they were placed in mailboxes from which students could retrieve them at the end of the school day. Yet, despite all these precautions, the court held that "the practice of distributing religious material to students could be construed as an endorsement of religion by the school."[46]

In another case, the singing of the Lord's Prayer by a high school choir was found to violate the establishment clause. According to the court, even the rehearsal of that song during choir practice was enough to constitute a violation. In a prime example of the jurisprudence of minutia, the court held that for a public school choir to sing just one religious song is to "advance the Christian religion."[47]

Outside the school setting, where endorsement is presumably less of a problem because the age of the audience is higher, a federal court ruled that a city's leasing of land to the Boy Scouts amounted to an unconstitutional establishment of religion. The city had first leased the land to the Boy Scouts in 1957 for the purpose of constructing and operating a headquarters. But in a 2002 lawsuit brought to invalidate this favorable lease as an unconstitutional establishment of religion, the court found that the Boy Scouts engaged in "religious, albeit nondenominational, instruction through its various Scout oaths, religious emblems program, chaplaincy program, Religious Relationships Committee, religious publications and the integration of religion in Scouting activities." According to the court, the Boy Scouts creed included a strong commitment to God, and its outreach work included ministry programs aimed at Catholic, Jewish, and Protestant youth. Thus the court held that a "reasonable observer would most naturally view" the city's lease arrangements with the Boy Scouts as an "endorsement" of the religious practices of that organization.[48]

Even a disclaimer of support has been construed as an unconstitutional establishment. A Louisiana school board required that its science teachers, before presenting the theory of evolution to their classes, read aloud an announcement stating that the board did not support or endorse that theory. There was no attempt to control what the teachers taught, or to present the religious beliefs of the board. Even so, the court found that the board's disclaimer endorsed religion "in such a manner as to convey the message that evolution is a viewpoint that runs counter to the religious belief of the Biblical theory of Creation."[49]

The endorsement test can often involve the judiciary in extensive oversight of private religious speech conducted on public property, so as to prevent the mistaken perception that the government is in fact sponsoring the speech. In *Capital Square Review and Advisory Board v. Pinette,* Justice O'Connor noted that "an impermissible message of endorsement can be sent in a variety of contexts, not all of which involve direct government speech or outright favoritism." Thus, the establishment clause imposes "affirmative obligations that may require a State, in some situations, to take steps to avoid being perceived as supporting or endorsing a private religious message."[50] The problem, of course, is how to determine when private religious speech becomes sufficiently associated with the government so as to cause an endorsement.

Although the endorsement test requires constant judicial oversight of religious speech, it does not seem to allow for any remedial action. For instance, a city that erected a crèche on the lawn of its civic center was not allowed to modify that display so as to comply with endorsement-test mandates. After receiving complaints from the ACLU, the city added to the crèche scene several reindeer, a large Santa Claus with a sack of presents, three-foot-tall candy canes, a snowman flanked by gift boxes, and various animals, including lambs and donkeys. Despite these changes, the court concluded that they "did not rescue the display from impermissible endorsement."[51] According to the court, the "context" of the display included the time period during which the original crèche stood; thus, the secular figures added later did not negate the earlier message of endorsement. The end result is: once an endorsement, always an endorsement. No matter what the city did, it could not remedy any constitutional defects.

As applied, the endorsement test renders remedial efforts nearly impossible. No matter what subsequent steps are taken to dissociate the governmental unit from the particular religious speech or symbol, the courts can always point to whatever endorsement may have occurred prior to that dissociation. In *Mercier v. City of La Crosse,* plaintiffs sued to force the removal from a public park of a monument bearing the Ten Commandments.[52] The monument had been placed in the park forty years earlier by the Fraternal Order of the Eagles. In an attempt to avoid the lawsuit, the city sold back to the Eagles the twenty-by-twenty-foot plot of land on which the monument stood. Subsequently, the Eagles installed a four-foot tall iron fence around the perimeter of the parcel, with signs at each corner of the fence stating that the monument was the private property of the La Crosse Eagles. Six months later the city erected a second iron fence around the monument. This fence was gated, and a sign was placed on it that read: "This property is not owned or maintained by the City of La Crosse, nor does the City endorse the religious expressions thereon." Yet, despite all these actions, the court held that the city had failed to cure the establishment clause violation and that a reasonable observer could still conclude that the city was sponsoring the monument.

The *Mercier* court acknowledged that the disclaimer sign might prevent a newcomer to La Crosse from perceiving any city endorsement of the religious message. The problem, however, lay with the longtime residents of the city. According to the court, those residents would know about the city's relationship with the monument, its desire to keep the monument on city property, and its efforts to resist removal of the monument. Yet what the court did not recognize was that these same residents would know that a federal judge had ruled the original monument a violation of the establishment clause and that the city was prohibited from endorsing the monument's religious message. Presumably, this knowledge would significantly reduce the feelings of alienation suffered by the plaintiffs who did not believe in or agree with the religious ideas conveyed by the Ten Commandments.

The endorsement test is grounded in part on Justice O'Connor's premise that the establishment clause prohibits the government from conveying ideas that divide the community into outsiders and insiders. In *Lynch,* Justice O'Connor wrote that "endorsement sends a message to nonadherents that they are outsiders, not full members of the political community, and an accompanying message to adherents that they are insiders, favored members of the political community."[53] But, under this interpretation, the endorsement test becomes a vehicle for ensuring equality of treatment between all religions—a kind of religious equal protection clause.[54]

Strict separationists argue that the endorsement test should even prohibit private religious speech that ostracizes nonadherents.[55] They claim that private religious speech on government property can marginalize religious dissenters, that a private religious group may so dominate a public forum that a dissenter may feel that he or she is not welcome as a full-fledged member of the political community.[56] In such a scenario the establishment clause would be used to protect anyone who might suffer a sense of alienation because of their nonbelief. If necessary, strict separationists argue, the establishment clause should impose special regulations (similar to time, manner, place restrictions) on religious speech in public forums, aimed at ameliorating any isolating effects of that speech.[57] Other suggestions include interpreting the establishment clause to include a kind of *Brown v. Board of Education*[58] element, imposing a sort of social affirmative action policy aimed at achieving equality between believers and nonbelievers.

In *Jewish War Veterans of U.S. v. United States,* one Jewish individual altered his travel route so as to avoid seeing a Latin cross on U.S. Navy property, alleging that the cross made him feel like an "alien."[59] According to proponents of a broadly empowered establishment clause, this sense of exclusion is what the First Amendment is all about. And the only way to combat the isolation that minority groups feel may be to ban all religious messages from public property.[60] But the First Amendment is all about freedom, not social engineering or individual feelings of exclusion.[61] Moreover, if government actions ever rise to the point of truly excluding minority beliefs from the public square, then the exercise clause should come into play.

Despite its shortcomings, however, Justice O'Connor's endorsement test deserves credit. It marked a crucial recognition that the *Lemon* test was overly hostile to religion, and it came as a necessary stage in the judicial rethinking of a rigid "wall of separation." Yet for all its accomplishments, the endorsement test tends to throw First Amendment jurisprudence into an inescapable morass of ambiguity.[62] It tends to elevate human emotions to the level of constitutional trump cards. In *Mercier,* for example, a privately financed Ten Commandments monument was successfully challenged on the grounds that it "emotionally disturbed" a plaintiff who viewed it, that it caused another plaintiff to feel "marginalized," that it distracted a third plaintiff and caused her emotional distress, that it "so upset" still another plaintiff that she became "sick to her stomach," and that it caused another so much "stress and disturbance" that she lost sleep.[63]

The endorsement test also diverts the courts from the essential focus of the establishment clause—state interference in the institutional autonomy of religious organizations—and turns it instead to all the possible perceptions of various religious expressions made on public property. But to rise to the level of a constitutional violation, endorsement should mean something more than the feelings of observers. It should mean that the government is backing up its "endorsement" with some type of legal sanction or penalty.

CHAPTER 4 • THE NEUTRALITY COMPROMISE

Neutrality has become the preferred approach for dealing with establishment clause cases. Given the confusion and contradictions of previous doctrines, neutrality may seem at first glance like a long-overdue solution. But, although it offers the appeal of simplicity, it falls short of fulfilling the underlying purpose of the First Amendment. The neutrality doctrine prevents the government from conferring any special benefits on religion in general, even though history demonstrates that the establishment clause was not intended to make democratic society indifferent to the special role and status of religion. The First Amendment framers did not intend to strip religion of its uniqueness, or to make it exactly equal to every secular institution in society. To the contrary, the establishment clause aims only to keep the government from singling out certain religious sects for preferential treatment, not from showing any favoritism to religion in general.

Instead of being a principled constitutional doctrine bolstered by historical precedent, neutrality is more of a compromise between competing forces—a means of ending all the conflicts and discriminations caused by the "wall of separation" approach. Mandating that religious groups be treated no differently from secular groups (despite their obvious differences), neutrality tries more to address the disadvantages imposed upon religion by the *Lemon* progeny than to express a comprehensive constitutional model governing the full range of relationships between state and religion. In a sense, neutrality was the ladder on which religion could start to climb out of the hole dug by *Lemon* and deepened by decades of separationist jurisprudence. But this ladder is just an escape route from the past discrimination visited upon religion; it does not lead to the ultimate destination, to a constitutional recognition of the special protection given to religion by the framers.

The Neutrality Approach to Religion Cases

In an effort to simplify establishment clause jurisprudence, the courts have moved toward a neutrality approach.[1] This approach is based upon the principle of equal treatment for both religion and nonreligion.[2] In *Good News Club v. Milford Central School,* for instance, an adherence to viewpoint neutrality led the Court to overturn a school board policy excluding religious groups from after-hours use of school facilities.[3] The *Good News* opinion, along with earlier decisions such as *Rosenberger v. Rector and Visitors of the University of Virginia,*[4] stands for the proposition that the establishment clause cannot be used to justify viewpoint discrimination against religious organizations seeking the same kinds of public benefits that secular groups receive.[5]

The neutrality doctrine has also allowed the courts to abandon the "no-aid" approach, which prohibited the flow of any governmental benefit to any religious organization.[6] To the strict separationists, a no-aid reading of the establishment clause requires the exclusion of religious institutions from generally available government aid programs, a position that essentially imposes a penalty on the free exercise of religion. This no-aid approach was largely responsible for the perceived conflict between the establishment and exercise clauses.[7]

By applying the neutrality doctrine to cases involving public funds going to religious organizations, the Supreme Court has finally rejected the "no-aid" approach. In *Zobrest v. Catalina Foothills School District,* the Court upheld the provision of a publicly funded sign-language interpreter for a deaf student at a religious school, noting that "governmental programs that neutrally provide benefits to a broad class of citizens defined without reference to religion" do not violate the establishment clause.[8] More recently, in *Zelman v. Simmons-Harris,* the neutrality doctrine was used to sustain Cleveland's school-voucher program. The Court ruled that the vouchers promoted private choice by giving money directly to students for their use at either religious or nonreligious schools. This scheme was found neutral because it gave private individuals the choice of whether to apply public funds to religious education.[9]

The neutrality doctrine sanctions government aid programs that are equally available to students of both public and private schools.[10] According to *Zelman,* so long as the programs exhibit governmental neutrality toward religion, indirect aid programs are permissible under the establishment clause, regardless of whether or not tuition money is ultimately diverted for religious purposes.[11] This ruling suggests that neutrality focuses only on the means of government programs, not the ends.[12]

The courts have also employed the neutrality doctrine in establishment clause cases involving religious expression, ruling that religious and secular groups must be treated similarly.[13] In *Lamb's Chapel v. Center Moriches Union Free School District,* the Court overturned a school district policy that permitted outside groups to use school facilities for everything but religious purposes. After a local church was denied permission to show a film series that discussed family and child-rearing issues from a religious perspective, the Court ruled that the establishment clause could not be used to single out and exclude religious groups.[14]

Likewise, in *Rosenberger v. Rector and Visitors of the University of Virginia,* the Court held that a public university's refusal to subsidize a religious periodical published by a recognized student organization constituted viewpoint discrimination, since the university provided subsidies to a wide variety of nonreligious student periodicals.[15]

Neutrality Governs Both Exercise and Establishment Cases

Although most legal scholars use neutrality in connection with the establishment clause, courts have also adopted a neutrality approach in exercise clause cases as well.[16] In the exercise realm, neutrality was employed in the landmark decision in *Employment Division v. Smith,* in which the Court was asked to recognize a religious exemption for the sacramental use of an otherwise illegal drug by members of the Native American Church. Not only did the Court refuse to do so, it also declined to apply the type of judicial scrutiny that earlier cases had required.[17] In *Sherbert v. Verner* and *Wisconsin v. Yoder,* the Court had held that any state action substantially burdening the free exercise of religion must be strictly scrutinized.[18] Thus, under the doctrinal framework of *Sherbert* and *Yoder,* the exercise clause provided greater protection for religious practices than for secular activities. But in *Smith,* the Court declared that neutral laws of general applicability affecting religious practices do not require any form of heightened judicial review and hence do not require any religious exemptions. Even if such laws burdened the exercise of religion, they would be upheld under a rational basis review.[19] Taking the neutrality approach, *Smith* essentially reduced the exercise clause to a prohibition on deliberate governmental discrimination against religion, holding that formal neutrality is sufficient to satisfy the demands of religious liberty.[20]

In the post-*Smith* era, the right to free exercise of religion exists only to the extent that the exercise does not violate a neutral law of general applicability. Such laws are now more or less immune to First Amendment challenges, whereas prior to *Smith* the government could enforce laws burdening religious exercise only if it could establish a compelling justification for doing so. However, this neutrality approach, insofar as a law of general applicability applies equally to both religiously inspired conduct and all other forms of conduct, appears inconsistent with the exercise clause,[21] which plainly elevates religiously inspired conduct to the status of a fundamental right.[22] In fact, *Smith* actually affords less protection to expressive religious conduct under the exercise clause than expressive political conduct receives under the free-speech clause.[23] Unlike laws of general applicability that inhibit religious exercise, which according to *Smith* do not merit any First Amendment scrutiny, a law of general applicability that incidentally inhibits expressive political conduct is subject to a high degree of First Amendment scrutiny, requiring the government to justify the regulation as necessary to serve important government interests.[24]

Persisting Formalisms

The resistance to the granting of any public benefit to religion is reflected in the *Lemon* legacy and its maze of rules governing the most intricate and minute aspects of church-state relations. In their establishment clause decisions, courts have too often looked at all the trivial distinctions of government aid—e.g., the number of religious recipients versus the number of nonreligious recipients; whether the aid is in the form of cash or in the much less visible form of tax breaks; whether the direct recipient is a religious institution or an individual who forwards the aid to a religious institution; whether the aid reaches religion "directly" from the state or as the result of a predictable choice by an indi-

vidual recipient; and whether the administration of the aid program results in any visible associations between government and
a religious institution.[25] Courts have also required that to be an
equal participant in a government program, a religious institution cannot be "too religious," whatever that might mean.[26]

This array of rules and formalities, all designed to prevent government from somehow advancing religion, has likewise seeped
into the neutrality approach. In its application of the neutrality doctrine, the Court has adopted the direct-indirect test, which
generally requires that government aid reaching religious institutions do so only indirectly through the private choices of citizens.[27] But the distinction between direct and indirect aid can often be irrelevant and formalistic.[28] As Justice O'Connor observed
in *Zelman,* even though the voucher program qualified as indirect aid, a significant portion of the government funds reached
religious schools without restrictions on the use of those funds."[29]
It has also been noted that a needless emphasis on the direct-
indirect distinction can deprive states of the legislative flexibility to create new types of education programs.[30] Furthermore, the
line between direct and indirect is not always easy to draw. A
perfectly neutral voucher program could be invalidated solely because the government's tuition checks are made out directly to
the religious school chosen by the parents rather than to the parents themselves.

Nonetheless, the direct-indirect distinction has greatly influenced the Court's attempt to refashion the *Lemon* rule. In *Agostini,* involving a federally funded program sending public school
teachers into private religious schools to give remedial instruction, the Court adopted a three-part test for determining whether government aid impermissibly advances religion: (1) the aid
must not result in indoctrination, (2) it must not define its recipients by reference to religion, and (3) it must not create an excessive entanglement of government and religion.[31] But just as the

Lemon test did, the *Agostini* test focuses too much on the government action and not enough on the actual occurrence of any religious coercion. The real concern of the first prong should not be whether some indoctrination can occur, since indoctrination can always occur in any program,[32] but whether the public has alternative options by which to receive the same government benefits, and hence the freedom to escape any indoctrination they might feel. The second prong of the *Agostini* test essentially addresses the nonpreferential factor—e.g., whether the government is preferring one sect over another—and the third prong is really concerned with whether government involvement with a religious organization infringes on the religious liberty and autonomy of that organization.

Recognizing some of the drawbacks of the direct-indirect distinction, *Agostini* abandoned the rigid rule that "all government aid that directly assists the educational function of religious schools is invalid." The Court stated that no establishment violation occurs when government money goes to sectarian institutions "only as a result of the genuinely independent and private choices of individuals."[33] After all, it was the parents and not the government who decided where to send the eligible children to school.

The Court reinforced its *Agostini* holding in *Mitchell v. Helms,* where it allowed the government to lend educational materials and equipment directly to both public and religious schools.[34] The quantity of materials lent was based on enrollment, and about 30 percent of the program's resources ended up going to religious schools. As in *Agostini,* the four-justice plurality in *Mitchell* downplayed the distinction between direct and indirect aid to religious schools as formalistic. In her concurring opinion, however, Justice O'Connor argued that this distinction should be maintained.[35]

Mitchell is distinguishable from *Agostini* in that it involved direct aid to religious schools in the form of library and media materials and computer software and hardware. Yet eligibility for the funds was still based on the private choices of parents as to where to enroll their children. The plurality opinion in *Mitchell* rejected the suspicious stance that had often been taken toward religious organizations. The possibility of a religious school using a state-funded overhead projector to show a film about Jesus Christ was deemed to be of no constitutional significance, since that same piece of equipment could be used to show a film about George Washington. Unlike the approach in *Aguilar,* the *Mitchell* Court did not believe that the mere potential for diversion was enough to establish a constitutional violation. Instead, challengers had to prove that the aid in question was actually used for sectarian purposes.

In *Mitchell,* the Court's decision rested on neutrality grounds: if all organizations (both public and private) were eligible for aid, then no one could reasonably conclude that government had favored any religious beliefs or institutions through its grants. As long as the aid was made available to all recipients on religion-neutral criteria, the plurality considered it unimportant that some of the aid was ultimately diverted to religious uses through the enrollment decisions of private individuals. Despite the fact that the majority of aid designated for private schools went to religiously affiliated ones, the Court concluded that the aid was "allocated on the basis of neutral, secular criteria that neither favor nor disfavor religion," and that the materials were "made available to both religious and secular beneficiaries on a nondiscriminatory basis."[36]

Mitchell seems to stand for the following propositions: that indirect aid flowing to religious organizations through the independent choices of private individuals does not violate the establishment clause, even when such aid is applied to religious uses; and that the establishment clause permits direct government aid to flow to religious organizations without first passing through the hands of private individuals, but only if such aid is not applied to religious uses or "used to advance the religious missions" of the organization.[37] Thus, under *Mitchell,* it is clear that government may in some circumstances enact policies and aid programs that directly benefit religious groups. However, also underlying the *Mitchell* decision was the Court's finding that the aid at issue neither favored nor disfavored religion in general.[38]

An issue at the heart of *Mitchell* was the "pervasively sectarian" issue: whether state aid could go to institutions that are so pervasively sectarian that their secular activities (which qualify for public funds) cannot be separated from their religious ones. In the plurality opinion, only four justices stated explicitly that the pervasively sectarian nature of a government aid recipient is no longer relevant.[39] But until a majority of the Court overrules the use of the pervasively sectarian test, the lower courts can continue to apply it. Consequently, the test is still being used in increasingly convoluted ways.

In *Steele v. Industrial Development Board,* the court ruled that a religious university was so pervasively sectarian that a tax-exempt bond issue aimed at helping the university expand its campus violated the establishment clause.[40] Not only did the court retain the pervasively sectarian test, it expanded it to include a complex consideration of all the following factors: (1) whether the school adheres to the American Association of University Professors statement of principles on academic freedom; (2) whether the school is sponsored by a religious organization; (3) whether the school teaches religious doctrine in its programs; (4) whether institutional documents state religious restrictions on what can be taught; (5) whether the board of trustees is elected by the church; (6) whether the church approves certain financial transactions; (7) whether a majority of students—or a percentage greater than the population in that area—are members of the church; (8) whether religion or theology classes are required; (9)

whether classes begin with a prayer; (10) whether admissions are restricted based upon the applicant's religion; (11) whether attendance is required at religious activities; (12) whether obedience to the doctrines and dogma of the faith is compelled; and (13) whether the school takes any action to propagate a particular religion.

The question under the establishment clause should not be whether religion in general is better off because of some government program, but whether the government has singled out certain religious sects for preference and in so doing has infringed on the religious liberty of others. However, the whole point of the direct-indirect distinction is to keep the government from providing any "direct" advancement to religion at all. In *Bowen v. Kendrick,* the Court stated that no government grants should go to "pervasively sectarian" organizations. But such a single-minded focus on not allowing the "advancement of religion" can often end up fostering discrimination against the expression of religious views by "pervasively sectarian" organizations—the kind of discrimination that was held in *Good News Club* to be a violation of the free-speech clause.[41]

The problem with the Court's emphasis on "advancement of religion" is that it looks only at whether religion has received a benefit, not at whether the government has somehow restricted religious liberty, which is after all the fundamental concern of the First Amendment. Illustrating this misplaced focus is the decision in *DeStefano v. Emergency Housing Group, Inc.,* holding that direct, unrestricted state funding of an organization whose staff members actively supervise Alcoholics Anonymous (AA) meetings and discuss AA literature with clients violates the establishment clause. This holding was based on the finding that AA meetings were religious in nature and that the staff's participation constituted indoctrination. But again, the rule that staff members can present all perspectives on a subject except religious perspectives raises a free-speech issue as well as a neutrality issue. In addition, the court essentially concluded that in every instance where direct funding is used for activities that could be characterized as religious indoctrination, the participants in those activities could attribute such indoctrination to official government policy.[42] Such a presumption, however, seems to violate the neutrality doctrine. Likewise, in *School District of Grand Rapids v. Ball*,[43] where the Court noted that a program sending public teachers into religious schools would create a "symbolic union" between the government and religion, such a presumption, made automatically about religious organizations, does not seem to square with a neutrality approach.

Drawbacks of the Neutrality Doctrine

Although neutrality aided religion in *Rosenberger* and *Good News Club* by eliminating state-sanctioned discrimination, the doctrine does not always work so well for religious practitioners. In the exercise realm, for instance, the *Smith* approach can be insufficiently protective of religious liberty.[44] Even neutral laws can infringe on fundamental religious practices: employment discrimination laws conflict with the Catholic male priesthood; laws against serving alcoholic beverages to minors conflict with the celebration of communion; regulations requiring hard hats in construction areas can effectively exclude Amish and Sikhs from the workplace; and the policies of public hospitals can conflict with the religious scruples of doctors and nurses in such matters as euthanasia and abortion.

In *Brownfield v. Daniel Freeman Marina Hospital,* the California court of appeals held that a rape victim can seek damages against a hospital that does not provide her with abortive contraception as part of her emergency care.[45] The court so held even though the hospital was a Catholic one, and even though Catholic beliefs oppose the morning-after pill. In addition, several states

have passed laws requiring hospitals to make emergency contraception available to rape victims.[46] Since the laws do not specifically target religious hospitals, they qualify under the *Smith*
rule as neutral and generally applicable. Nonetheless, providing
emergency contraception violates fundamental Catholic beliefs;
in essence, requiring Catholic hospitals to supply the morning-after pill is akin to forcing them to perform abortions.

Laws regulating the type of benefits that all employers must
provide to all employees are prime examples of neutral laws. However, in *Catholic Charities of Sacramento, Inc. v. Superior Court,*
a Catholic Church affiliate brought a constitutional challenge to
a California law requiring that employer-provided health insurance programs cover prescription contraceptives.[47] Catholic Charities, which did not provide coverage for prescription contraceptives to its 183 full-time employees because of moral and religious
opposition, claimed that the statute violated the exercise clause.
But the California Supreme Court rejected this claim and held
that the statute was a neutral law of general applicability, even
though the statute substantially infringed on the religious beliefs
of Catholic Charities. This holding occurred despite the court's
acknowledgment of Catholic moral opposition to prescription contraceptives. The court also recognized that the work of Catholic
Charities, and hence of its many employees, was not just a secular or fund-raising activity unrelated to the Catholic religion. Basic Catholic doctrine, according to the court, compels its followers to "engage in corporal works of mercy" of the kind engaged in
by Catholic Charities. Thus the court's holding directly interfered
with a basic tenet of the Catholic faith. It penalized the Catholic
Church for employing people to provide such religiously inspired
services as counseling, low-income housing, and immigration assistance. As the dissenting judge wrote, the law amounted to a
"purposeful intrusion into a religious organization's expression of
its religious tenets and sense of mission."

The *Catholic Charities* decision illustrates Jesse Choper's claim that the neutrality approach is "inadequately sensitive to religious freedom by flatly prohibiting all religious exemptions from general regulations no matter how greatly they burden religious exercise." In adhering so rigidly to the goal of impartiality, the neutrality approach "downgrades the positive value that both Religion Clauses assign to religious liberty."[48] It also ignores the fact that religious organizations operate much differently from secular organizations; hence, to treat the two equally may in fact be to treat religion unfairly. In 2005 a Milwaukee court held the Catholic archdiocese liable for the negligent driving of a volunteer who was delivering a statue of the Virgin Mary to an invalid.[49] The imposition of liability hinged on the fact that the volunteer organization (the Legion of Mary) held its meetings on church property, even though the volunteer was driving her own car and even though the archdiocese did not control the activities of the Legion of Mary. Perhaps such a ruling is appropriate for private business organizations that use very few volunteers, but it places a substantial burden on religious organizations that depend heavily on volunteerism.

Another illustration of neutrality's inadequacy is found in laws giving historical preservation commissions authority over building expansion or modification. Given the close link between a house of worship and the religious expressions of its congregation, law imposing building restrictions on churches, synagogues, mosques, and temples might well constitute infringements on religious speech.[50] Because they qualify as neutral laws, land-use ordinances governing houses of worship rarely receive rigorous judicial scrutiny under free-exercise review.[51] Under New York's land-marking statute, for example, several religious structures in New York City have been "landmarked" against their will. The problem with these laws is that, by designating a building a historic landmark, the city can require a congregation to maintain the façade at whatever cost, regardless of whether the church has any money left to carry out its religious work.[52]

In *Grace United Methodist Church v. City of Cheyenne*, city zoning laws prohibited a church from operating a religious instruction center. The church argued that even though the zoning laws were neutral and of general applicability, they substantially burdened the church's ability to propagate its religious message through the operation of its religious education program. But the court refused to look any further than the facial neutrality of the zoning statutes. Furthermore, the court concluded that the statutes imposed only "an incidental burden on the church's religious conduct." The church could always operate its religious education program somewhere else, in another part of the city; or it could scale back the program at its current location, so as not to be on "such a grandiose scale" that it violated zoning laws.[53] But a change of venue would not only impose significant financial costs, it would move the religious education program away from the church building, the unifying and spiritual focus of the congregation.[54]

The judicial willingness to dismiss what some judges call "incidental burdens" on religious exercise is reflected in another zoning case, in which a church was denied the right to conduct worship services at property owned by the church within a particular zoning district.[55] The church argued that because it could not use its property to hold worship services—the most important activity engaged in by a religious congregation—it was forced to spend a considerable amount of money to rent space where worship services could be held. But the court refused to recognize this argument, holding that financial burdens do not rise to the level of infringement of religious freedom. The court further stated that the zoning law restricted nothing more than the location of religious conduct, and hence did not substantially burden the free exercise of religion. According to the court, the inability to hold worship services at church-owned property amounted to a mere incidental burden, even though throughout history religious exercise has occurred primarily at the site of a church or synagogue or mosque.

The neutrality doctrine's tolerance for "incidental" burdens was highlighted in a recent U.S. Supreme Court decision, *Locke v. Davey,* in which a student pursuing a major in theology was specifically excluded from a state's general scholarship program. Under that program, Washington State provided scholarships to assist academically gifted students with postsecondary education expenses. All majors or degrees were included in this program, except for theology. In its ruling, the Supreme Court admitted that the program discriminated on its face against religion, but nonetheless found that the state's "disfavor of religion" was only of a "milder kind."[56] Even though the state imposed an economic penalty on anyone choosing to study theology, the Court held that the scholarship program "does not require students to choose between their religious beliefs and receiving a government benefit." The dissent, on the other hand, argued that the program blatantly discriminated against religion, and that it was no defense to find that the discrimination was merely of a mild kind.[57] Indeed, few parents in America would call the deprivation of college tuition scholarships "incidental."[58]

A similar ruling occurred in *Bagley v. Raymond School Department,* where the Maine Supreme Court held that a voucher program expressly excluding religious schools did not violate the exercise clause. The exclusion did not burden the plaintiffs' religious freedom, the court ruled, because they were still free to send their children to a religious school, even though they had to pay the entire tuition bill themselves.[59] However, to a great number of people, the payment of a full tuition bill constitutes a substantial burden on the freedom of exercising religious beliefs through religious education.

The neutrality approach has also been unsuccessful in completely eliminating deliberate discrimination against religion. Following the sexual abuse scandal in the Catholic Church, the California legislature passed a special law specifically extending the statute of limitations for anyone who wanted to make such a claim for any injury ever suffered.[60] Courts have even allowed lawsuits against churches for negligent ordination, negligent training, and negligent supervision of clergy. But such suits strike at the heart of the sectarian and ministerial functions of religious organizations. They intrude into the very freedom of religious organizations to choose whom to appoint as ministers or priests and how to train or supervise those ministers and priests. In the words of one observer, clergy sexual misconduct litigation gives "hundreds of juries around the United States almost complete freedom to act against churches out of religious animus, even when that animus has nothing to do with the evidence in the case."[61]

Another problem with the neutrality approach is that it seems easily eroded. In *KDM ex rel. WJM v. Reedsport School District,* the Ninth Circuit Court of Appeals conditioned the level of constitutional scrutiny on the magnitude of the burden imposed rather than on the neutrality of the law. In *KDM,* a legally blind schoolchild with cerebral palsy received special equipment from a publicly funded vision program while enrolled in a religious school; however, the public school district refused to provide a vision specialist to meet with the student at the student's school. Upholding this refusal, the court cited an Oregon regulation prohibiting any special-education services from being provided in a religious setting. Even though this regulation was not neutral, since it specifically singled out religious venues, the court found no impermissible burden, because the law's purpose was not the "suppression of religion or religious conduct."[62] Under this interpretation, the court essentially applied the neutrality standard only to the law's purpose, and not to its effect. Thus the Ninth Circuit held that strict scrutiny does not apply even to a facially nonneutral law that burdens religion, unless there is evidence of an impermissible intent to suppress religion.[63]

Despite all these drawbacks, the courts, after decades of religion-clause confusion, have eagerly embraced the neutrality doctrine.[64] One reason for this embrace is that neutrality eases the burdens on courts by limiting their involvement in certain issues. Unlike the *Lemon* test, neutrality permits courts to avoid intricate questions regarding the precise uses made by religious groups of public funds. Instead, all a court must ask is whether religious groups are being treated the same as secular groups. Another reason for the embrace of neutrality is that it reflects the concepts of equality and nondiscrimination so ingrained in the legal culture of contemporary America. Ever since the Supreme Court's 1954 decision in *Brown v. Board of Education,*[65] there has been an ever-increasing emphasis on formal equality under the equal protection clause of the Fourteenth Amendment and in the legal culture generally.

This emphasis on equality, however, can work against religion's constitutionally elevated role, since any preferential treatment of religion can be classified as discriminatory. If, as the neutrality approach dictates, government must be neutral between religion and nonreligion, then government cannot provide any benefits to religion unless they are made equally available to nonreligious groups. But this approach also prevents the state from accommodating particular religious practices or from granting to religious organizations exemptions from generally applicable laws, no matter how greatly those laws burden religious exercise or how insubstantial the competing state interest may be.[66] As one scholar has noted, "the immediate impact of formal neutrality may seem beneficial for religion, but its long-term effect . . . may be to contaminate and secularize religion."[67]

Under the neutrality approach, the exercise clause has been essentially transformed into a subspecies of equal protection, with the focus not on the religious practitioner but on whether the government is making some distinction between religion and nonreligion. But in the process, the religious practitioner can be harmed, because a person punished by a neutral law is just as punished as one who is targeted.

The neutrality doctrine implies that religion is neither distinct nor distinctly important, despite that fact that religious liberty is the first freedom mentioned in the Bill of Rights. By leveling religion on the same plane as the secular, neutrality ignores constitutional text and history. It ignores the unique aspects of religion, as well as the role that the framers envisioned for it in American society. Those who wrote the First Amendment did not think that the government should adopt a position of indifference or neutrality toward religion.[68]

CHAPTER 5 • THE HISTORICAL RELATIONSHIP
BETWEEN RELIGION AND GOVERNMENT

In eighteenth-century America, religion was practiced as publicly as politics was, and civil laws often reflected religious values.[1] Public accommodations of religion were frequent, and few
people believed that they constituted any kind of establishment
of religion.[2]

A substantial influence in the settling of America was the
quest for religious freedom. Massachusetts, Rhode Island, Pennsylvania, and Maryland were all founded for religious reasons,
by people seeking relief from the dictatorship of state-established
religions in Europe. But the new Americans were not trying to
abandon a world in which religion and government were inter-
connected. They were simply attempting to make the New World
into a better image of God's kingdom.[3] To them, the lesson of religious intolerance in Europe was not that church and state should
be strictly separated, but that a corrupt government had poisoned
a state-created religion.

The religious inspiration of the earliest colonies can be seen in
their charters. The first charter of Virginia described the colony
as serving "the Glory of his Divine Majesty." The fundamental or-

ders of Connecticut vowed "to maintain and preserve the liberty and purity of the gospel of our lord Jesus which we now profess."[4] And of course there was the well-documented Puritan desire to create a city on a hill in Massachusetts, a commonwealth committed to the truths of the gospel.[5]

The Supreme Court has said that the religion clauses of the First Amendment are heavily grounded in the history surrounding their adoption.[6] It is a full and rich history, for religion provided the first political blueprints for many of the new colonies. And yet, throughout much of the modern establishment clause jurisprudence, the courts have largely ignored this history. Instead, as revealed in Chapter 2, they have focused almost single-mindedly on only one historical figure—Thomas Jefferson—and only one concept—the "wall of separation."[7]

It is impossible to cover thoroughly the history of the religion clauses of the First Amendment in just one chapter. Hundreds of volumes have been written on this subject. Yet, despite all this research and debate, contemporary disagreements over the framers' intent remain as contentious as ever. One reason for these continuing disagreements is that the framers never stated in a clear and unanimous voice their precise intention behind the general, broad language of the First Amendment. Perhaps that was because they considered the language clear and their intentions obvious. At any rate, the constitutional debates surrounding the drafting of the First Amendment are relatively sparse and somewhat meandering. Therefore, it is possible for different minds to have differing interpretations of what was said during those proceedings, just as it is possible to find within the literature of eighteenth-century political thought a wide array of beliefs and arguments concerning the public role of religion in a democracy.

Given this ambiguity in the literature, some historians and constitutional scholars claim that any attempt to reach a conclusion regarding the framers' intent is futile. Hence, because of this futility, constitutional history becomes irrelevant and the meaning of the First Amendment becomes simply what modern judges say it is. But this argument possesses two major shortcomings. First, even though the literature may be ambiguous on the framers' views of religion and democracy, the historical record is not. Abundant evidence exists on how eighteenth-century Americans actually structured and maintained the relationship between democratic government and religion. Presumably, since it has never been seen as a constitutional provision of radical change, the First Amendment was intended to preserve this relationship that had evolved over nearly a century and a half.

The second shortcoming to the argument asserting that ambiguity renders constitutional history irrelevant is that it ignores the benefit-of-the-doubt requirement. Unquestionably, the framers were intensely protective of religious freedom. They not only valued the public influence of religion, but they grounded their legal and political institutions on this influence. Furthermore, the First Amendment is unquestionably more pro- than antireligion. Any doubts or ambiguities in the historical record should therefore be resolved in favor of religion.

Even though there was a wide spectrum of beliefs on the relationship between state and religion in late eighteenth-century America, and even though these beliefs underwent change throughout the colonial, revolutionary, and constitutional periods, it is possible to outline those ideas which received a broad consensus. It is also possible to illustrate certain historical patterns and trends that existed throughout all the colonies and states of eighteenth-century America.

Eighteenth-Century Views on the Need for Religion in a Democracy

More than any other single concept, the "wall of separation" metaphor has shaped the direction of establishment clause doctrines in the modern era. However, not only does the metaphor have almost no historical basis, it actually contradicts the relationship between religion and government that existed in eighteenth-century America.

To Americans of the constitutional period, religion was an indispensable ingredient of self-government.[8] Political writers and theorists emphasized the need for a virtuous citizenry to sustain the democratic process.[9] John Adams believed there was "no government armed with power capable of contending with human passions unbridled by morality and religion."[10] He wrote that "religion and virtue are the only foundations not only of republicanism and of all free government but of social felicity under all governments and in all the combinations of human society."[11]

The constitutional framers "saw clearly that religion would be a great aid in maintaining civil government on a high plane," and hence would be "a great moral asset to the nation."[12] A 1788 New Hampshire pamphleteer expressed the prevailing view: "Civil governments can't well be supported without the assistance of religion."[13] This was why George Washington urged his fellow Virginians to appropriate public funds for the teaching of religion.[14] His objective was not to establish a religion but to maintain a democratic government.

According to Washington, religion was inseparable from good government, and "no true patriot" would attempt to weaken the political influence of religion and morality.[15] As a general in the revolutionary army, he required church attendance by his soldiers.[16] At his urging in 1777, Congress approved the purchase of twenty thousand Bibles for the troops.[17] And in his farewell address to the nation at the end of his presidency, he warned that "reason and experience both forbid us to expect that national morality can prevail in exclusion of religious principle."[18]

Late eighteenth-century Americans generally agreed that the only solid ground for the kind of morality needed to build a virtuous citizenry lay in religious observance. Consequently, it was expected that the state "would treat religious questions as issues of civil order" and that the "courts would foster the observance of religion."[19] In early America, churches were the primary institutions for the formation of democratic character and the transmission of community values.[20] As Professors Richard Vetterli and Gary C. Bryner have explained, "There was a general consensus that Christian values provided the basis for civil society. Religious leaders had contributed to the political discourse of the Revolution, and the Bible was the most widely read and cited text. Religion, the Founders believed, fostered republicanism and was therefore central to the life of the new nation."[21] The notion that the First Amendment was intended to foster a strict policy of state neutrality or indifference toward religion would have been met with, to use Justice Story's words, "universal disapprobation, if not universal indignation." It was the separation of a specific church from state, not the separation of all religion from the state, that was the aim of the framers. Since law was an expression of morality, and since morality derived from religion, it was seen as both impossible and undesirable to completely separate the state from religion.[22] The constitutional principles of church-state relations arose out of a "framework wherein Protestant Christianity and American culture intertwined."[23]

By the 1780s, the justification for governmental support of religion had ceased having any real theological component. The need to glorify or worship God did not explain the late eighteenth-century belief in the value of religion for the new republic. Instead, there was only "the civic justification that belief in religion would preserve the peace and good order of society by improving men's morals and restraining their vices."[24]

Government Recognition and Support of Religion

Government during the founders' generation consistently supported religion.[25] It donated land for the building of churches and religious schools. It collected taxes to support ministers and missionaries. It outlawed blasphemy and sacrilege, as well as unnecessary labor on the Sabbath.[26] Indeed, as of 1789, six states still maintained some formal system of public-supported religion.[27]

Stating that the "good order and preservation of civil government" depended upon "religion and morality," the Massachusetts constitution of 1780 provided for the "support and maintenance" of teachers of "piety, religion and morality."[28] In Pennsylvania, civil law prohibited blasphemy and enforced Sabbath observances.[29] The Maryland constitution of 1776 authorized the state legislature to "lay a general and equal tax for the support of the Christian religion," leaving to each individual the power to designate which cause or denomination should receive his tax money.[30] Similar provisions were included in the original constitutions of Connecticut and New Hampshire, the latter also stating that no person of one sect would have to pay for the support of any other sect.[31]

Although the framers rejected the idea of an established church, they did not perceive any real tension between government and religious organizations.[32] To the contrary, the Bill of Rights was ratified in an age of close and ongoing interaction between government and religion.[33] Congress appointed and funded chaplains who offered daily prayers, presidents proclaimed days of prayer and fasting, and the government paid for missionaries to the Indians. In the Northwest Ordinance, Congress even set aside land to endow schools that would teach religion and morality.[34]

The Public Expression of Religious Views

Religious beliefs found frequent expression in the acts and proceedings of early American legislative bodies. Five references to God appear in the Declaration of Independence. In setting up a government for the Northwest Territory in 1787, the Continental Congress charged it with furthering "religion, morality and knowledge" in the territory.[35] Early in its first session, the Continental Congress resolved to open its daily sessions with a prayer, and in 1782 it supported "the pious and laudable undertaking" of printing an American edition of the Scriptures.[36] Indeed, the proceedings of the Continental Congress are filled with references to God and religion.

When the First Congress, the very same Congress that created the Bill of Rights, reenacted the Northwest Ordinance in 1789, it declared that religion and morality were "necessary for good government."[37] This language was taken from the Massachusetts constitution of 1780 and later copied into the New Hampshire constitution of 1784,[38] and it indicates that the First Congress did not believe the First Amendment to prohibit public encouragement of religious exercise. Congress also consistently permitted invocations and other religious practices to be performed in public facilities.[39] Even Thomas Jefferson, who was probably the most separationist of any of the founding generation, supported a proposal inviting religious sects to conduct worship services at the University of Virginia, a state institution.[40]

On September 26, 1789, the day after the final language of the First Amendment was adopted by Congress, and in a spirit of jubilation over passage of the Bill of Rights, the House and Senate both adopted a resolution asking the president to "recommend to the people of the United States, a day of public fasting and prayer, to be observed, by acknowledging with grateful hearts, the many signal favors of the Almighty God."[41] Thus, the First Congress obviously did not intend to render all public prayer unconstitutional under the establishment clause.

In the years following ratification of the First Amendment, Presidents George Washington and John Adams continued to issue broad proclamations for days of national prayer.[42] James Madison likewise recognized that the government could designate days of solemn observance or prayer. When he served in the Virginia legislature, he sponsored a bill that gave Virginia the power to appoint "days of public fasting and humiliation, or thanksgiving." Later, during his presidential administration, Madison issued at least four proclamations recommending days of national prayer and thanksgiving.[43] He also oversaw federal funding of congressional and military chaplains, as well as missionaries charged with "teaching the great duties of religion and morality to the Indians."[44]

The Eighteenth-Century Understanding of Establishment

According to historian Thomas Curry, the classical concept of an exclusive state church pervaded the American image of an establishment of religion throughout the colonial and constitutional periods.[45] A state preference for one denomination over others was what was primarily thought to be an establishment of religion, because the framers did not want to duplicate the English experience with the established Anglican Church.[46]

Separation of church and state was a concept focused on ensuring the institutional integrity of religious groups, preventing government from dictating articles of faith or interfering in the internal operations of religious bodies.[47] As Elisha Williams wrote, every church should have the "right to judge in what manner God is to be worshipped by them, and what form of discipline ought to be observed by them, and the right also of electing their own officers" free of interference from government officials.[48] In the American view, the most repressive aspect of establishment involved government intrusion into religious doctrines and liturgies.[49] Under the Anglican system in England, for instance, the law mandated the type of liturgies and prayers to be used during worship services, as well as the fundamental articles of faith.[50]

Although modern jurisprudence focuses on the "advancement

of religion" as a key element of establishment, in eighteenth-century America the key element taken from the Anglican experience was "control."[51] In England it was the state that controlled the church, not the other way around; government officials dictated the appointment of ministers, and civil law controlled religious doctrine and articles of faith.[52] Thus, to the framers, an "establishment of religion" was understood to refer to "a church which the government funded and controlled and in which it used its coercive power to encourage participation."[53]

The ways in which the English establishment exerted control were twofold. It prohibited public religious worship outside of the Anglican Church, and it dictated the ecclesiastical doctrines of the Church of England.[54] From the time of Elizabeth I, people not attending Anglican services were subject to monetary fines, the amount of which depended on the length of their absence.[55] Marriages could be lawfully performed only by ministers of the Church of England, and the law refused to recognize the offspring of marriages performed outside the Church.[56] Based on this English experience, Americans hinged their opposition to establishment not on any disagreement with government support of religion but on an opposition to state tyranny over religious exercise.[57]

The Tradition of Nonpreferential Aid to Religion

During the constitutional period, opinion was divided on whether states could support and promote an individual Christian denomination. However, there was overwhelming agreement that government could provide special assistance to religion in general, as long as such assistance was given without any preference among sects.[58] Both before and after the Revolution, Americans made a conscious distinction between two types of state action: the granting of exclusive privileges to one church, and nonexclusive assistance to all churches. Only the former was considered to be an "establishment" of religion.[59] For instance, Maryland Catholics who opposed any state-established religion nonetheless supported state aid to religion if conferred without preference between sects.[60] According to Thomas Cooley, the establishment clause prohibited only "discrimination in favor of or against any one Religious denomination or sect."[61]

The framers recognized that granting exclusive privileges and monopoly status to one religious sect would only weaken religion, not strengthen it.[62] Madison, for one, declared that established religion tends toward "indolence in the clergy and servility in the laity."[63] The widespread eighteenth-century view was that establishment exerted corrupting effects on the ministries of the established church.[64] Religious establishments were seen to "pervert rather than advance true religion."[65] Just as free markets were seen as producing a strong economy, disestablishment and free exercise were believed necessary to produce strong religions. It was thus for the purpose of strengthening religion that the establishment clause was drafted.[66]

During the constitutional debates, Governor Samuel Johnston explained his support for the First Amendment and attempted to allay the fears of opponents by arguing that "there is no cause of fear that any one religion shall be exclusively established."[67] His wording was clear in its reference to the "exclusive" establishment of "one religion." To the Virginia ratifying convention of 1788, James Madison stated that religious liberty existed in America because of "that multiplicity of sects which pervades America, and which is the best and only security for religious liberty in any society."[68] Richard Henry Lee, who thought any religion should be supported so as to foster public morality, did not consider disestablishment to mean the removal of government's "general ability to promote all religion."[69]

The framers' generation firmly embraced the nonpreferentialist tradition.[70] "It is revealing," one historian has noted, "that in every state constitution in force between 1776 and 1789 where 'establishment' was mentioned, it was equated or used in conjunction with 'preference.'"[71] North Carolina's constitution of 1776 stated that there "shall be no establishment of any religious church or denomination . . . in preference to any other." Both the Delaware and New Jersey constitutions provided that "there shall be no establishment of any one religious sect . . . in preference to another."[72] (Later, over the course of the nineteenth and twentieth centuries, thirty-two different state constitutions would contain a "no preference" clause. The Arkansas constitution of 1874 provided a typical example: "No preference shall be given, by law, to any religious establishment.")[73]

According to the nonpreferentialist tradition, the religion clauses were designed to foster a spirit of accommodation between religion and the state, as long as no single church was officially established and governmental encouragement of religion did not deny any citizen the freedom of religious expression.[74] The very text of the First Amendment supports this view. The use of the indefinite article *an,* rather than definite article *the,* before the phrase "establishment of religion," indicates that the drafters were concerned with government favoritism toward one sect, rather than a general favoritism of religion over nonreligion.[75] This notion is further supported in the congressional debates over the establishment clause. On August 15, 1789, Madison stated that he "apprehended the meaning of the words to be that Congress should not establish *a* religion, and enforce the legal observation of it by law."[76] This view was repeated in 1803 by Chief Justice Jeremiah Smith of New Hampshire, who, subscribing to the view that an establishment constituted an exclusive government church, declared that New Hampshire had no establishment, even though the state's tax system provided financial support to all denominations.[77] Neither Connecticut, Massachusetts, nor Vermont considered its financial support of all churches to be an establishment of religion.[78] That was because, in the early American view, nothing in the language of the First Amendment foreclosed governmental promotion of religion in general, provided that it did so in a nonpreferential manner.[79]

James Madison repeatedly stressed that government could accommodate or facilitate religious exercise, so long as it did so in a nonpreferential way.[80] When he spoke of the proposed establishment clause as pertaining only to the establishment of a particular "national religion," he implicitly endorsed governmental "nondiscriminatory assistance" to religion in general.[81] At the Virginia ratifying convention, where delegates debated and voted on the First Amendment, Madison spoke of the establishment clause in terms of an exclusive government preference for one religion. Edmund Randolph likewise spoke of "the establishment of any one sect, in prejudice to the rest." And Patrick Henry, arguing on behalf of the establishment clause, insisted that "no particular sect or society ought to be favored or established, by law, in preference to the others."[82] As Thomas Curry notes in his history of the First Amendment, "by emphasizing the exclusive favoring of one particular sect, Americans appeared to draw a careful distinction between such an exclusive establishment and a favoring of all sects."[83]

The eighteenth-century adherence to nonpreferentialism hinged on the belief that the exercise clause is preeminent to the establishment clause. Throughout the debates on the First Amendment, the prevailing view was that "the Establishment Clause should not be considered more important than the exercise of one's equal rights of conscience," and that the establishment clause "was to be treated merely as a means of facilitating the free exercise of one's religious convictions."[84] The preeminence of the exercise clause was also reflected in the belief that government should not be hindered in accommodating people's efforts to practice their religious beliefs.[85] Daniel Webster, for one, believed that government could actually promote religious exercise in the public square.[86]

Coincidental with their belief in the doctrine of nonpreferentialism, early Americans were almost universally opposed to the kind of strict separation of church and state that modern-day separationists espouse. Because of the fear that such separation would hinder the free exercise of religion, the strict separationist view was almost nonexistent during the constitutional period.[87] This view, in fact, was wholly rejected by "every justice on the Marshall and Taney courts."[88]

Prior to the 1947 decision in *Everson v. Board of Education,* the "wall of separation" metaphor had never appeared in establishment clause jurisprudence.[89] Its appearance in *Everson,* however, resulted more from cultural attitudes and beliefs than from constitutional precedent.[90] As Justice Rehnquist would later argue, "the greatest injury of the 'wall' notion is its mischievous diversion of judges from the actual intentions of the drafters of the Bill of Rights."[91]

The Framers' View of Religion's Public Role

At around the time of the drafting of the First Amendment, individual states were ratifying their own constitutions and passing their own laws governing religion. In 1785 a bill for the "support of the public duties of religion" passed the Georgia legislature by a vote of forty-three to five.[92] The Delaware legislature declared in 1787 that it was their "duty to countenance and encourage virtue and religion by every means in their power."[93] In 1789 the New Jersey legislature appointed a committee to "report their opinion on what may be proper and competent for the Legislature to do in order to promote the Interest of Religion and Morality among all ranks of People in this State."[94] And throughout the constitutional period, a system of compulsory financial support for religion continued to prevail in Massachusetts, Connecticut, New Hampshire, and Vermont.[95]

The religion clauses of the First Amendment provide for a legal separation between church and state, not a moral separation.[96] The framers no more intended a government isolated from religious influence than they did a civil government devoid of moral influences.[97] The notion that the constitutional framers were afraid of religious influences over the state, in Stephen Carter's words, "is nonsense."[98] The whole justification for the Revolution had been interwoven with claims that freedom was a God-given right.[99]

According to the most eminent nineteenth-century constitutional scholars, the framers did not intend to expunge religious influence from society or even foster a climate of detached neutrality towards religion.[100] A primary objective of the First Amendment was not to insulate society from religion but to advance the interests of religion.[101] The framers wanted to create an environment in which the strong moral voice of religious congregations could influence the federal government and where the clergy could speak out boldly, without fear of retribution, on matters of public morality and the nation's spiritual condition.[102]

Drafting and Debating the First Amendment

The framers' principal concern in drafting the establishment clause was to ensure equality among religions, not between religion and nonreligion. They did not think that the government "should adopt a position of being areligious or certainly antireligious." To the contrary, they believed that government had a duty to affirmatively support religion.[103]

During the years immediately preceding enactment of the First Amendment, interest in some form of official support for religion was on the rise. Many leaders were convinced that public virtue was declining, and this led to a loss of confidence in democracy.[104] The decline was attributed to the paucity of public religious worship and teaching, a result of the collapse of the established Anglican Church.[105] Consequently, nearly every state witnessed a movement to strengthen religious institutions and practices within its borders. Just as the creation of the American Republic coincided with a dismantling of the monarchical Church of England, it simultaneously inspired a concern for strengthening religion in general, which in turn would promote republican virtue.[106] As Tocqueville wrote: "Religion is much more needed in the republic they advocate than in the monarchy they attack, and in democratic republics most of all. How could society escape destruction if, when political ties are relaxed, moral ties are not tightened? And what can be done with a people master of itself if it is not subject to God?"[107]

On April 15, 1789, before beginning debate on the religion clauses, the First Congress voted to appoint two chaplains of different denominations to serve in each house for the duration of the debates.[108] During the ensuing proceedings on the establishment clause, one framer voiced his fear "that it might be thought to have a tendency to abolish religion altogether."[109] Mr. Gerry thought the amendment would be better if it stated that "no religious doctrine shall be established by law." Madison said he understood the amendment to mean that Congress "should not establish a religion and enforce the legal observation of it by law." Benjamin Huntington worried that the establishment clause "might be taken in such latitude as to be extremely harmful to the cause of religion." He specifically feared that the public support of ministers or the building of churches "might be construed into a religious establishment." Finally, he hoped that the amendment would be interpreted so as "not to patronize those who professed no religion at all." Madison, in explaining the term "establishment," stated that the primary fear of the drafters was that "one sect might obtain a preeminence, or two combine together, and establish a religion to which they would compel others to conform."

Much of the debate focused on the prohibition of government favoritism of one sect over any others. But there is another aspect of those debates worth noting, an aspect that encompasses the whole eighteenth-century dialogue over religious establishment. As one historian has noted, a remarkable feature of the religion debates was that the advocates of the existing state establishments "tended to offer secular justifications grounded in the social utility of religion, whereas the most prominent voices for disestablishment often focused more on the theological objections."[110] In other words, the state needed religion more than religion needed the state. This was why governmental support of religion during this period "had nothing to do with religious belief."[111]

None of the twenty drafts of the First Amendment's religion clauses in 1788 and 1789 ever included the principle of separation of church and state.[112]

The Postratification Environment

Scholars have noted that "close ties between religion and government continued . . . even after the adoption of the Bill of Rights."[113] The first four presidents included prayers in their first official acts as president.[114] Indeed, these prayers and religious messages set a tradition that continued to endure for another two hundred years.[115] Lincoln's famous and pervasively religious second inaugural address has been called a "theological classic," containing "fourteen references to God, many scriptural allusions, and four direct quotations from the Bible."[116] During the D-Day invasion of World War II, President Roosevelt read to the nation a prayer for the success of the mission.[117] And following the terrorist attacks of September 11, 2001, President Bush's speeches to the nation were filled with references to Scripture and calls to prayer.

In an 1811 case affirming a conviction for blasphemy, the chief justice of the New York Supreme Court stated that in America "the morality of the country is deeply ingrafted" upon religion.[118] A year earlier, Massachusetts chief justice Theophilus Parsons, in a religious establishment case, noted the connection between the public good and the state of public morality: "The object of a free civil government . . . cannot be produced but by the knowledge and practice of our moral duties."[119] To Justice Parsons, civil laws were not sufficient to achieve order and justice. He argued that society depends upon behavior that cannot be legally enforced—behavior like charity and hospitality, benevolence and neighborliness, familial responsibility and patriotism. The best way to inculcate such values, according to Parsons, was to support religion. Later, in 1844, the U.S. Supreme Court noted the close relation between church and state when it recognized that "religion is a part of the common law."[120]

Even the 1833 Massachusetts state constitutional amendment, which abolished the mandated payment of tithes for religion, left intact the provisions that commended religious ceremony and morality. The preamble of the constitution continued to assert that it was "a covenant" between God and the people of Massachusetts. Similar endorsements of religious morality appeared in other state constitutions. Connecticut, Delaware, and Maryland stated that it was the duty of citizens to worship God. Another six constitutions repeated the language of the Northwest Ordinance that "religion, morality and knowledge" were necessary for good government.[121]

During the postconstitutional period, federal statute mandated the refunding of import duties paid on vestments, paintings, and furnishings for churches, and on plates for printing the Bible.[122] In 1819, New Hampshire passed a law authorizing towns to support Protestant ministers, a law that remained on the books for the rest of the century.[123] However, education was the area involving perhaps the closest ties between church and state. The school system was largely overseen by the clergy, usually with the support of local taxes.[124] In New York in 1805, for instance, schools run by Presbyterian, Episcopalian, Methodist, Quaker, and Dutch Reformed groups all received public support. Later, these groups were joined by Baptists, Catholics, and Jews.[125]

Tocqueville observed in 1833 that in America "almost all education is entrusted to the clergy."[126] During the nineteenth century, it was common practice for religious schools in New Jersey, Connecticut, Massachusetts, and Wisconsin to be supported by state-generated revenue.[127] In 1850, the California legislature gave religious organizations control over a large part of the state's education budget, as it was those organizations that were educating the burgeoning immigrant population.[128] Up until 1864, education in the District of Columbia was provided entirely through private and religious schools, which received public support.[129] And many of the nation's first public schools and state universities had mandatory courses in religion and required attendance at daily chapel and Sunday worship services.

Aside from education, the other social welfare systems existing in the community also had a strong religious character.[130] Government depended on churches and religious organizations to provide most social services in the community.[131] Even at the end of the nineteenth century the federal government was financing the construction of religiously affiliated hospitals.[132]

Remaining Vestiges of Religion's Public Role

Many signs of America's historical religious identity survive today. Witnesses in courts swear on the Bible and take an oath that concludes with the words "so help me God." Presidential proclamations invoke God. The Supreme Court opens its sessions with the invocation "God save the United States and this honorable Court," and overlooking the Court's chamber is a frieze depicting the Ten Commandments. In the House and Senate chambers, and on U.S. currency, appear the words "In God We Trust." The figure of the crucified Christ is painted on the capitol rotunda. The Great Seal of the United States proclaims "Annuit Coeptis," which means "God has smiled on our undertaking," and under the seal is inscribed the phrase from Lincoln's Gettysburg Address, "this nation under God." Adorning the walls of the Library of Congress are the words of Psalm 19:1 and Micah 6:8, and engraved on the metal cap of the Washington Monument are the words "Praise be to God." Both houses of Congress, as well as many state legislatures, precede their daily work with a prayer given by a publicly funded legislative chaplain. Children in public schools across the nation pledge allegiance to "one nation under God" every weekday morning.

Up until the latter part of the twentieth century, state and local governments continued to support religious ceremonies and symbols. The Ten Commandments and various Bible verses were inscribed on the walls of public buildings. Christmas and Easter were official holidays. Government-sponsored chaplains were appointed to state legislatures, prisons, and hospitals. Thanksgiving Day prayers were offered by governors and mayors. States and municipalities donated land, services, and materials to struggling churches. Property grants and tax subsidies were furnished to religious schools and charities. Tax exemptions were accorded to the real and personal property of many churches, clerics, and charities.[133] And the courts did not interfere in these arrangements. They gave each state and locality great leeway to determine for itself the proper relationship between state and religion.

Eventually, however, the Court began turning away from history as a guide to its religion decisions. In a 1963 opinion, Justice Brennan warned against a "too literal quest for the advice of the Founding Fathers."[134] This warning soon became reality, as the Court began constructing its high and impregnable "wall of separation" between church and state. Instead of protecting religion and preserving the nation's religious heritage, the Court used this wall of separation to institutionalize a growing social animosity to religion. And in doing so, the Court inverted the status of religion. When the Constitution was written, crèches were permitted on public property and blasphemy was punishable by law. Two centuries later, crèches are banned and blasphemy is being publicly funded, as exemplified by the financial support given by the National Endowment of the Arts for Andre Serrano's "Piss Christ."

CHAPTER 6 • THE CULTURAL SUSPICION

With First Amendment freedoms, the courts act as guardians, protectors from the cultural and political forces that threaten those freedoms. In the area of religion, however, the courts have been somewhat tentative and wavering in this role. According to a study completed by legal scholars at the University of Virginia, political attitudes and conflicts have shaped the Supreme Court's establishment clause opinions more than have original intent or constitutional precedent.[1] Consistent with this finding, liberal justices tend to find establishment violations more often and more readily than do other justices.[2]

Overall, the Supreme Court has been "far more comfortable" with free-speech cases than with cases involving religious expression or exercise.[3] In the speech area, as discussed in Chapter 1, the courts have taken a fairly monolithic approach, protecting the speech no matter what the argument for censorship is. Everything from sexually explicit speech to hateful insults to flag burning to offensive art to profanity is protected, all under the theory that the marketplace of ideas requires the most speech possible. Judges almost never look into what discomfort or antagonism the speech might cause, or into how valuable the speech is for a democratic society. And yet, in establishment clause cases, courts justify religious-expression restrictions on any number of grounds, many of which relate to perceptions of the social divisiveness or alienation that such expression might cause. But, as Alan Schwarz has written, "if avoidance of strife were an independent constitutional value, no legislation could be adopted on any subject which aroused strong and divided feelings."[4]

The Critics

Religious beliefs and crusades have always encountered opposition, just as controversial or opinionated speech has. History has not changed on that point. What has changed is the growth of more institutionalized opposition to religion in general. This opposition is not confined to or focused on a particular issue or belief; it extends more generally to the very existence of religion, and it is perpetuated by groups that have become increasingly entrenched in modern society. The nature of this institutionalized opposition to religion can be seen in contrast to the public opposition to certain types of speech (e.g., indecency). When the public becomes sufficiently outraged to rise up in protest against indecent speech that crosses the line of tolerance, such as Janet Jackson's breast-baring incident at the 2004 Super Bowl, it tends to confine that outrage to a specific incident. There are no institutional forces in American society that continually oppose free speech in general. And because of this absence of institutionalized opposition, free speech has enjoyed a more solid legal and constitutional foundation than religion has.

Since the 1960s, and in stark contrast to the views of the constitutional period, opponents have based their drive for a complete separation of church and state on the argument that religion should be an entirely private matter. But such privatization can end up eliminating religion totally from the public sphere.

The case of *Sechler v. State College Area School District,* for instance, shows how far school administrators have gone in trying to rid holiday celebrations and displays of any Christian content. In *Sechler,* the school's winter holiday program was filled with symbols for Kwanzaa, Chanukah, and the Swedish festival of St. Lucia, but no Christian symbols were allowed. A reflection of how a once religious holiday has been almost completely consumerized, the song sung during the school's program was called "Bruno's Christmas at the Mall."[5]

Critics claim that religion is undemocratic and encourages a blindly obedient herd mentality. According to Ira Lupu, religion does not foster a citizenry capable of exercising independent and critical judgment; it undermines the "habits of mind necessary for democratic decision making." In a similar vein, Steven Gey states that religion is "fundamentally incompatible" with the "intellectual cornerstone of the modern democratic state," which is the realization that "there can be no sacrosanct principles or unquestioned truths." Religion, according to Professor Gey, fails to inculcate the "anti-authoritarian mind set" on which democracy depends.[6] (But there are also those who say that religion, instead of creating a passive society, fosters one in which dissent from the prevailing secular norms is nourished, as reflected in the prominent role played by religious organizations in such social revolutionary causes as the civil rights movement.)[7]

Political theorist Amy Gutman, now the president of the University of Pennsylvania, argues that education must serve as a mechanism to "convert children away from the intensely held [religious] beliefs of their parents." Educator John Goodlad agrees that schools "should liberate students from the ways of thinking imposed by religions and other traditions of thought."[8] As philosopher Richard Rorty sees it, religion fosters intolerance and extremism;[9] in *Truth and Progress,* Rorty argues that the highest achievements of humanity are incompatible with religion. Rogers Smith in *Liberalism and American Constitutional Law* claims that religion should receive constitutional protection only when it completely transforms itself into something more "rational" or "self-critical." And Steven Macedo, in *The New Right Versus the Constitution,* insists that government should be free to punish "illiberal" churches, since to do so would be to promote greater overall freedom.[10]

These views, according to Frederick Mark Gedicks, reflect an "American cultural elite" that believes individuals should be "shielded from the regressive and superstitious influence of traditional religious beliefs and practices." Gedicks argues that this elite views religion as "a cynical, disintegrating force bent on subverting" the civil rule of law through "the irrational, passionate, and violent overthrow of rationality, reason and peace."[11] In the secularist mindset, religious adherents are often seen as violent revolutionaries.[12]

These secularist accusations reflect an intolerance toward religious fundamentalists—an intolerance that is especially ironic in that it occurs during an age of mandated acceptance of every other kind of social, ethnic, cultural, and racial group.[13] Despite the fact that the religiously devout are expected to tolerate society's views on sex, birth control, abortion, and evolution, there is little attempt to tolerate devoutly religious views on those subjects. Yale University has refused to allow any on-campus recruiting by the Christian Legal Society on the grounds that the CLS disapproves of homosexual conduct. A float proclaiming "Merry Christmas" was banned from Denver's Parade of Lights. And when the New York City board of education decided as part of its sex education program that every student in public school be taught how to use a condom, even though the practice violated the religious beliefs of Catholics, Orthodox Jews, and Muslims, families who were offended by the practice were not initially even given a chance to opt out of the program.[14]

Judicial Reflections of the Hostility toward Religion

The cultural criticisms of religion have been echoed by judges. Supreme Court Justices Stevens and Breyer have argued that public aid to religion, in the form of school vouchers, will in turn foster political discord and tear the social fabric underlying American democracy. They see a danger in religious expression that is too public, too openly displayed. They see religion as a divisive force, with the Court's role being to quell any conflicts that might arise from the religious practices of a diverse people, even though such a position seems to run counter to the idea of free exercise. Consequently, judges holding these views employ a broad reading of the establishment clause in an effort to confine religion to a tightly bounded private realm within society. They see the establishment clause as a kind of social regulator, minimizing any discomfort or conflict caused by a vibrant religious presence.

The problem with using the establishment clause to prevent any citizen from feeling alienated is that, because of the reality of human social life, someone will always feel alienated from the larger group.[15] Furthermore, social strife is inevitable in a society that values and protects individual rights. People are free to burn the American flag in front of a gathering of war veterans; artists are free to display desecrating art in galleries next door to religiously conservative churches; Nazis can march in Jewish neighborhoods. In any culture where free speech reigns and individualism rules, social strife is guaranteed.

A degree of alienation is also inevitable in a society that is as diverse and divided as America. In *One Nation, Two Cultures,* historian Gertrude Himmelfarb argues that the United States is deeply divided between a conservative population in the heartland that adheres to a somewhat strict moral code and a liberal urban population that lives by a looser one. As journalist Michael Barone notes, the nation is split between an observant, tradition-minded, moralistic America, and an unobservant, liberation-minded, relativistic America.[16] But when the courts use the establishment clause to try to ease these divisions, they end up favoring one side, the secular, thereby forcing the religious to mute their beliefs.

Despite the nation's inherent potential for conflict, and contrary to the claims of the separationists, there is little evidence that religion is in fact a source of serious cultural strife in America. Even though, according to polls, the United States is one of the most religious countries on earth, there is almost none of the kind of sectarian conflict that plagues much of the rest of the world.[17] Although Americans are more likely than citizens in other democratic countries to express a belief in God and attend church regularly, they are reluctant to impose their religious views on their neighbors.[18] Furthermore, the claim that religion is divisive ignores the fact that it is often a source of individual and social healing. The way individual victims and the nation as a whole turned to prayer after such tragedies as the Columbine shootings and the September 11 terrorist attacks reflects this healing role. Following September 11, for instance, members of Congress gathered together on the Capitol steps to sing "God Bless America."

Yet even if one does accept the premise that religion is divisive, that alone is not sufficient to single it out for more restrictive treatment than other forms of expression. In *Searcey v. Harris,* for instance, the court held that a public high school could not prevent an organization with a controversial ideological mission from participating in career day.[19] The organization at issue was the Atlanta Peace Alliance, and it wanted to participate in career day so as to dissuade students from entering the military. However, because of the alliance's controversial position on the military, the school board denied its request. And if the court had approached the case in the same way that it sometimes approaches religion cases, it might have upheld the exclusion of the group, reasoning that its presence could cause strife and outrage from students who were ardent military supporters.

When courts are not casting religion as a powerful source of social discontent, they can swing to the other extreme, when they trivialize religion by expanding its definition to include virtually any kind of philosophical or pop-culture orientation with which people wish to identify themselves. Judges have so watered down the definition that, in a constitutional sense, religion has ceased having any real meaning. Religious beliefs become simply matters of self-definition, with one's emotional needs rising to the level of religious callings. For the framers of the First Amendment, religious obligations were obligations to God, paramount over any needs of the self.[20] But modern courts have increasingly factored God out of religion.[21] In *Abington Township v. Schempp,* for instance, the Court referred to a "religion of secularism," essentially equating those who believe in a religion with those who do not.

In *United States v. Seeger,* involving military service exemptions granted to religious objectors, the Court expanded the definition of religion to include any "sincere and meaningful" belief that "occupies a place in the life of its possessor parallel to that filled by the orthodox belief in God." The Court concluded that religion did not require a belief in God, only a belief that was taken "seriously without reservation."[22] Under such a definition, just about any worldview or personal belief or lifestyle could qualify as a religion, thereby depriving religion of any real special role or status.[23] In *Welsh v. United States,* the Court even ruled that a person could be religious and not know it; because, unknown to the person, his life philosophy might actually qualify as a religion.[24]

By defining religion in a way that strips it of any essential meaning, courts blur the distinction between religion and non-religion. Not only have judges stated that "Ethical Culture" and "Secular Humanism" qualify as religions, but Alcoholics Anonymous, a therapeutic mutual assistance program, was declared a religion in at least six cases in 2001.[25] Furthermore, in *Alliance for Bio-Integrity v. Shalala,* a group of scientists' objections to the Food and Drug Administration's policy on genetically modified foods were treated as religious beliefs akin to Roman Catholicism.[26] And in *Yusov v. Martinez,* where a prisoner refused to comply with prison regulations, the court accepted his statement that obtaining a sample of DNA would violate his religious beliefs, even though the prisoner never presented any specific religion as the basis for his objection.[27]

The Cultural Rebellion against Religion

Establishment clause jurisprudence has been complicated by the way courts have incorporated into it various cultural suspicions that emerged in the latter part of the twentieth century. It has been complicated by the way courts have used the clause to try to confine religion's presence in the public arena.

The 1960s witnessed the most widespread cultural revolution ever experienced in the United States, a revolution that sought to completely transform American cultural values. It had many targets, among them religion, which was seen as the bastion of traditional moral values. Religion stood for everything that the sixties revolution opposed: self-restraint and self-discipline, the concept of sin, the power of moral judgment, and the elevation of virtue over self-actualization. And religious institutions came to be seen as perpetrators of repression and injustice.

Aside from being a direct object of the sixties rebellion, religion was also swept up in the wake of other social movements, the most prominent being the sexual revolution. Much of the liberal opposition to the Catholic Church, in fact, revolves around the church's condemnation of artificial birth control and abortion. And, to a significant degree, the crusade for abortion rights has evolved out of and now cloaks a larger crusade against religion, a crusade for the complete liberation of the individual from any subservience to a higher authority. In 1987, for example, Abortion Rights Mobilization filed a lawsuit challenging the tax-exempt status of the Catholic Church, claiming that the Church had violated that status by taking a public stand against abortion.[28] Indeed, the movement for sexual freedom has become a movement aimed at the dismantling of a much broader array of traditional values. This was particularly evident during the impeachment of President Clinton, where the president's defenders quickly moved from a defense of the specific charges to an attack on the legitimacy of traditional notions of virtue and morality.

The degree to which religion has become caught up in cultural conflicts over sexual mores can be seen in the findings of political pollsters. Early in the 1996 presidential election campaign, Bill Clinton's advisors discovered a polling technique that proved surprisingly determinative of whether a person was going to vote for Clinton or Bob Dole. Respondents were asked five questions, all dealing with attitudes on sex and religion. The questions were: Do you believe homosexuality is morally wrong? Do you ever personally look at pornography? Would you look down on someone who had an affair while married? Do you believe sex before marriage is morally wrong? Is religion very important in your life?[29] According to the pollsters, these questions were better voting indicators than anything else except party affiliation and race. Four years later, following the 2000 election, a correlation was shown between people's propensity to view adult videos, their frequency of attendance at religious services, and their choice of presidential candidate.

Another social movement into which an attack on religion has been swept is the multicultural movement. By undermining the legitimacy of all "Western" values and institutions, the multiculturalists have inevitably turned on religion, especially Christianity. And at the other end of the ideological spectrum, the self-actualization movement has cast religious beliefs as unhealthy and repressive causes of psychological dysfunction. The culture of the self has placed self-gratification above subservience to God or any moral authority.

Unquestionably, American culture has become more secular. But this shift in cultural values, by putting religion in a more precarious position, should give the courts all the more reason to protect religion and create constitutional doctrines that provide a bulwark against social hostility.

Institutional Hostilities to Religion

Apart from groups and individuals who confront religion on specific issues like abortion and divorce, there are institutional elements in American culture that have adopted an ongoing adverse stance toward any public expressions of religion. Even though these elements may not represent the majority viewpoint, they do reflect the voices of a social leadership that has influenced the judicial treatment of religion. One such institutional voice emanates from the field of journalism.

It is a common accusation that the "liberal media" are hostile to conservative religious values.[30] Polls and surveys show that journalists are overwhelmingly secular in their viewpoints. A Lichter-Rothman study found that 86 percent of journalists rarely or never attend religious services or meetings, and that 50 percent claimed no religion at all.[31] Apart from this general accusation, however, a more concrete example of journalistic hostility can be found in the 2002 press coverage of sex abuse allegations levied against certain priests in the Catholic Church. For months, that coverage dominated the front pages of the nation's newspapers, even though the alleged abuse had largely occurred decades earlier. The degree to which it so dominated the news can be seen through an examination of the front page of the *New York Times*.

As perhaps the most prominent newspaper in the world, the *Times* covers both national and international news. Hence, as readers know, it is quite unusual for any one story to appear on the front page frequently or consecutively over an extended time. But this was not the case with the problems of the Catholic Church. From March 3 to March 19, the story appeared on page one for eight consecutive days. (Meanwhile, during this most intense time of the war on terror, headlines concerning President Bush appeared on only three of the eight days.) From March 22 to March 25, stories on the sexual abuse scandal in the Catholic Church again appeared on four consecutive days, during which time no headlines on President Bush ran. From April 4 to April 10, seven consecutive days of front-page stories on the scandal in the Catholic Church ran—and from April 13 to April 29, seventeen consecutive front-page stories appeared. During the days between these periods of coverage, front-page stories continued to appear, though not consecutively; and whenever a front-page story did not appear, an article almost always appeared on an inside page of the newspaper. And the stories persisted for months. From May 3 to May 26, a total of sixteen front-page stories critical of the Catholic Church appeared in the *New York Times;* and from May 31 to June 17, a total of eleven front-page stories ran.

Throughout all this media coverage, the impression was given that a significant number of priests had been abusing children for years and that the Church hierarchy had not only covered up the crimes but had done nothing to stop the future commission of them. A survey for NBC News found that 64 percent of the public believed that Catholic priests frequently abused children.[32] But in February 2004 a study by the John Jay College of Criminal Justice reported that only 4 percent of Catholic priests had even been accused of such abuse, and more than half of all the accusations had been made against just seven priests.[33] In addition, the majority of abuse incidents had occurred prior to 1982, twenty years before the scandal erupted in the media. What the study also found was that the Church had made steady progress over nearly three decades in eliminating this problem. The percentage of priests accused each year of abuse had consistently declined since the mid-1970s, and the number of alleged abuses had fallen dramatically from the 1970s to the 1990s.[34] For instance, the number of boys aged eight to ten alleged to have been abused dropped by more than 90 percent during that time period.

Another study of the sexual abuse scandal revealed that fewer than 1 percent of all contemporary priests had charges pending against them.[35] In comparison, in the New York City public school system one child is sexually abused by a school employee every day, and more than 60 percent of employees accused of sexual abuse had remained at jobs within the schools where the alleged abuse occurred.[36] In 1994 Hofstra University professor Charol Shakeshaft conducted a study of 225 cases of teacher-student sexual abuse in the New York City school system. All of the accused admitted to the abuse, but none of the abusers had ever been reported to the police, and only 1 percent of them had lost their license to teach.[37] Shakeshaft also found that as many as 5 percent of the teachers had sexually abused children.[38]

What seems so hypocritical about the coverage of the clergy abuse scandal is that a sex-drenched media that often criticized the Church for being one of the few social institutions to say no to unrestrained sexual freedom relentlessly chastised it for the few individual priests who engaged in licentious sexual behavior. A media that condemned the Church for its moral opposition to homosexuality did a quick about-face, berating the Church for not rooting out homosexual conduct between priests and teenage boys.

A second area of American society that has become almost monolithic in its opposition to religion is Hollywood. Not that many decades ago, the Catholic Church was celebrated in American movies. Caring and dedicated priests were played by Spencer Tracy in *Boys Town,* Pat O'Brien in *Angels with Dirty Faces,* Bing Crosby in *Going My Way* and *Bells of St. Mary's,* and Frank Sinatra in *Miracle of the Bells.* Movies like *Ben-Hur, The Robe, The Ten Commandments,* and *The Greatest Story Ever Told,* all made between 1953 and 1965, were both respectful and celebratory of religion. But then the tide turned. On the rare occasions when religion did appear as the subject of a movie, as it did in *The Last Temptation of Christ* in 1988, it was portrayed in a way that offended the sensibilities of religious believers. More recently, films like *Dogma* and *Stigmata,* both released in 1999, were vehemently anti-Catholic. And most recently, though in an entirely different way, *The Passion of the Christ* revealed just how antireligious Hollywood has become.

The Passion depicts the life and death of Jesus Christ. The historical accuracy of its portrayal of the crucifixion was endorsed by the Vatican. It is respectful of Christian religious beliefs, and was made by a man who practices a conservative brand of Catholicism. But even though it was directed and produced by Mel Gibson, one of the biggest stars in Hollywood, it was met with immediate outrage and condemnation from that community. Heads of major studios said they would avoid ever again working with Mr. Gibson.[39] People who worked on the film were told that it would be a "career wrecker."[40] Critics charged the film with being too violent, at the same time that the gratuitously violent *Kill Bill: Vol. 2* was being released to rave reviews.

Called "a joy ride for sadomasochists," *The Passion* was described as being "constructed like nothing so much as a porn movie." Critics accused the film of anti-Semitism and argued that it would endanger Jews and subject them to violence and harassment. As one reviewer noted, the film "has made me feel less secure as a Jew in America than ever before."[41] Many predicted an outbreak of religious violence. Others accused Mel Gibson of harboring serious anti-Semitic views. Still others said that the film was the kind of thing that "tends to bring out the worst in people."[42] But the widely forecast violence and harassment of Jews never did occur.

In addition to accusing Mel Gibson of bigotry, detractors of the film slandered him as a religious zealot and, contrary to the Hollywood code of privacy regarding personal issues, reminded audiences that Gibson had once been an "abuser of various substances."[43] Even Mr. Gibson's father was dragged into the mudslinging, charged with being a Holocaust denier and anti-Semite. This backlash against Mr. Gibson had all the earmarks of a smear campaign, just because he made a movie that bucked the trend of the past thirty years and portrayed Christianity in a positive and even reverential light.

Perhaps *The Passion* raised the ire of Hollywood because it brought religious traditionalism back into a media spotlight that had long had an almost exclusively secular focus. So often the churches and synagogues and mosques that dot the American landscape are depicted in the media not as symbols of freedom but as incipient threats to the American way of life. Such an attitude was reflected in the characterization of President Bush's faith-based initiative as an ayatollah-type act, and in Ted Turner's comment that employees who had ashes on their forehead on Ash Wednesday were "Jesus freaks."[44] Within the American media, devout religious belief is often associated with people who are obsessed with destroying secular freedoms, the chief one of which is the right to an abortion.[45]

The belittling and demeaning attitude of Hollywood toward devout religious beliefs was particularly evident in a "reality" television series called "Amish in the City." In that series, five Amish youths were placed into "an extended sleepover in a Hollywood mansion," during which they were exposed to a host of temptations that violated their religious beliefs. As one commentator noted, the purpose of the show was "to peep at religiously raised children sampling the delights" of modern life.[46]

Education is yet another area of American society in which suspicion of religion has become systemic. In the field of higher education, diversity is the most celebrated of values: racial diversity, ethnic diversity, gender diversity, sexual preference diversity—every kind of diversity except religious diversity. As one commentator noted, "it's appalling that evangelical Christians are practically absent from entire professions, such as academia, the media and filmmaking."[47] But this absence is not entirely surprising, given the view, not infrequent among university faculty, that one of "the worst features of the American character" is its "toxic religion."[48]

With respect to racial discrimination, numbers often provide the strongest evidence. If the racial composition of a company's workforce is dramatically out of line with the racial composition of the community, there is almost always a presumption of racial discrimination. The same approach ought to be taken regarding the religious composition of university faculty. According to survey data, the devoutly religious are grossly underrepresented in those ranks.[49] One study reports that "the lack of religious diversity at many schools is at least as severe as the lack of racial diversity." Another study focusing on the religious makeup of law faculties found that law professors are more than three times as likely as the general population to have no religious beliefs or affiliation.[50]

The tension between higher education and traditional religious beliefs shows itself in the way the expression of those beliefs can be ridiculed and derided as "hate speech." After a professor at Indiana University wrote an essay on why conservative Christians oppose hiring homosexuals in certain "moral exemplar" positions such as schoolteachers, university officials called the comments "deplorable."[51] They accused the professor of engaging in hate speech and creating a dangerous and discriminatory environment for gay students. But whereas religious viewpoints critical of gay rights are labeled hate speech, harsh condemnations of devout Christians rarely suffer the same treatment.[52]

Even in the nation's elementary schools, religion is frequently treated with suspicion or disparagement. One study of widely used textbooks found that religion's historical role was often slighted, that Protestantism was almost entirely excluded, and that the religious motives of America's founders were extirpated.[53] In the teaching of ethics, public schools not only ignore religion but often preach a moral relativism that denigrates religious beliefs.[54] The presence of religious symbols in public schools are sniffed out like illegal drugs hidden in backpacks. In a Texas school district, for instance, parents complained that school authorities, prior to a holiday party, searched student "goody bags" for religious items, which were then confiscated until after the school day had ended.[55] And an Alabama sixth-grader was admonished for wearing a cross necklace to school.[56]

On social and cultural issues, which to the religiously devout can also be moral issues, educators can display a blatant intolerance toward religious viewpoints. Such was the case at a Michigan high school that, as part of its diversity week activities, scheduled a panel discussion on homosexuality and religion. The panel organizers deliberately chose gay-friendly religious leaders as presenters. A Catholic student who held contrary religious views on the subject, believing homosexuality to be a sin, was refused a position on the panel. She was also prevented from giving a speech on the subject. A faculty advisor explained that allowing people "hostile to homosexuality on the panel would be like inviting white supremacists on a race panel,"[57] and school authorities readily admitted that the panel was created to convey only one viewpoint regarding the issue of homosexuality. Any opposing religious view was deemed "negative" and summarily excluded.

The Politicization of Religion

The United States is the most religiously active society of the Western democracies. According to a 2003 Harris poll, 79 percent of Americans said they believed in God.[58] A poll by the Pew Research Center for the People and the Press found that 81 percent said that prayer was an important part of their lives.[59] Another poll found that 14 percent of Americans belong to a Bible-study group.[60] Nearly 40 percent of adults in the United States attend religious services at least once a week, and 60 percent attend at least once a month.[61] But despite this widespread religious affiliation, religion has become politically polarized. According to the Pew Research Center poll, people who attend church more than once a week vote Republican 63 percent of the time; and people who seldom or never attend church vote Democratic by a margin of 62 to 38 percent.[62]

The political polarization of religion is also reflected in the religiously based attacks on President Bush, who is a devout Christian. During the 2004 campaign, Bush opponents warned voters "of the danger of a theocratic president." Conservative Christian supporters of Bush were likened to Islamic fanaticists.[63] Liberal groups even filed complaints with the Internal Revenue Service against tax-exempt religious organizations whose members were actively supporting President Bush's re-election.[64]

The degree to which hostility toward religion has seeped into the ideological orientation of one end of the political spectrum can be seen in the litigation strategy of the American Civil Liberties Union.[65] The ACLU claims to defend all First Amendment freedoms; yet, as the chart below illustrates, over the past four decades the organization has become increasingly obsessed with a one-sided view of the establishment clause alone. It is an obsession that in turn has caused the ACLU to devote its energies to preventing or stopping any public display or expression of religion.

ACLU Cases

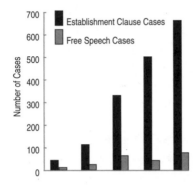

	1950–1959	1960–1969	1970–1979	1980–1989	1990–1999
Establishment Clause Cases	43	112	331	502	664

From 1950 to 1999, the number of free-speech cases per decade in which the ACLU involved itself grew by a factor of seven, whereas the number of establishment clause cases in which the ACLU tried to quash some kind of religious expression grew by a factor of nearly sixteen. Although the ACLU has fought for the speech rights of pornographers, convicted criminals, child molesters, occultists, Nazis, and illegal aliens, it has consistently tried to deny those same rights to religious believers.[66] Indeed, "removing religion from the womb of culture has become the practiced virtue of the ACLU over the past several decades," according to commentator William Donohue. [67] When Pope John Paul II traveled to Poland in 1983, the Communist authorities provided him with an altar built atop a stadium in Warsaw. But during the pope's visit to America in 1979, the ACLU tried to prevent public officials from accommodating him in any way.[68]

Not only does the ACLU rarely rise to the defense of religious liberty, it has tried to restrict religious expression in a way it would never allow other forms of speech to be restricted. According to Lawrence Freedman, a former ACLU lawyer, the ACLU has grown increasingly hostile to religious expression of any kind.[69]

Even such a staunch separationist as historian Leonard Levy recognizes that attempts by the ACLU to eliminate every cooperative relationship between government and religion can appear "ridiculous." Writing nearly a decade before just such a lawsuit was heard by the U.S. Supreme Court, Levy argued that "silly suits, such as those seeking to have declared unconstitutional the words 'under God' in the pledge of allegiance" only cause more social division and conflict. According to Levy, the Court had the good sense in 1993 to refuse to hear a case in which an atheist, with ACLU support, sought to prevent the daily recitation of the Pledge of Allegiance because of its "one nation under God" language. As Levy noted, "Public opinion, which is extremely conservative in matters involving public recognition of God, should not be tempted to retaliate on such an inconsequential issue."[70] And yet the ACLU continues to pursue the kind of blind retaliation against religion that was evident in a lawsuit in which the ACLU sued a Catholic youth center for refusing to open its doors to rock singer Ozzy Osbourne.[71]

A glaring hypocrisy has arisen in the political left's hostility to fundamentalist Christians. Liberals denounce stereotypes of Muslims but not of "Christian nuts."[72] They avoid racially sensitive expressions like "ghetto blaster," yet routinely call conservative Christians "fanatics." T-shirts proclaim "So Many Right-Wing Christians, So Few Lions." Choice is exalted in connection with the right to abortion, but not with the right of poor children to use education vouchers to attend inner-city religious schools. School boards order the removal of books on Christianity from classrooms, while books on Native American religious traditions and the occult are allowed to remain.[73] And when presented with the conflict between the First Amendment rights of the Ancient Order of the Hibernians and the desire of a group of gays and lesbians to march in the New York City St. Patrick's Day parade, city officials chose the side of the latter.

The Secularization of America's Civil Religion

Religious morality is being steadily replaced by what has become a political morality. It could even be called a materialistic morality. Guilt feelings now arise not because of some moral shortcoming but because of missing three straight days of working out, or deviating from a low-fat diet, or buying a new suit before it goes on sale. The moral issues of the day are not those relating to the spiritual soul of humanity but to various political agendas. The selling of tobacco products is cast in a moral light. Tax codes are discussed in moral terms. Environmental policies are called moral imperatives. Yet traditional moral issues are no longer accepted as such. In their place, moral relativism has taken root. Thus morality colors political issues but not personal issues. Opposing the expansion of welfare is immoral, whereas drug use and gang violence and illegitimacy are not immoral.

An increasingly law-based culture has pushed aside the morality-based culture that once prevailed in America. This was most acutely demonstrated during the 1999 impeachment controversy, during which President Clinton waged war on traditional notions of moral character and religious values—notions that the framers considered vital to a healthy democracy. But this assault on America's historic notion of virtue spawned an unsustainable double standard. Although it is immoral for tobacco companies to lie about the addictive power of cigarettes, there is apparently nothing immoral about a president lying to the country about how he has conducted himself in office. And even though President Clinton was brimming with ideas concerning the morality of children—e.g., V-chips, curfews, and campaigns against truancy—he could not admit to any moral boundaries on his own sexual behavior.

A crusade has evolved to create a kind of civil religion out of a particular political agenda. The quest for virtue has moved from the Scriptures to the legislative committee rooms. The word "values" no longer applies to morality, but is used to describe policy positions. Political correctness has come to epitomize this new brand of civil religion. It is a religion that preaches the evils of Western civilization. It is a religion that fosters a kind of national guilt, and transfers moral authority to the demands of certain sanctioned victims, as if victimization in itself conferred moral superiority. And if there is a devil in this new civil religion, it is the moral dictates of a religious order rooted in the past.

CHAPTER 7 • A THEORY OF THE ESTABLISHMENT CLAUSE

There is a simplicity to the First Amendment that has been lost in all the polarizing social attitudes about religion. The secularization of American culture, as well as all the religious turmoil around the world, has injected a constitutionally unintended suspicion into the judicial interpretations of the establishment clause. And instead of remaining steadfast in its protection of religion, particularly in the face of frequent social and political attacks, the courts have wavered, issuing conflicting and inconsistent opinions. This inconsistency has led one court to describe establishment clause case law as suffering "from a sort of jurisprudential schizophrenia."[1] But if the courts had focused more on the historical underpinnings of the First Amendment and less on all the cultural criticisms of religion, perhaps they could have avoided half a century of tortured jurisprudence. The simple fact is that, in the framers' experience, religion was the most important social institution in America, and the exercise of religious beliefs was the most sacred of personal freedoms. It was out of these experiences and beliefs that the First Amendment arose.

Focusing on the historical background of the religion clauses, as well as on the unequaled status of religion in eighteenth-century America, it is easy to see at least what the establishment clause is *not*. It is not an equal protection clause, immunizing the nonreligious from any feelings of discomfort or alienation that might arise from the religious practices of others. Nor is the establishment clause, as Kathleen Sullivan puts it, a constitutional mandate for "a secular public order," protecting it from any incursion of religious expression.[2] The establishment clause is not a door that was intended to be shut on the closet of religious exercise. Instead, it is the framers' constitutional recognition that American democracy cannot survive without the active influence of free and vibrant religious organizations.

The only way to preserve religious liberty and uphold the spirit of the First Amendment is for the courts to articulate an enduring and consistent theory of the religion clauses. Because of decades of inconsistent jurisprudence, however, the courts have failed to settle religion disputes in a way that provides the stability necessary for freedom. Consequently, doctrinal inconsistencies and ambiguities have served as weapons in the hands of those social and political forces trying to shove religion further to the sidelines of society.

The Unitary Nature of the Religion Clauses

Over the past several decades, courts have tended to see the exercise and establishment clauses as being "at war with each other."[3] Whereas the exercise clause is used to protect religious beliefs, the establishment clause is used to place boundaries on the public expression of those beliefs.[4] Not surprisingly, this checks-and-balances approach has bred a continual cycle of litigation over the proper role of religion in the nation's public life.[5]

In a 1948 opinion, Justice Jackson warned of the consequences resulting from too broad a view of the establishment clause.[6] He warned that the wall of separation could become a winding and convoluted wall—and sure enough, it did. In the ensuing years, the Supreme Court upheld the federal funding of Catholic teenage pregnancy counseling centers, but struck down a state tax exemption for sales of religious periodicals.[7] It approved a federal law exempting religious employers from Title VII prohibitions on religious discrimination, but overturned a state law allowing religious employees to claim exemptions from working on their sabbath.[8] And it upheld the constitutionality of a state-funded chaplain who opened each legislative session with prayer, but struck down a county's policy of allowing a privately funded Christmas display in the foyer of its courthouse.[9]

As reflected in many of the religious expression cases, the establishment clause has "become the enemy of the free exercise of religion."[10] But such a result makes no textual sense, because the free-exercise clause is then nullified or negated by the establishment clause.[11] Textually, the Constitution provides greater protection to religious practices than to any secular belief-related activities.[12] Therefore, to apply the establishment clause in a way that limits religion makes no sense. Nor does it make sense that secular, nonreligious speech should be more protected than religious speech. Thus, any tension or conflict that has been perceived between the two religion clauses is contrary to the spirit of the First Amendment.[13] In the constitutional scheme, the exercise and establishment clauses work together to create a proreligion constitutional command.

Some scholars argue that the establishment clause is entirely in the service of free exercise, that forbidding establishment is just one means of achieving complete free exercise for those who "might dissent from whatever religion is established."[14] Thus, taken together, the two clauses protect a single liberty—religious liberty—against two different threats to that freedom: on one hand, government action that restricts the religious practices of individuals or minority sects; and on the other, government action that interferes in the institutions freely chosen and shaped by the various religious denominations.[15] While the establishment clause guarantees that the government will not give preference to any one religious sect, the exercise clause guarantees that it will not restrict the religious practices of any individual.[16]

The Exercise Clause Is the Primary Clause

Freedom to practice their religious beliefs was what brought the Puritans to America, and a vibrant religious life came to define colonial life in the eighteenth century. The first and foremost concern of the framers of the First Amendment was not to create a separation of church and state, but to guarantee religious freedom. And the absence of an established church was just one aspect of achieving freedom of religion.

The free-exercise clause defines a fundamental individual liberty and articulates what the framers saw as a natural right. The establishment clause, on the other hand, simply provides a negative check on certain governmental actions;[17] it addresses what the framers perceived from their experience with England as one of the gravest threats posed to religious liberty by a centralized government. As such, the establishment clause plays a supporting role to the exercise clause.[18]

Any establishment of religion ultimately affects religious exercise, because it forces people into supporting a religion they do not espouse or causes government intrusion into the religion they do espouse. Establishments of particular religions are distinctly repugnant to those who adhere to other religions. To the irreligious, however, the injury caused by an establishment of religion is no worse than an injury caused by governmental adoption of some secular doctrine that they reject.[19] As scholars have noted, religious liberty was "the only concern of the authors of the religion clauses."[20] Consequently, the free-exercise clause, which directly protects religious liberty, is the primary clause within the First Amendment. According to Professor Laurence Tribe, whenever tension exists between the two, "the free exercise principle should be dominant in any conflict with the anti-establishment principle."[21] As Professor George Dent argues, "one can justify a greater sensitivity to establishment claims than to free exercise claims only if the religion clauses are viewed as promoting secularism."[22] In *McDaniel v. Paty,* where the Court overturned a Tennessee prohibition on ministers serving in political office, Chief Justice Burger wrote that establishment concerns regarding separation of church and state cannot "overbalance legitimate claims to the free exercise of religion."

Contrary to current notions, the establishment clause does not act as a kind of veto or check on the exercise clause. Instead, given the primacy of the exercise clause in the First Amendment hierarchy, the establishment clause occupies a subordinate position. It elaborates on the exercise clause; it makes specific reference to one particular protection granted to religious liberty. Consequently, the establishment clause can never properly negate or counteract the exercise clause—it can apply only in a specific subset of religious freedom cases in which the applicability of the exercise clause may not be discernable. This is not, however, the way the clause has been interpreted.

Over the past decade and a half, the establishment clause has been at the focal point of First Amendment jurisprudence, with free exercise having been "left on the sidelines of the rights revolution." It has been the establishment clause that has assumed primacy in the First Amendment hierarchy. The exercise clause, meanwhile, has taken a beating from judges who have given an expansive interpretation to the notion of 'establishment,' while at the same time ignoring the restrictions being inflicted "on the associational aspects of free exercise."[23] In this way, the constitutionally privileged status of religion been turned into a disability.[24]

This expansive interpretation of "establishment" has encouraged litigation over just about every occurrence of public-associated religious expression. A lawsuit was filed after a Chicago park district refused to allow a family to inscribe a religious message on a brick they had purchased as part of a fund-raising effort for a new playground. The bricks, used for paving the center of the playground, could be inscribed with whatever message the purchaser wanted, as long as it did not have any religious content.[25] In another brick-fund-raiser case, a New York public school ended up removing from a front walkway all bricks containing a religious messages.[26] Elsewhere, a brick inscribed with the message "For All the Unborn Children" was removed from a city park, as were bricks inscribed with a student's name and a cross from a flagpole plaza.[27] The basis of these removals was that a few privately composed religious messages, included among many more nonreligious messages, were enough to connote an official government establishment of religion.

As Stephen Carter has observed, an overly broad view of the establishment clause has led to a long line of court cases trying to dictate which specific government programs amount to forbidden "establishments" and which do not.[28] Moments of silence in schools, for instance, have been held to be such establishments. But if these moments amount to a state compulsion to engage in a particular religious exercise, then they violate the exercise clause; they in no way rise to the level of an establishment within the historical meaning of that term.[29] An establishment of religion occurs only when the government has involved itself, in a permanent or ongoing way, within the institutional integrity of an existing or created religious denomination.[30] Consequently, the establishment clause applies only on an institutional level, governing the relationship between governmental entities and religious organizations. And because of this narrow scope, it is the exercise clause that should actually cover many of the controversies currently being decided under the establishment clause.

In the area of public prayer or religious expression, the establishment clause has often been used to negate free exercise. Refusing to allow students to engage in a moment of silence during
an entire school day sends the message that prayer is something
best kept hidden, out of the public square.[31] It suggests, contrary
to the beliefs of most religious people, that religion should be kept
separate from the rest of human existence. Furthermore, to deny
group prayer to students who want a moment to pray together
is to deny "the associational aspects of free exercise."[32] Using the
establishment clause in this way, the Court invalidated a state
program that allowed public school students to read Bible verses
to their fellow students as part of the school day, a state law that
required the posting of the Ten Commandments (albeit privately
financed) in public school classrooms, and a state policy setting
aside a moment of silence for meditation and prayer by public
school children.[33]

Distinctions between the Exercise and Establishment Clauses

The exercise clause looks to protect individual freedom. It is
geared to members of minority religious sects, to protect them
from any kind of religious censorship or restrictions imposed by
the majority. It guarantees to the individual that the state will
not infringe on the practice of his or her religious beliefs, and that
the state can neither prescribe nor proscribe any religious practices. The establishment clause, on the other hand, works at the
institutional level. It seeks to protect religious freedom by guard-
ing against state interference in the institutional autonomy of religious organizations, and in so doing it serves as a subset of the
exercise protection.[34]

In *Bradfield v. Roberts,* the Court's first establishment clause
case, a challenge was made to a congressional allocation of
$30,000 to a hospital in Washington, D.C., operated by the Catho-

lic Church. In rejecting this challenge and upholding the grant, the Court stated that "a law respecting a religious establishment" is not necessarily "a law respecting an establishment of religion." Moreover, the recipient of the public funds was not a religious establishment but a hospital that just happened to be run by a religious group. The Court had it right. The establishment clause is not concerned with whether some individual denomination receives a temporary, one-time benefit. It is concerned with preventing permanent institutional alignments between the government and a particular religion. As an 1878 decision in *David v. Boget* stated, the use of public buildings for religious meetings—a use that is inherently *occasional and temporary*—does not amount to an establishment violation. But a century later, this notion of permanent alignment had become almost completely obscured. In *Elrod v. Burns* the Court ruled that any kind of perceived alignment or sponsorship between government and religion, "even for minimal periods of time," qualifies as an "irreparable injury."[35]

Employing the individual/institutional distinction between the two clauses, most if not all of the cases concerning religious speech on public property can be seen as more properly falling under the jurisdiction of the exercise clause than of the establishment clause. In these cases it is more appropriate to look at the compulsion test of the exercise clause, not the endorsement test of the establishment clause. The core concern is whether a person's religious exercise is being coerced, not whether some agency of government has made some perceived endorsement of religion. Consider, for instance, the case of *Lee v. Weisman,* where the Supreme Court held unconstitutional the inclusion in a public high school graduation ceremony of a prayer given by a local rabbi. Since the prayer was initiated by the school, the Court concluded that it violated the establishment clause and held that the government cannot coerce people into participating in a religious act.[36] But this case should have been decided under the exercise

clause, since the government, according to the Court, was interfering with free-exercise rights by compelling people attending a
public event to participate in a religious ceremony, even if that
ceremony lasted only seconds. Furthermore, there was nothing
in the school's behavior that amounted to an establishment of religion. To extend a constitutional provision, aimed at preventing
the federal government from creating an American equivalent of
the Church of England, to apply to religious speech uttered during a public ceremony is to stretch constitutional meaning to the
breaking point.

The Court's decision in *Santa Fe Independent School District
v. Doe* also reveals how the judiciary has been applying the establishment clause where it should be using the exercise clause.
At issue in *Santa Fe* was a Texas school district's practice of having a student, who was annually elected to the office of student
council chaplain, deliver a prayer over the public address system
before each varsity football game. This practice was held by the
Court to be a violation of the establishment clause. The Court
also found that the prayer practice was coercive, insofar as objecting witnesses were put into the position of either attending
a personally offensive religious ritual or foregoing a traditional
gathering of the school community.[37] But this finding shows that
the case should have been analyzed under the exercise clause. If
compulsion was exerted on the exercise or nonexercise of an individual's religious beliefs, the exercise clause was the proper one
under which to judge the matter.[38]

Under this view of the First Amendment, nearly all of the religious expression cases of the past sixty years, stretching back
to *Engel v. Vitale,* should have been decided under the exercise clause, not the establishment clause.[39] In *School District of
Abington Township v. Schempp,* for instance, the Court used the
establishment clause to invalidate a state law requiring, at the
opening of each school day, a reading of verse from the Bible and

the recitation of the Lord's Prayer.[40] But again, *Schempp* should have been decided under the exercise clause, because the state-mandated prayers were in effect telling children how to "exercise" certain religious beliefs. These mandated prayers may have intruded into the free-exercise rights of both students and parents, but there was nothing "establishment" about them. Indeed, a state-sponsored religion, with all the regulatory bureaucracy needed to maintain such a religion, cannot be formed merely by permitting or encouraging prayer in public schools.[41]

Recent cases show that courts continue to apply the establishment clause to disputes that should be governed by the exercise clause. In *Westfield High School L.I.F.E. Club v. City of Westfield,* high school officials imposed suspensions on Bible club members who, in violation of school policy, distributed religious literature to other students during noninstructional time, with the resulting litigation being decided on establishment clause grounds.[42] In *Donovan v. Punxsutawney Area School Board,* a dispute involving a meeting of a high school Bible club during noninstructional time was also judged under the establishment clause.[43] But the case should have been decided on the issue of whether, by allowing to group to meet, the school effectively denied or infringed upon someone else's free-exercise rights.

The problem with state-organized classroom prayer is not that it amounts to an establishment of religion but that it "represents a profound interference with the freedom of the family" to exercise its own religious beliefs.[44] Because children should not be forced to adhere to a creed contrary to the moral or religious teaching of their family, school prayer cases should only be analyzed under the exercise clause.

With the establishment clause focusing on the relationship between government and religious institutions, not between government and the individual, there is something of an analogy between the exercise/establishment clauses and the speech/press clauses of the First Amendment.[45] Just as the speech clause protects individual freedom, the press clause protects the institutional integrity of the press.[46] The press, like religion, is made up of nongovernmental institutions formed for the purpose of exercising constitutional freedoms. Hence they are institutions whose autonomy the government needs to respect. In *Lee v. Weisman,* Justice Kennedy stated that the "Free Exercise Clause embraces a freedom of conscience and worship that has close parallels in the speech provisions of the First Amendment, but the establishment clause is a specific prohibition on forms of state intervention in religious affairs with no precise counterpart in the speech provisions."[47] Kennedy, however, ignores the individual-institutional distinctions present in both the speech/press and exercise/establishment clauses.

In many respects, a state establishment of religion has the same purpose as state licensing of the press. Both enable the government to control private institutions and their dissemination of ideas. In late eighteenth-century America, long before the development of the modern mass media, churches were the foremost institutions for the formation and dissemination of opinion. It is estimated that about 80 percent of the published political pamphlets in the 1770s were reprints of sermons.[48]

The individual/institutional distinction between the two religion clauses also reveals ways in which the exercise clause is applied where the establishment clause should be. In *Jimmy Swaggart Ministries v. Board of Equalization of California,* the Court ruled that the imposition of sales and use taxes on religious articles sold by a religious ministry did not violate the exercise clause. Upholding the taxes under the neutrality doctrine, Justice O'Connor doubted whether there was even a free-exercise burden, since the collection of taxes did not appear to violate any "sincere religious beliefs." As O'Connor noted, the only burden was a reduction in income to the religious organization. But this is just the type of injury the establishment clause seeks to prevent—not an injury to individual beliefs but an injury to the institutional integrity and autonomy of religious organizations. Thus, in *Swaggert Ministries,* the Court's use of the neutrality doctrine completely blinded it to the institutional focus of the establishment clause. Perhaps payments of money do not directly infringe on an individual's religious beliefs, but they do affect the autonomy and viability of institutions that can survive only if they avoid financial debt.

The Establishment Clause and Accommodation

In the past, the establishment clause has been used to constrain governmental accommodations of religion.[49] But since the exercise clause is the dominant clause, it must determine the propriety of governmental accommodations; so if free exercise requires accommodation, the establishment clause cannot deny it.[50] Accommodation cannot rise to establishment, as long as the government is merely accommodating.[51] Unlike accommodation, establishment occurs when the government uses its authority and resources to support one religion over another. Far from enacting into law certain religious dictates, accommodations simply seek to tolerate religious dissent from the secular policies adopted by the political majority. Accommodations do not amount to permanent alliances between government and selected religious sects. With accommodation, the individual decides for herself how or what to practice, and then the government simply facilitates.[52]

When addressing issues of government accommodation, the Court has often examined the matter from the perspective of the outsider, the opponent of the governmental programs. Instead, the concern should be with the religious liberty and institutional autonomy of those who have now become involved with the government. Unless, for instance, the government is actually taxing citizens specifically for the support some religious sect, the focus should be on those inside the program being financed, not on the outsiders.[53]

Accommodation is often attacked as benefiting religion, but there is nothing in the First Amendment that prevents even-handed benefits for all religions. As Professor Conkle notes, "there is nothing approaching a consensus, historical or contemporary, for the proposition that government should be precluded from favoring religion generally, as against irreligion."[54] In fact, inherent in the very text of the First Amendment is a constitutional favoritism for religion, as long as that religion is not run or dictated by the government. The First Amendment not only protects religious exercise in a way that most secular activities are not protected, it also protects religious institutions from government interference in a way most secular institutions are not.

The establishment clause protects the autonomy of religious institutions. But autonomy is not the same as separation; it does not require complete independence, only the absence of coercion.[55] The notion of autonomy relating to religious institutions can be likened to the autonomy of the family. Whereas families are autonomous from the state, the state is not autonomous from families. The state is shaped and influenced by family concerns; and although the state cannot coerce the family, it may give aid and assistance to families. Likewise, the intent of the establishment clause was to free religious institutions from ecclesiastical coercion by the government, but not to free the state from accommodating religion and taking advantage of the unique social contributions of religion.[56] To the framers, "government noninvolvement in the province of the church did not mean total government separation from general religious ideas and affirmations relevant to civic life."[57]

Government support of religion over nonreligion is not an establishment problem.[58] Contrary to the separationist position, nonreligion receives no constitutional protection. This is not the case, however, with the nonexercise of religion, against which the government may not discriminate. The exercise clause grants equal protection to both the exercise and nonexercise of religion. Individuals are free to exercise (or not) as they see fit, but under the establishment clause courts are not free to elevate the secular to the same constitutional status as religion. There is a significant difference between religion and nonreligion, on the one hand, and exercise and nonexercise, on the other. Whereas the exercise clause protections belong to the individual, the establishment clause does not belong to a secular society.

In *Texas Monthly v. Bullock,* the Court held that a sales-tax exemption for periodicals published by a religious faith violated the establishment clause because similar exemptions were denied to nonreligious publications.[59] There was no allegation that Texas discriminated among different religious sects, only that a benefit was given to religion generally that was not otherwise available to nonreligious organizations; nor was there any allegation that this benefit had any effect on anyone's free-exercise rights. The only issue before the Court was essentially whether religious organizations in general could be given benefits not accorded to nonreligious organizations, or whether the establishment clause required mandatory indifference to the impact of government action (e.g., sales taxes) on religious institutions. Even though Justice Brennan noted that "we in no way suggest that all benefits conferred exclusively upon religious groups or upon individuals on account of their religious beliefs are forbidden by the establishment clause unless they are mandated by the Free Exercise Clause," that is exactly how the Court ended up ruling.[60]

By focusing its inquiry in *Texas Monthly* on whether the benefits flowed exclusively to religious groups, the Court took the position that the establishment clause forbids the government from favoring religion in general over other secular organizations.[61]

But this approach deprives the legislative branch of needed flexibility; for if a legislature concluded that religious organizations were more successful than secular ones at certain social welfare functions, such as drug rehabilitation, then there should be nothing to stop that legislature from providing nondiscriminatory funding to religious organizations that is not provided to secular organizations. Short of the state's imposition of a national religion, the establishment clause should not prevent a democratic government from being responsive to the beliefs and values of its citizens. And in a society in which more than 90 percent of the citizens claim to be religious, to say that government should not be responsive to religion is to say that government should not be responsive to the opinion of the people.[62]

Accommodation is particularly needed because of the pervasive reach of government in contemporary society. The regulatory web of government can ensnare religious organizations in ways unheard of in previous generations. In *Corportation of the Presiding Bishop of the Church of Jesus Christ of Latter-day Saints v. Amos,* for instance, churches were exempted from the antidiscrimination requirements of Title VII, thereby allowing them to favor members of their own faith when hiring for ministerial positions within the church. If it were not for this accommodation, the government would end up getting deeply entangled with religiously sensitive church decisions. A similar need for accommodation was highlighted in a case holding that enforcement of laws requiring property owners to rent to unmarried couples violated the religious freedom of owners who were devout Christians. As the court stated, exercise clause exemptions "do not as a general matter violate the Establishment Clause."[63]

Accommodation is also necessary because of how deeply the government has become involved in the kind of social work that was once the exclusive province of religion. The post–New Deal expansion of government's social welfare role has put it in direct competition with an age-old function of religion. And if the establishment clause is read as broadly as separationists wish it to be read, it will create the perverse condition that "wherever government goes, religion must retreat."[64] Moreover, the broader the reading of the establishment clause, the more necessary it becomes for the judiciary to take an aggressive role in monitoring government acts or policies for violations of the establishment clause.

The accommodation doctrine reflects, as does the nonpreferential aid model outlined in the following chapter, the belief that the exercise clause has supremacy over the establishment clause. Since the purpose of the First Amendment is to maximize religious liberty, and since every presumption should be made in expanding that liberty, the establishment clause should apply only when government accommodation of religion reaches the point where one or more sects have been singled out for special benefits, or when that accommodation begins to infringe on religious exercise rights.[65] The separationists, however, see the establishment clause as protecting a secular society and keeping the public presence of religion in check. Thus, whenever a perceived conflict arises between the establishment clause and the exercise clause, they give priority to the former and make every presumption in favor of limiting the public role of religion.

Texas Monthly v. Bullock presented the question of which religion clause is subordinate to the other. In Justice Brennan's view, the sales-tax exemption was unconstitutional because it gave to religion an accommodation not required by free exercise. This approach subordinated the exercise clause to the establishment clause, whereas upholding the exemption would have reversed that relationship. Since the Court viewed the exemption as nothing but a benefit to religion, it did not even consider whether that benefit would expand or diminish exercise rights. This decision is a classic example of the Court simply refusing to allow the government to assist religion affirmatively. Thus, under *Texas Monthly,* government benefits to religion can be sustained only if they flow to nonreligious groups as well, or if the accommodation is aimed only at alleviating an unquestioned free-exercise infringement.

In *Estate of Thornton v. Caldor,* the Court similarly subordinated free-exercise rights when it struck down a Connecticut law requiring employers to recognize the right of any employee not to work on a day he designated as his Sabbath.[66] The law violated the establishment clause, Justice O'Connor wrote in her concurring opinion, because it singled out Sabbath observers for special protection, even though that protection would greatly serve religious exercise.

Contrary to what *Texas Monthly* might suggest, nonmandatory accommodations of religion occur quite frequently. Municipalities, for instance, frequently adopt ordinances that protect churches.[67] In these ordinances, certain types of establishments, such as theaters, fire stations, and bars are not allowed within a certain distance of religious houses of worship. The presumption is that religious exercise is a valuable activity deserving of protection, and that minimizing the types of businesses that might be "demoralizing or annoying" to churchgoers is one way to protect it.[68] Despite this presumption, however, and in an opinion focusing more on a rigid rule of neutrality than on the protection of religious liberty, the Court in *Larkin v. Grendel's Den* invalidated a law that gave a church the right to veto the grant of a liquor license to an establishment within a five-hundred-foot radius of the church.[69]

Secular Society Is Not the Focus of the Establishment Clause

In its establishment clause jurisprudence, the Court's focus has often been disproportionately on the government. Relying upon the "advancement" element of the *Lemon* test, the Court has been too concerned with whether government might be extending some benefit to religion. Consequently, too much emphasis has been put on the government side of the equation and not enough on the religious liberty side. But in connection with the First Amendment, a governmental action is only relevant when it is infringing upon the autonomy of religious institutions or coercing individuals in their religious exercise.

Even though religious liberty should be at the center of judicial inquiry, too often the courts drift off into examining government action or intent, as if the whole point of the establishment clause is to maintain some pure type of religiously indifferent government. Many of the establishment clause doctrines focus on what the government does or how it acts, rather than on whether individual religious liberty is actually expanded or restricted. This mistaken focus occurs when courts try to determine the legislative intent of the challenged statutes, as directed by the first prong of the *Lemon* test, requiring that "a statute must have a secular legislative purpose." In *Wallace v. Jaffree,* for instance, the Court noted the possibility that some state legislatures might use false pretenses to disguise religious intentions.[70] In *Santa Fe,* the court likewise stated that it should not stop at an analysis of the text of the school district's prayer policy but should also examine whether the policy was enacted with some intent regarding the promotion of religion. But not only is the mental state of elected officials difficult to ascertain, legislative motivations should be irrelevant to establishment clause inquiries, since only the actual legislative mandates can affect religious liberty.

The only concern of the religion clauses is the effect of governmental action on the freedoms of religious believers and on the institutional autonomy of religious groups. It is religion that is the beneficiary of the First Amendment, not government or a secular society. Neither government nor secular society has any independent rights under the First Amendment religion clauses; hence, neither government nor secular society can have an equal constitutional status with religion. Unfortunately, however, the courts have become so focused on whether government is giving away any benefit to religion that they have lost sight of the only concern that really matters—the government's effect on religious liberty. Perhaps this blindness has resulted from an overemphasis on the establishment clause over the exercise clause. Perhaps it has resulted from religion's periodic trespass across a preconceived social boundary, inside of which the religious presence in society is meant to be confined. Or perhaps an overbroad interpretation of the establishment clause, extending over decades, has dulled the court's sensitivities to exercise issues. But because the two clauses must be complementary, and because the exercise clause is the primary of the two, all establishment clause cases must be decided with an eye toward the exercise element, with a focus on whether religious institutions are having their liberty restricted.

CHAPTER 8 • IF NOT NEUTRALITY, THEN WHAT?

The Case for Nonpreferential Favoritism of Religion

Some of the earliest American colonies were started as havens for religious believers. Nearly the entire educational system in eighteenth-century America was operated by religious institutions. The first liberty mentioned in the Bill of Rights is religious freedom. During the presidency of Thomas Jefferson, religious services were held in the U.S. Capitol.

There is absolutely no historical evidence to suggest that the framers of the First Amendment intended religion to be treated in the same way as any secular institution or activity. Yet, under the neutrality doctrine currently being employed in religion cases, that is exactly how the courts are interpreting the First Amendment. The neutrality doctrine prevents the government from showing any favoritism at all to religion. But this is just the opposite of what the framers wanted to achieve. The historical record indicates that the framers intended the establishment clause only to keep the government from singling out certain religious sects for preferential treatment, not to prevent the government from giving nonpreferential aid to religion in general.[1]

The modern Court has so far rejected this nonpreferential aid model of the establishment clause.[2] Although it has moved away from the separationist mindset of *Lemon,* it has refused to go any further than the neutrality approach.

Nondiscriminatory Aid to Religion

The Court has repeatedly ruled that the establishment clause prohibits the government from giving preference to certain religious sects, as well as from showing any preference to religion over nonreligion.[3] But this rule, so long asserted that it has become almost unquestioned, is only half true. History reveals that the framers intended religion to hold a special place in society and government to extend whatever support was needed to preserve that special place.

The first step in discrediting the rule forbidding any favoritism toward religion in general is to show that government does indeed have the power to assist religion. Such power has long been recognized; it is reflected in the Supreme Court's decision in *Roemer v. Board of Public Works of Maryland,* upholding a state grant program that included religious schools among its recipients. In dismissing the establishment clause arguments, the Court counseled against an overzealous application of separationist principles, stating that a "hermetic separation" of church and state is "an impossibility" and has "never been required."[4] More recently, the Court ruled that a state program does not violate the Constitution simply because it aids a religious institution.[5] Furthermore, America's "unbroken" history of giving tax exemptions for religious property—a history reaching back to colonial times—reflects a long-standing tradition of government aid to religion.[6]

The next step in analyzing the rule against nonpreferential favoritism is to ask whether, in the course of aiding religion, government may assist some religions more than others. Such a scenario would be called preferential and would obviously violate the framers' intent, and so ruled the Court in *Larson v. Va-*

lente. In that case, the Supreme Court struck down on establishment grounds a Minnesota statute that effectively discriminated against the Reverend Sun Myung Moon's Unification Church. For years, Minnesota had exempted religious organizations from state laws governing charitable solicitations. Then, in 1978, the legislature amended the law to exempt only those organizations that received more than 50 percent of their contributions from members or affiliated organizations. The legislature defended the law with the argument that it was trying to prevent abusive solicitations of the public, but the Court held that the 50-percent rule violated the establishment clause command "that one religious denomination cannot be officially preferred over another."[7] According to the Court, the statute drew an explicit distinction between religious denominations based on their sources of income, and then used that distinction to impose regulatory burdens only on certain denominations.

The final step in examining the rule against nonpreferential favoritism is to examine whether the First Amendment mandates that the government refrain from showing any favoritism to religion in general. A recent case involving a city's lease of land to the Boy Scouts shows how counterproductive a rigid application of this rule can be. In *Barnes-Wallace v. Boy Scouts of America,* a group of lesbian and agnostic parents and their scouting-aged sons sued the city of San Diego for leasing public-park land to the Boy Scouts. The lease was first executed in 1957 and provided an eighteen-acre section of land to the Boy Scouts to construct a headquarters and youth activities facility. In 2002 the lease was renegotiated and extended. Plaintiffs argued that this lease reflected an impermissible government endorsement of religion, since the Boy Scout creed included adherence to generalized religious beliefs, and since the lease to the Boy Scouts was made on favorable terms not available to every other person or organization in society.

Although the Boy Scouts did engage in religious activities, the court found that they did so from a nondenominational standpoint. The Court also found that the Boy Scouts recognized and supported all the major faith denominations. Consequently, the case was not about whether, by granting a lease to the Boy Scouts, the city was favoring one religion over another; it was about whether the city could essentially favor religion over nonreligion. And yet, despite all the educational and youth developmental programs run by the Boy Scouts, despite all the benefits conferred by the Boy Scouts on a wide range of city youth, the court struck down the lease and held that, because it constituted preferential treatment of an organization with religious programs and practices, the lease carried "the appearance" of a governmental endorsement of religion.[8]

The Special Value of Religion

Contained within the neutrality approach is the assumption that the First Amendment protects secularism and atheism as much as it does religion. What neutrality ignores is the special value of religion, a value that prompted the framers to specify religious freedom as the first liberty in the Bill of Rights.

Religion is the oldest, most enduring institution in American social life. In this role, it has often provided the social capital necessary to overcome the atomizing force of individualism. Communities fostered by religion create a valuable buffer between the state and the individual.[9] They advance the flourishing of moral principles, and they promote cultural diversity.[10] Not only does religion tend to promote voluntary compliance with secular laws, but it strengthens the American political community by fostering the bonds of connectedness.[11] Religion has also contributed to the character of democratic institutions by inculcating values essential to self-government—values that stem from a deep belief in the dignity of all human beings created in God's image.[12]

Since America's founding, religion has provided the primary

foundation for civic virtue. Yet, as American culture has become more secular, with ethical codes becoming more law-based than morality-based, a minimum level of public ethics has become both more difficult to maintain and less frequently achieved. Experience has shown that without a religious foundation ethical codes lose their strength and authority. This lesson is illustrated by the U.S. Army's experience in the ethical and moral training of its troops. In an attempt to improve troop behavior and military image, the army in 1947 instituted "Character Guidance," a program grounded on moral and religious values that trained soldiers in morality and citizenship. During the late 1960s, however, the ACLU complained about the religious nature of the army program. As a result, the army tried to diminish the religious component, and in 1971 changed the name of the program to "Human Self-Development." But its attempt to establish moral codes that were not religiously based was unsuccessful, and in 1977 the entire program was officially discontinued.[13]

A healthy democracy cannot survive without a social value system that supports the communal interests and bonds of that society.[14] Religion helps counteract the destructive urges of individual narcissism that elevate self-centeredness to the point of drowning out any sense of public responsibility. It is the strongest known antidote to a culture of the self that belittles duty to others and to the public good. According to recent studies, a large majority of Americans believe that religion helps improve individual behavior and conduct, and that "more religion" is the best way to decrease crime, greed, and materialism.[15] Conversely, Americans often name the loss of religion as a leading cause of such social problems as drugs and crime.[16] Not surprisingly, with the distancing of religious influences from the public sphere over the past several decades, society has witnessed dramatically higher levels of violence, sex abuse, illegitimacy, and other manifestations of cultural dysfunction.[17]

In addition to its social role, religion plays a vital political role. It is not only an important source of viewpoints in the process of democratic self-government[18] but has been a powerful political motivator behind some of the nation's greatest crusades. Political movements motivated by religious inspiration and supported by religious belief and institutions include the Social Gospel movement, women's suffrage, nearly all the peace movements, the child welfare campaign, and the demand for freer immigration of refugees. Religious organizations energized both the abolitionist movement of the nineteenth century and the civil rights movement of the twentieth. In the Southern Christian Leadership Conference, the organization that provided the leadership and infrastructure of the civil right movement, twenty-one of the twenty-five original officers were ordained ministers, including its president, Dr. Martin Luther King Jr.[19] And as exemplified by King's renowned "God is Marching On" speech, religious imagery infused the movement. The religious principles and character of the civil rights movement, perhaps more than any other factor, inspired the majority culture to oppose racial segregation.[20]

Religion also adds to the vitality of a democracy by serving important public functions such as health, welfare, and education. Religious organizations operate hospitals, nursing homes, halfway houses, counseling and rehabilitation programs.[21] Even courts ruling against the free-exercise claims of religious groups have recognized that the missions of certain churches compel them "to engage in corporal works of mercy, which consist especially in feeding the hungry, sheltering the homeless, clothing the naked, visiting the sick and imprisoned and burying the dead."[22]

Long before government bureaucracies became involved in providing social welfare services, religious institutions performed that role. They continue to do so, often achieving goals that the state cannot.[23] This ability was highlighted in *Zelman v. Simmons-Harris,* the Cleveland school-voucher case. Prompting the voucher program was a recognition of the "crisis of magnitude" that existed in the Cleveland public school system, where only 10 percent of ninth graders were able to pass a proficiency test and more than two-thirds of high school students failed to graduate.[24] The voucher program passed with the strong support of inner-city minorities who hoped to escape the chronically failing urban schools.[25]

Studies have revealed that most urban public school students around the nation are failing to perform at even the most basic level of achievement and that black parents strongly support school choice, with 66 percent saying they would switch their children from public to private school if money were not an obstacle.[26] An investigation commissioned by the National Center for Education Statistics shows that private schools produce better cognitive outcomes (even after controlling for the family background of the students), provide a safer and more structured learning environment, and have less racial segregation. For instance, minority students who attend Catholic schools do better than their public school peers, and are more likely to graduate, go on to college, and earn a degree. Numerous studies have found that Catholic schools can successfully educate the same minority populations that urban public schools could not.[27]

In *Zelman,* Justice Thomas observed that "failing urban public schools disproportionately affect minority children most in need of educational opportunity." He warned that the "failure to provide education to poor urban children perpetuates a vicious cycle of poverty, dependence, criminality, and alienation that continues for the remainder of their lives." He cited data from Cleveland showing that religious schools are more educationally effective than public schools. Whereas 95 percent of the eighth graders in Catholic schools passed a state reading test, only 57 percent of their public school peers did; similarly, whereas 75 percent of the Catholic school students passed a math proficiency test, their public school peers had only a 22 percent passage rate.[28] Furthermore, the average cost of sending a child to a religious school was considerably lower than the cost of public school. In the Cleveland program, for example, religious schools received a maximum of $2,250 per student in public funding, whereas public schools were allocated $7,746 per student.[29]

In addition to education, prison operation and offender rehabilitation has been an area in which religious organizations have proved especially effective. Take, for instance, the case of Prison Fellowship Ministries (PFM), a nondenominational group founded in 1976 by former Nixon aide Charles Colson, who embraced evangelical Christianity while serving time in a federal prison in Alabama for his part in the Watergate cover-up. PFM volunteers and staffers operate in prisons across the country. Among other functions, they teach faith-based courses that show inmates how religious conviction can help them stay off drugs, care for their children, and hold down a steady job.[30] A civil liberties group, Americans United for Separation of Church and State, filed suit to stop a PFM operation in Iowa, but a barrier to the lawsuit "was finding a prisoner who wanted to complain." Another obstacle to the suit was that PFM does a far better job rehabilitating prisoners than the government does. Studies show that PFM inmates, once released, are half as likely to return to the criminal justice system than other inmates.[31]

Reasons to Favor Religion

By encouraging a diverse political landscape composed of many competing groups and interests, James Madison hoped to achieve pluralism and avoid the threat of majority tyranny;[32] he believed a thriving pluralism would make it difficult for any one group to dominate politics. He saw religion in much the same way. The way to guard against the oppression of minority religions, Madison believed, is to promote a robust religious pluralism, with a "multiplicity of sects."[33] And the way to achieve such a "multiplicity of sects" is to accommodate and support them. As one legal scholar has noted, accommodations "do not constitute an establishment of religion, which tends toward unification of authority in state and church, but rather they foster diversity of nongovernmental organizations."[34]

Religion should be encouraged and favored because it provides important social benefits and discharges various state burdens. Religious organizations cultivate public-spiritedness. As recognized by the courts, religious organizations foster in citizens the virtues of benevolence, charity, generosity, love of neighbor, sympathy for those in trouble and distress, and beneficence to the poor.[35] Polls show that evangelical Christians, for instance, are more likely to contribute to charities that help the poor; and in the traumatized countries of Africa, religious groups are the bulwark of the health care system.[36] Religion also inculcates public morality and instructs officials on social justice and ethical standards.[37] Religious organizations even fulfill burdens of foreign aid through their programs for foreign missions and disaster relief.[38]

By giving special recognition to religion, the government does not just help a useful social institution to survive, it adheres to one of the most fundamental laws of sovereignty. The framers considered religious duties more important than secular duties.[39] As the Declaration of Independence states, the duties owed to God transcend those owed to any temporal authority.[40] To the religious believer the duty to God is supreme, and religious claims precede and transcend any claims of the state.[41] Thus, even though the state cannot determine the truth of religious beliefs, it should respect them and afford them every possible benefit of the doubt. As the philosopher Blaise Pascal once argued, the risk of not respecting religious beliefs is a risk not worth taking.[42] However, the state cannot simply ignore religious claims without essentially treating them as false.

The state should be able to support religion in general because of religion's ability to solve problems that the government cannot solve. In *Zelman,* the Court recognized that "any objective observer familiar with the full history and context of the Ohio program would reasonably view it as one aspect of a broader undertaking to assist poor children in failed schools, not as an endorsement of religious schooling in general." As Justice O'Connor declared in her concurring opinion, the Court should not "ignore how the educational system in Cleveland actually functions." Even the challenging parties conceded that the voucher program was "enacted for the valid secular purpose of providing educational assistance to poor children in a demonstrably failing public school system."[43] Consequently, the establishment clause should not deny to government the flexibility to let religion address certain social problems. The First Amendment was not intended to exclude religious approaches to social problems, or to deny society the benefit of religious contributions to secular projects.

Operating as it must with a kind of religious blindness, the neutrality doctrine can deprive democracy of one of its strongest institutions. In *American Civil Liberties Union of Louisiana v. Foster,* an establishment clause challenge was brought against religious organizations participating in a federal program that allocated funds for teaching and promoting sexual abstinence among youth. The objection was that these organizations, in teaching abstinence, incorporated certain religious messages and values.[44] But then, if abstinence is a real social goal, no one can teach it like religion can.

Even though religion-based programs have been noticeably successful in addressing drug and alcohol addiction, the courts have often refused to allow public funding of those programs. In *Warner v. Orange County Department of Probation,* the plaintiff, who had committed three alcohol-related driving offenses within approximately one year, was ordered by a sentencing judge to attend an Alcoholics Anonymous program.[45] But because AA possesses a religious nature—stressing the concept of a "higher power" and that recovery from alcoholism requires a "spiritual awakening"—the plaintiff brought an establishment clause challenge to the judge's order. Even though the reviewing court found that much of the religious component of AA was nondenominational and that the effectiveness of the AA program was beyond doubt, it nonetheless held that the requirement of attendance at AA meetings amounted to an establishment of religion.

Another example of a court's refusal to allow the government to take advantage of the special talents of religious organizations is found in *Freedom from Religion Foundation, Inc. v. McCallum.* At issue in *McCallum* was a state grant to an organization called Faith Works, which provided long-term residential treatment to drug and alcohol addicts in Milwaukee, Wisconsin. As a Christian faith-based treatment center, Faith Works incorporated a voluntary religious component in its recovery program. Counselors welcomed discussions regarding participants' spiritual issues but never required such discussions. Nor did counselors try to convert participants to any particular religious sect. Faith Works served people of all religious backgrounds; it did not impose any religious tests or preconditions on the participants. Notwithstanding these voluntary aspects, however, the spiritual component of Faith Works was seen as a significant factor in achieving the program's high rate of success. Yet, despite the fact that Faith Works was the only program in Milwaukee offering a long-term residential program, and that all participants were free to choose whether to accept treatment at Faith Works or to attend some alternative facility, the court still ruled that government funding of Faith Works was a violation of the establishment clause.

In *McCallum,* the court found that the public funding amounted to governmental indoctrination of religion, even though participation in religious activities was not required and even though potential residents were informed of the spiritual component of Faith Works prior to their being admitted. This finding relied on the formalistic direct/indirect distinction of the neutrality doctrine. Because the government funds went directly to Faith Works, instead of indirectly through some kind of voucher system, the court held that an establishment of religion had occurred. The court ruled that an organization's "religious indoctrination" (resulting merely from its staff members' "encouraging participants to integrate spirituality into their recovery program") is attributable to the government whenever that organization receives direct, unrestricted public funds.[46] However, this attribution element is yet another diversion from the essential nature of the establishment clause, which serves two primary functions: to protect the institutional autonomy of religions from governmental interference; and to prevent the government from singling out certain denominations for preferential treatment. If "religious indoctrination" does occur as a result of some governmental action, then it is the exercise clause that should come into play.

The Accommodation Doctrine and Nonpreferentialism

Unlike the neutrality doctrine and its religious blindness, accommodation tries to understand the special needs of religious exercise and support governmental efforts to facilitate that exercise. In *Zorach v. Clauson,* Justice Douglas articulated the constitutional basis for accommodating religion and the religious needs of citizens:

> We are a religious people whose institutions presuppose a Supreme Being. . . . When the state encourages religious instruction or cooperates with religious authorities by adjusting the schedule of public events to sectarian needs, it follows the best of our traditions. For it then respects the religious nature of our people and accommodates the public service to their spiritual needs. To hold that it may not would be to find in the Constitution a requirement that the government show a callous indifference to religious groups. That would be preferring those who believe in no religion over those who do believe.[47]

Accommodation is a concept the courts have long accepted, though to varying degrees; but inherent within any accommodation is a preferential treatment for religion. In *Arver v. United*

States, the Court upheld certain religious exemptions contained in the Selective Service Act. This spirit of accommodation continued in *Zorach v. Clauson,* where the Court upheld a public school program allowing students release time to attend religious classes off the school's premises. In *Walz v. Tax Commission,* the Court sustained a state tax exemption of church property, ruling that it did not constitute an establishment of religion. *Transworld Airlines v. Hardison* upheld Title VII provisions that required employers to make reasonable accommodations to their employees' religious needs, and *Presiding Bishop v. Amos* exempted religious organizations from liability for religious discrimination in hiring decisions.

Governmental accommodation of religion provides a foundation for nonpreferential favoritism of religion, because the former cannot exist without accepting the basic premise of the latter. In *Stark v. Independent School District No. 640,* the court held that a school district's arrangement with a small religious group, whereby religious parents were allowed to send their children to a public school containing one multiage classroom that conformed to the group's religious tenets opposing the use of computers, did not amount to an unconstitutional establishment.[48] The religious group provided the building to be used as a public school, open to anyone who wanted to attend, on the condition that the state provide the books and a teacher. The accommodation made by the state, and approved by the court, involved the state's agreement to operate the school in accordance with the group's religious objection to the use of technological devices such as computers and televisions.

Another example of accommodation occurred in *Children's Healthcare Is a Legal Duty, Inc. v. Min De Parle,* where the court upheld provisions in the federal Medicare and Medicaid Acts that gave nonmedical benefits to patients treated in religious nonmedical health care facilities.[49] These provisions, opponents argued, were designed to accommodate Christian Scientists. But perhaps there is no clearer example of nonpreferential favoritism of religion than in the special accommodations made by the military, which employs more than fourteen hundred ministers of eighty-six different religious denominations and operates some five hundred chapels.[50]

Throughout American history, courts have endorsed various types of accommodations. However, they were generally more prone to do so prior to *Lemon*. In the wake of the separationist influence of *Lemon*, they have been far more guarded in their willingness to accommodate.[51] But this hesitancy often lacks a logical consistency, other than a blind devotion to the neutrality doctrine. For instance, in *Barense v. Town of Barrington*, the court held that a town's sixty-year practice of providing free snowplowing and trash collection for all churches and synagogues violated the establishment clause.[52] By providing a benefit to religious entities that was not available to nonreligious entities, the town unconstitutionally preferred religion to nonreligion. But this singular focus on whether religion in general was receiving some benefit diverted the court's attention from the fundamental issue of whether free snowplowing could ever rise to the level of an establishment of religion.

Although the accommodation doctrine recognizes the special nature of religion in general, its application tends to be specifically focused on clearing away obstacles to the free-exercise needs of religious groups. The nonpreferential aid model, on the other hand, goes one step further and allows completely discretionary benefits to be given to religion (such as free snowplowing), as long as those benefits are given without discrimination among sects.

The separationists argue that accommodation is just establishment in disguise.[53] But as Justice Rehnquist once wrote, "governmental assistance which does not have the effect of inducing religious belief, but instead merely accommodates or implements an independent religious choice does not . . . violate the Establishment Clause."[54] And as Justice Brennan admitted in his *Texas Monthly* opinion, the courts should be able to uphold some accommodations that are not actually mandated by the exercise clause.[55] Yet the Court has never clarified the relation between permissible and mandatory accommodations.[56] This is where nonpreferentialism comes into play—under this doctrine, all nonpreferential accommodations, whether mandatory or voluntary, are constitutional unless they have a coercive effect on someone else's religious exercise.

Although accommodation is usually employed to prevent a free-exercise violation, the legislative branch should be given the flexibility to address and alleviate burdens that the courts have not yet held to be free-exercise violations. The focus should be on how best to achieve religious liberty. And the presumption should be to accommodate, up until the point that such accommodation begins to coerce the free-exercise rights of others. A government committed to religious pluralism must be able to recognize and accommodate religious needs, even if those needs do not fit within the judiciary's definition of "burden" under the exercise clause.[57]

Contrary to the religious blinders worn by the neutrality doctrine, accommodation seeks to discern the social and political realities of modern life that affect religious practices. Indeed, given the pervasiveness of government in modern society, favoritism may need to be given to religion just to preserve its relative status or role in society. For instance, the government should not be allowed to crowd out religious organizations from their historic involvement in social welfare work; yet such a result could easily occur if the government funds only nonreligious approaches to social problems.

When the First Amendment was ratified, government had little or no involvement in education or social welfare. These functions were predominantly left to the private sphere, where religious institutions played a leading role. But with the rise of the welfare-regulatory state, the spheres of religion and government were no longer distant and distinct. The state had now "extended its regulatory jurisdiction over broad aspects of life that formerly had been private and frequently religious, creating conflicts with both religious institutions and the religiously motivated activity of individuals." This takeover of religion's traditional functions, without a corresponding approach of accommodation, constricts the ability of religious groups to perform the social duties that their religious beliefs command them to perform.[58]

The Logic of Accommodation Refutes Neutrality

Accommodation and neutrality are two concepts fundamentally at odds. Adhering to the neutrality doctrine, while at the same time trying to accommodate religion, can only lead to illogical and confusing results. Such confusion is illustrated in a comparison between the decision in *Stark v. Independent School District No. 640,* where the court allowed the state to set up a separate school catering to a religious sect's opposition to technology, and *Barense v. Town of Barrington,* where the court ruled that a town's provision of free snowplowing to all religious institutions amounted to an unconstitutional establishment of religion.

There are several types of accommodation. The first type involves seemingly mandatory accommodations—those required by the exercise clause.[59] But a strict application of the neutrality doctrine prohibits even this kind of accommodation, because it grants to religion certain benefits not given to nonreligion. Yet if this kind of accommodation is not allowed, then free-exercise rights will be sacrificed merely for the sake of some establishment clause theory.

A second type of accommodation involves the permissive kind; these are accommodations not required by the exercise clause but also not prohibited by the establishment clause. For example, regarding tax exemptions for religious property, the Court has generally concluded that while they are neither proscribed by the establishment clause nor prescribed by the exercise clause, they are nonetheless constitutionally permissible.[60] Again, however, without a constitutional model permitting nonpreferential aid to religion, such accommodations will be on shaky ground. The safer and more constitutionally consistent approach would be to make every presumption in favor of religious exercise. Such a presumption would mean that nonpreferential favoritism of religion in general is constitutional unless it violates free-exercise rights. The crucial issue here, in terms of limitations on government action, is not whether benefits have been granted to religion in general, but whether government has actually coerced religious actors.

Another way to look at this issue is to consider the costs of not accommodating. It may often be impossible to know if in fact the exercise clause demands a particular accommodation. Or perhaps it is impossible to know just how much a nonmandatory accommodation may actually expand free-exercise rights. But the First Amendment mandates that religion be given every benefit of the doubt; it suggests that the costs of not accommodating religion may be too high even to risk. Take, for instance, the case of *Leebaert v. Harrington,* where parents of a seventh-grade student sought for religious reasons to have their child excused from a mandatory sex education course.[61] The parents' religious principles were opposed to various subjects covered in the health and sex education course, and they did not want to have their child exposed to such material. They did not seek to alter the course, they simply wanted their child excused from it. But the court refused to grant such an exemption, claiming that to do so would be to give parents a kind of veto power over the decisions of school authorities. According to the court, the parents could always send their child to private school, even if the cost might be prohibitive.

A similar refusal to accommodate, and one in which the neutrality doctrine was used to prejudice religious exercise, occurred in *Smith v. Fair Employment and Housing Commission*, involving a lawsuit brought against a landlord whose religious beliefs prevented her from renting a duplex to an unmarried couple. The landlord, a devout Christian who believed it a sin to lease her units to cohabitating couples, was charged with violating a state law prohibiting discrimination on the basis of marital status. The lower court had sided with the landlord, finding that the statute imposed a substantial burden on the landlord's religious exercise. But the California Supreme Court overruled that decision, holding the statute to be both generally applicable and neutral toward religion. The court acknowledged that the law imposed burdens on the landlord's religious beliefs, but argued that to rule in favor of the landlord would be to deny the prospective tenants "the full choice of available housing accommodations enjoyed by others in the rental market."[62] Thus, in the court's judgment, it was better to give a prospective renter the full option of renting every one of hundreds or thousands of available rental units in the locale than it was to protect the religious beliefs of a single landlord who rented out only two duplex buildings. Clearly, this was not a decision in which every benefit of the doubt was given to religious liberty.

The Danger of Nonpreferential Aid

The issue of whether the First Amendment permits nonpreferential aid to religion is a constitutional one. Settling this issue, however, does not necessarily answer an even more basic and profound question: namely, whether it is sound policy for the government to extend particular kinds of aid to religion, and whether such aid might corrupt religious organizations that become addicted to it. Indeed, governmental support of religion could be a wolf in sheep's clothing. In many European countries, nonpreferential support is the standard practice; but in nearly all those countries, religion is in decline, in part because people perceive that it could never make it on its own without such government support. In America, on the other hand, religion is strong because it has had to survive on its own; it has not become dependent on government, nor has it become corrupted by the demands of government. Nonetheless, the issue of whether to seek and accept government aid is for religious institutions to make—it is not for the First Amendment to prohibit outright.

CONCLUSION

Equal protection is in vogue, and the judicial use of neutrality in religion cases coincides with a larger social trend toward equality and away from any discriminatory treatment. Yet, while neutrality marks a welcome change from *Lemon* and its hostility toward religion, it still does not capture the spirit and intent of the First Amendment.

As the historical record demonstrates, the First Amendment does not place religion and nonreligion on the same level. It does not give the same importance to each, nor does it command the government to treat them the same way. Given the framers' belief in the value of religion to a democracy, the First Amendment was certainly not intended to create or protect a secular state; it was meant to preserve the vibrant religious life of the nation and the public expression of religious values.

In the latter half of the twentieth century, courts began turning away from the historical roots of the First Amendment, even though virtually every member of the Supreme Court "has subscribed to the view that political and moral traditions are relevant to defining constitutional rights."[1] But this disregard for historical tradition has called into doubt every judicial ruling on religion. As Robert Bork wrote, constitutional freedoms do not depend upon the pronouncements of judges, they depend "upon their acceptance by the American people, and a major factor in that acceptance is the belief that these liberties are inseparable from the founding of the nation."[2]

The neutrality approach confines religion to a role defined by secular institutions. It puts false boundaries around the public space allotted to religion. But nothing in the text or history of the First Amendment suggests that it was intended to prevent society from taking advantage of the special services and talents of religion, which provide a valuable alternative to the secular state. Under neutrality, there is much less outright discrimination against religion than there was under *Lemon,* but there is also no recognition of the special value or role of religion in our constitutional scheme. In a way, neutrality is an attempt to sterilize religion, to make it just like every other institution or activity in society. The neutrality doctrine reflects a simplistic compromise on the religion question—an attempt not to fulfill the true spirit of the First Amendment but simply to minimize conflict.

The establishment clause model presented in this book advocates a much narrower reach than do any of the models currently being used by the U.S. Supreme Court. It does not apply to any point of interaction between the state and religion or religious expression. Instead, it focuses strictly on state interference in the *institutional* autonomy of religious organizations. This interference must have some kind of permanent or ongoing institutional effect in order to constitute an improper establishment of religion. Absent this effect, the exercise clause will probably be the appropriate measure of the governmental action.

One of the mistakes of establishment clause jurisprudence has been the separation of the clause from religious liberty. Rather than seeing the clause as an institutional complement to the individual protections of the exercise clause, rather than interpreting the clause as prohibiting a different type of religious coercion, the courts essentially took the establishment clause away from religion and gave it to an amorphous entity called "secular society." In doing so, the courts turned the establishment clause from a protector of religious liberty to a check on religious liberty.

Since religious liberty is the foremost concern of the First Amendment's religion clauses, and since the exercise clause is the one more broadly focused on religious liberty, that clause is the primary one. Therefore the establishment clause can never properly be employed to limit the free exercise of religion; it can only cover those institutional settings in which the exercise clause might not be discernibly applicable. This theory, as set forth in Chapter 7 above, articulates the positive reach of the establishment clause—what it strives to achieve within the scheme of the First Amendment. The nonpreferential aid model outlined in Chapter 8 simply describes what the establishment clause was not meant to do. Contrary to how it has been applied in the past, the establishment clause should not be used to prevent the state from giving preferential aid to religion in general, as long as that aid is not discriminatory among individual sects. Under the First Amendment, the government is not prohibited from favoring religion over nonreligion; all the establishment clause is meant to ban is governmental coercion of institutional religious freedom. It is the religious, not the nonreligious, who are the beneficiaries of the establishment clause; it does not guarantee to secular groups that they will always receive any and every benefit given to religion.

The courts have come partway toward recognizing the nonpreferential favoritism model. They have ruled that government-funded programs are not unconstitutional just because these programs may aid religion, but they have never specifically endorsed the idea of nonpreferential favoritism of religion in general, even though history shows a clear difference between establishing a religion and supporting a preexisting religious presence in society. The essential distinction in government funding cases should not be whether the funds are given directly or indirectly to the religious organization but whether the aid is to finance the *status* or *institutional survival* of a religion, or whether the aid finances a particular *function* performed by a religious organization. And in the latter respect, it is the *goal* (secular) of the function that is important, not the *means* (religious) used to achieve it.

After decades of confusing jurisprudence on this subject, the courts should abandon such formalistic establishment tests as the "perception of endorsement" and "attribution of indoctrination." The religion clauses are about coercion, not perception. If perception is a problem, then it needs to be a matter of education. It needs to be openly debated in the legislatures. When there exists a misperception about government's motives or actions, the solution is to educate. Religious presence should be tolerated, not banished. If anything, the French experience should be instructive enough. The French government's attempts to curtail public religious expression are causing severe tension with its growing Islamic population.

Under the spirit of the First Amendment, it is better to favor all religion than to risk discriminating against one or more religions, or to risk eliminating a religious presence from the nation's public life. It is better to risk the incidental occurrences of some religious proselytizing than to censor religious viewpoints. Consequently, the government should make it easier to exercise religious beliefs than not. The burden should be on challengers to prove an impermissible establishment of religion, not on religious practitioners to prove that no establishment has taken place.

One advantage of the more limited establishment clause model proposed here is that it would end the accommodation conflict and all the endless disputes over how "religious" an organization is, or whether that organization receives some "advancement" through a government program, or whether some aid might result in some perception of attribution, or whether some religious organization receiving aid is somehow conveying some religious message, or whether the nonreligious recipients of a government program are sufficiently numerous in comparison to the religious recipients. As the post-*Lemon* legacy has shown, a confusing and inconsistent case law can easily be exploited by antireligion forces to bring about infringements on religious liberty that would not be allowed with any other fundamental freedoms, such as freedom of speech.

According to Robert Nagel, the purpose of judicial review in constitutional cases is to articulate clear and enduring principles and to avoid endless controversy and uncertainty. "Ultimately, the rule of law requires more than official compliance with judicial decrees; it requires widespread habits of mind that conceive of the announced law as being authoritatively settled even as it evolves."[3] It is for precisely this reason that the courts need to adopt more tolerant religious doctrines that are well grounded in history and consistent with the nation's constitutional experience.

American identity is intertwined with its religious heritage. The nation's political values and social mores are rooted in religious principles. It is not within the province of the courts to effect a cultural transformation in America similar to that which has occurred in much of Europe. There, amid a tidal wave of secularism, churches have been reduced to tourist stops. In *The Cube and the Cathedral,* George Weigel describes a European culture that has become almost hostile to Christianity. Indeed, the drafters of the European Union's seventy-thousand-word constitution refused even to acknowledge Europe's Christian tradition or influence. Perhaps not surprisingly, this radical secularism is coinciding with growing anti-Semitism and anti-Islamic sentiments in Europe, along with an increasing hesitancy to take any bold stand or significant sacrifice for freedom and democracy around the world.

NOTES

Notes to Introduction

1. *Walz ex. rel. Walz v. Egg Harbor Township Board of Education,* 187 F.Supp.2d 232 (D.N.J. 2002).

2. *Oxford v. Beaumont Independent School District,* 224 F.Supp.2d 1099 (E.D. Tex. 2002).

3. *Rusk v. Crestview Local Schools,* 220 F.Supp.2d 854 (N.D. Ohio 2002).

4. *Skarin v. Woodbine Community School District,* 204 F.Supp.2d 1195 (S.D. Iowa 2002).

5. *Barense v. Town of Barrington,* 955 F.Supp. 151 (D.N.H. 1996).

6. Stephen L. Carter, "Reflections on the Separation of Church and State," 44 *Arizona Law Review* 293, 299 (2002).

7. George W. Dent Jr., "Of God and Caesar: The Free Exercise Rights of Public School Students," 43 *Case Western Reserve Law Review* 707, 720 (1993).

8. Mary Ann Glendon, "Law, Communities, and the Religious Freedom Language of the Constitution," 60 *George Washington Law Review* 672, 679 (1992). But nowhere, according to Professor Glendon, have the "deleterious effects of an excessively narrow view of free exercise and an inflated concept of establishment been more apparent than in the cases involving education." "In a judicial pincer movement, one line of decisions requires the public schools to be rigorously secular, while another has struck down most forms of public assistance to parents of private school students who desire to protect their children from a public educational system that is often actively promoting values that are profoundly at odds with the family's religious convictions" (679). The contorted, confusing, historically contradictory course of establishment doctrine in the twentieth century began with the decision in *Everson v. Board of Education,* 330 U.S. 1, 16 (1947), which was the Court's first formal foray into what would become a jungle of establishment clause jurisprudence. This marked the first judicial appearance of the phrase "wall of separation between church and state." It was a phrase that

has proved to be the curse of establishment clause jurisprudence over the past half-century.

9. Mark E. Chopko, "Religious Access to Public Programs and Governmental Funding," 60 *George Washington Law Review* 645, 654 (1992). "Each of the three prongs of the test . . . invite distrust of one or the other of the actors in the church-state drama" (656).

10. *Wolman v. Walter*, 433 U.S. 229, 248–51 (1977); *Meek v. Pittenger*, 421 U.S. 349, 362–66 (1975).

11. *Wolman*, 433 U.S. at 252–55.

12. One scholar has referred to this distinction as the "two plastic reindeer rule." Richard S. Myers, "Reflections on the Teaching of Civic Virtue in the Public Schools," 74 *University of Detroit Mercy Law Review* 63, 64 (1996).

13. *Sante Fe Independent School District v. Doe*, 530 U.S. 290 (2000). For a discussion of this case, see Douglas Kmiec, "Free Speech, Religion, and the Gridiron: The Supreme Court Tackles School Prayer," *Preview U.S. Supreme Court Cases*, March 8, 2000, 324.

14. *Adler v. Duval County School Board*, 250 F.3d 1330 (11th Cir. 2001).

15. Andrew Koppelman, "No Expressly Religious Orthodoxy: A Response to Steven D. Smith," 78 *Chicago-Kent Law Review* 729 (2003).

16. Linda Greenhouse, "Justices Consider Religious Displays," *New York Times*, March 31, 2005, A18.

17. John Fonte, "Manifesto of Hope," *National Review*, Dec. 31, 2004, 41.

18. *Lee v. Weisman*, 505 U.S. 577, 594 (1992).

19. *Engel v. Vitale*, 370 U.S. 421 (1962).

20. The prayer composed by the regents read: "Almighty God, we acknowledge our dependence upon Thee, and we beg Thy blessings upon us, our parents, our teachers and our Country." Ibid., 422.

21. *Roberts v. Madigan*, 921 F.2d 1047, 1059, 1049 (10th Cir. 1990).

22. *Bishop v. Aronov*, 926 F.2d 1066, 1068–69 (11th Cir. 1991).

23. For religious prayer and symbol cases, the coercion test of the free-exercise clause, and not the endorsement test of the establishment clause, is appropriate. "An analysis of the propriety of state compulsion traditionally has been central to any understanding of claims surrounding the Free Exercise Clause." Stanley Ingber, "Religious Children and the Inevitable Compulsion of Public Schools," 43 *Case Western Reserve Law Review* 773, 776 (1993).

24. *Church on the Rock v. City of Albuquerque*, 84 F.3d 1273 (10th Cir. 1996); *C.H. v. Oliva*, 990 F.Supp. 341, 353–54 (D.N.J. 1997); and *Nichol v. Arin Intermediate Unit 28*, 268 F.Supp.2d 536 (W.D. Pa 2003), respectively.

25. *Everson*, 330 U.S. 1, 8 (stating that the "establishment of religion clause of the First Amendment means at least this: neither a state nor the Federal Government can set up a church").

26. Dean Murphy, "God, American History and a Fifth-Grade Class," *New York Times*, Dec. 5, 2004, Week in Review sec., 4.

27. Michelle Malkin, "Grace, Gratitude and God," *Washington Times*, Nov. 25, 2004.

28. *Zelman v. Simmons-Harris*, 536 U.S. 639, 686 (Stevens, J., dissenting); ibid., 717 (Breyer, dissenting).

29. Just as the establishment and exercise clauses are but two aspects of a single First Amendment religion mandate, there is but a single concern of both clauses: the protection against government coercion of individual and institutional religious conduct.

30. Washington quoted in Walker P. Whitman, *A Christian History of the American Republic* (Boston: Green Leaf Press, 1948), 42; Webster and Lincoln quoted in Harold K. Lane, *Liberty! Cry Liberty!* (Boston: Lamb and Lamb Tractarian Society, 1939), 31 and 32, respectively; Theodore Roosevelt, *The Foes of Our Own Household* (New York: Charles Scribner's Sons, 1926), 134.

Notes to Chapter 1

1. *Reynolds v. United States,* 98 U.S. 145, 161 (1878) (stating that religious beliefs are inviolate); *Prince v. Massachusetts,* 321 U.S. 158, 166 (1944) (stating that a parent's right to raise his or her children according to the parent's religion is fundamental); Rodney K. Smith and Patrick A. Shea, "Religion and the Press: "Keeping First Amendment Values in Balance," 2002 *Utah Law Review* 177, 179 (2002) (stating that the "exercise of conscience . . . [is] of the greatest highest priority").

2. *Lee v. Weisman,* 505 U.S. 577, 591 (1992).

3. *Minersville School District v. Gobitis,* 310 U.S. 586 (1940).

4. *Virginia State Board of Education v. Barnette,* 319 U.S. 624 (1943).

5. *Sable Communications v. FCC,* 492 U.S. 115 (1989).

6. *United States v. Playboy Entertainment Group, Inc.,* 529 U.S. 803 (2000).

7. *Roberts v. Madigan,* 921 F.2d 1047 (10th Cir. 1990).

8. *C.H. v. Oliva,* 226 F.3d 198 (3d Cir. 2000).

9. *Aguilar v. Felton,* 473 U.S. 402 (1985) (ruling that the provision of the program to religious school students constituted an illegal establishment of religion).

10. *Sante Fe Independent School District v. Doe,* 530 U.S. 290 (2000).

11. *Everson v. Board of Education,* 330 U.S. 1 (1947).

12. Daniel O. Conkle, "Toward a General Theory of the Establishment Clause," 82 *Northwestern University Law Review* 1113, 1134 (1988).

13. Carl Esbeck, "Dissent and Disestablishment: The Church-State Settlement in the Early American Republic," 2004 *Brigham Young University Law Review* 1385, 1576. The establishment clause "was never meant to restrain the residual power of the states" (1578). Professor Hamburger also discusses why the Fourteenth Amendment did not incorporate the establishment clause; see Philip Hamburger, *Separation of Church and State* (Cambridge: Harvard University Press, 2002), 436.

14. Charles Fairman was one of the first scholars to make this argument. See Charles Fairman, "Does the Fourteenth Amendment Incorporate the Bill of Rights? The Original Understanding," 2 *Stanford Law Review* 1, 5 (1949).

15. Conkle, "General Theory of the Establishment Clause," 1137.

16. Ibid.

17. Stephen L. Carter, "Reflections on the Separation of Church and State," 44 *Arizona Law Review* 293, 299 (2002).

18. George W. Dent Jr., "Of God and Caesar: The Free Exercise Rights of Public School Students," 43 *Case Western Reserve Law Review* 707, 720 (1993).

19. Richard John Neuhaus, "A New Order of Religious Freedom," 60 *George Washington Law Review* 620, 630 (1992).

20. Esbeck, "Dissent and Disestablishment," 1586.

21. Michael Paulsen, "Lemon Is Dead," 43 *Case Western Reserve Law Review* 795, 798 (1993). Paulsen goes on to argue that if "nonestablishment and free exercise are understood as correlative rather than contradictory principles, it is logical to read the clauses as mirror-image prohibitions on government prescription and proscription, respectively, of the same thing—religious exercise" (808).

22. Ibid., 798.

23. Carl Esbeck also argues that the exercise and establishment clauses do not collide with each other; they reinforce each other. Esbeck, "Dissent and Disestablishment," 1389.

24. *Wisconsin v. Yoder,* 406 U.S. 205, 214 (1972).

25. Neuhaus, "New Order of Religious Freedom," 627.

26. Ibid. Neuhaus further argues that "once we forget that the establishment provision is a means and instrument in support of free exercise, it is a short step to talk about the supposed conflict or tension between the two provisions. From there it is a short step to the claim that the two parts of the Religion Clause are pitted against one another and must somehow be balanced. . . . [and t]hus establishment becomes the master of the free exercise that it was designed to serve" (628).

27. Michael W. McConnell, "Accommodation of Religion: An Update and a Response to the Critics," 60 *George Washington Law Review* 685, 690 (1992) (stating that "the concern of the Religion Clauses is with the preservation of the autonomy of religious life").

28. Under *Boy Scouts of America v. Dale,* 530 U.S. 640, 648 (2000), the right of expressive association is impaired if the government "affects in a significant way the group's ability to advocate public or private viewpoints."

29. Rodney A. Smolla, *Smolla and Nimmer on Freedom of Speech* (Deerfield, Ill.: Clark Boardman Callahan, 2003), 2–66.

30. *Sable Communications,* 492 U.S. 115 (holding that a ban on indecent telephone messages violates the First Amendment since the statute's denial of adult access to such messages exceeds that which is necessary to serve the compelling interest of preventing minors from being exposed to the messages).

31. *Arkansas Writers' Project, Inc. v. Ragland,* 481 U.S. 221, 228 (1987).

32. *Clarkson v. Town of Florence,* 198 F.Supp.2d 997, 1006 (E.D. Wis. 2002) (stating that such "laws by no means receive a free pass under the First Amendment").

33. *Turner Broadcasting System, Inc. v. FCC,* 512 U.S. 622 (1994). This standard, though not as rigorous as strict scrutiny, does impose meaningful limits on government; and under it challengers have a reasonable chance of getting the law struck down. Smolla, *Freedom of Speech,* 3–4.

34. In cases involving both free-speech and free-exercise claims, a noticeable disparity exists between the depth of the courts' free-speech analysis and

that of their free-exercise analysis. *Daniels v. City of Arlington*, 246 F.3d 500 (5th Cir. 2001) (engaging in more thorough free-speech review of police department prohibition on the wearing of a cross on police uniform); *Watchtower Bible and Tract Society v. Village of Stratton*, 240 F.3d 553 (6th Cir. 2001) (undergoing a more exhaustive free-speech analysis of regulation restricting door-to-door soliciting); *Quental v. Connecticut Commission on the Deaf and Hearing Impaired*, 122 F.Supp.2d 133 (D. Conn. 2001) (scrutinizing sanctions placed on a public employee making religious statements to public more closely under free-speech analysis).

35. *Employment Division v. Smith*, 494 U.S. 872 (1990), 878–79, 886.

36. Prior to *Smith*, free-exercise cases had been governed by the doctrine of *Sherbert v. Verner*, 374 U.S. 398, 403 (1963) (holding that laws burdening religious exercise had to be justified by a compelling state interest).

37. *Smith*, 494 U.S. 872, 888–90, 878.

38. *Hernandez v. Commissioner*, 490 U.S. 680, 699 (1989).

39. *Strout v. Albanese*, 178 F.3d 57, 65 (1st Cir. 1999). Unlike free-exercise doctrines, "free speech doctrine is not limited in its application to laws that directly and exclusively regulate speech." Brownstein, "Protecting Religious Liberty: The False Messiahs of Free Speech Doctrine and Formal Neutrality," 28 *Journal of Law and Politics* 119, 154 (2002). General laws that encompass "both expressive and non-expressive activity may in some circumstances be challenged on its face as violating the Free Speech Clause" (*Strout*, 65).

40. *KDM v. Reedsport School District*, 196 F.3d 1046 (9th Cir. 1999), 1051.

41. Ibid., 1050–51. This holding was based on the *Hernandez* decision, in which the Supreme Court ruled that heightened scrutiny was required only if a law imposed a "substantial burden" on a "central religious belief or practice." *Hernandez*, 490 U.S. 680, 697–700. Using a similar approach, the First Circuit held that Maine's practice of providing funding to private secular schools, but not to religious schools, did not violate the exercise clause. *Strout v. Albanese*, 178 F.3d 57, 59 (1st Cir. 1999). The *Strout* holding was based in part on the court's finding that the program did not reflect a "substantial animus" toward religion (65); *Bagley v. Raymond School Department*, 728 A.2d 127 (Me. 1999) (holding that Maine's tuition-funding program did not violate the exercise clause).

42. Dent, "Of God and Caesar," 712; Ira C. Lupu, "The Trouble with Accommodation," *George Washington Law Review* 743, 755–59 (1992).

43. Michael W. McConnell, "Free Exercise Revisionism and the Smith Decision," 57 *University of Chicago Law Review* 1109, 1142–43 (1990) (listing several long-used activities that might be forbidden if *Smith* were so construed).

44. *Smith*, 494 U.S. 872, 881–82. The Court stated that when a neutral law of general applicability burdening religiously motivated conduct invokes "not the Free Exercise Clause alone, but the Free Exercise Clause in conjunction with other constitutional protections, such as freedom of speech and of the press," strict scrutiny would be applied to such a "hybrid situation" (881). Thus a hybrid rights situation "involves a neutral law of general applicability that substantially burdens the exercise of religion and sufficiently burdens some other constitutionally protected interest to invoke the application" of some higher standard of review. Brownstein, "Protecting Religious Liberty," 191.

45. *Smith,* 494 U.S. 872, 881. A hybrid case, according to the Court, is one that implicates multiple fundamental rights (881–82).

46. *Heffron v. International Society for Krishna Consciousness, Inc.,* 452 U.S. 640 (1981).

47. *City of Lakewood v. Plain Dealer Pub. Co.,* 486 U.S. 750, 759 (1988).

48. *Barnes v. Glen Theatre, Inc.,* 501 U.S. 560, 578n4 (1991).

49. Brownstein, "Protecting Religious Liberty," 152.

50. As Professor Brownstein argues: "It is hard to imagine a more conventionally accepted place and means for conducting religious assemblies than a house of worship. Even if the zoning of houses of worship does not constitute content or viewpoint discrimination, at a minimum it should receive intermediate-level scrutiny. Churches are among the primary places where religious expression occurs, and limits on the size, structural features, and accessory uses of a house of worship influence the manner of the expressive activities that may occur there. Thus, the zoning of churches should be reviewed as a regulation of the place and manner of religious assembly. . . . Unfortunately, courts do not always comply with these standards or apply this form of review. Religious land uses often receive less protection that the Free Speech Clause would seem to require" (ibid., 153n123).

51. Smith and Shea, "Religion and the Press," 178 (arguing that judicial decisions have "created an imbalance between the freedom of the press and religious freedom").

52. William P. Marshall, "The Case against the Constitutionally Compelled Free Exercise Clause," 40 *Case Western Reserve Law Review* 357, 360 (1990).

53. Note, "Neutral Rules of General Applicability: Incidental Burdens on Religion, Speech and Property," 115 *Harvard Law Review* 1713, 1717–18 (2002).

54. *Cohen v. California,* 403 U.S. 15, 25 (1971).

55. *Playboy,* 529 U.S. 803, 817–18, 813.In *Playboy,* the Court found that confining the Playboy Channel's programming to the hours of 10:00 P.M. to 6:00 A.M. posed too great a burden on adults who wanted to view indecent material (817–18). This was the only side of the speech equation at which the Court looked. The programming confinement was intended to help shield children from indecent programming, but the Court did not (other than with assumptions) consider any burden to a parent's right or ability to so shield, other than stating that it was the duty of viewers to "avert their eyes" (813); *Erznoznik v. Jacksonville,* 422 U.S. 205 (1975) (striking down an ordinance prohibiting drive-in movie theaters from exhibiting nudity). The Court placed the burden of eluding exposure on the viewer, opining that "the burden falls upon the viewer to . . . avert [her] eyes" (210).

56. *Lee,* 505 U.S. 577, 580, 588.

57. Ibid., 641 (Scalia, J. dissenting).

58. *Santa Fe Independent School District v. Doe,* 530 U.S. 290, 294, 312 (2000).

59. *Lassonde v. Pleasanton Unified School District,* 320 F.3d 979 (9th Cir. 2003).

60. *Lynch v. Donnelly,* 465 U.S. 688 (1984) (O'Connor, J., concurring).

61. *Capital Square Review and Advisory Board v. Pinette,* 515 U.S. 753 (1995), 773, 778 (O'Connor, J., concurring).

62. Steven G. Gey, "When Is Religious Speech Not 'Free Speech'?" 2000 *University of Illinois Law Review* 379, 444 (2000).

63. *Tinker v. Des Moines School District,* 393 U.S. 503, 508–9 (1969) (holding that students could not be punished for wearing a black armband to school to protest the Vietnam War, even if their symbolic speech caused fear or apprehension or discomfort to their fellow students).

64. *Cohen,* 403 U.S. 15, 26 (1971).

65. *Lamont v. Postmaster General,* 381 U.S. 301, 305 (1965).

66. *Boler v. Youngs Drug Products Corp.,* 463 U.S. 60, 61 (1983).

67. *Hedges v. Wauconda Community Unit School District No. 118,* 9 F.3d 1295 (7th Cir. 1993) (rejecting a public school policy prohibiting distribution of any religious pamphlets containing religious advocacy); *Hemry v. School Board,* 760 F.Supp. 856 (D. Colo. 1991) (upholding the application to a religious newspaper a public school rule prohibiting distribution in any school of material disruptive of normal school activity or discipline or inconsistent with the district's educational mission); *Muller v. Jefferson Lighthouse School,* 98 F.3d 1530 (7th Cir. 1996) (rejecting a student's challenge to a public school requiring religious handbills to be submitted to the principal and approved in writing). Another set of cases has upheld public school limitations on student religious speech in the classroom. *DeNooyer v. Livonia Public Schools,* 799 F.Supp. 744 (E.D. Mich. 1992) (upholding a school district's order prohibiting a student from showing a videotape of herself singing a proselytizing religious song to a second-grade class during show and tell); *Duran v. Nitsche,* 780 F.Supp. 1048 (E.D. Pa. 1991) (denying an injunction against school officials who prohibited a student from distributing a survey on God and giving an oral presentation on God to a fifth-grade class).

68. *Community-Service Broadcasting of Mid-America v. FCC,* 593 F.2d 1102, 1122 (D.C. Cir. 1978).

69. *Riley v. National Federation of the Blind of North Carolina,* 487 U.S. 781, 808 (1988).

70. *Thomas v. Anchorage Equal Rights Commission,* 165 F.3d 692, 713 (9th Cir. 1999).

71. *Edwards v. Aguillard,* 482 U.S. 578 (1987). The Louisiana statute that required equal treatment for creationism if evolution were taught in a public school, which was struck down in *Edwards,* was triggered by such an event (593). A legislator's son recited in school that "God created the World, and God created man." The teacher graded this answer "unsatisfactory." Alan Freeman and Betty Mensch, "Religion as Science/Science as Religion: Constitutional Law and the Fundamentalist Challenge," *Tikkun* 64, no. 2 (1987): 64–65.

In *Lee v. Weisman,* Justice Kennedy argued that the state may not use the coercive power of government to enforce a particular religious or antireligious orthodoxy. But since school attendance is mandatory, the teaching of viewpoints antagonistic to religion, according to the reasoning of *Lee,* can rise to the level of government coercion and "an attempt to employ the machinery of the State to enforce a religious [or antireligious] orthodoxy." *Lee,* 505 U.S. 577, 592.

Furthermore, the forbidding of the teaching of creationism or intelligent design in public schools because "it lends support to a religion, while exclusively permitting or requiring the teaching of evolution, might be construed by a court as viewpoint discrimination." Francis J. Beckwith, "Public Education, Religious Establishment, and the Challenge of Intelligent Design," 17 *Notre Dame Journal of Law, Ethics and Public Policy* 461, 489 (2003).

72. Commentators argue that *Lee v. Weisman,* which holds that public schools cannot offer prayers at graduation, also means that schools "must excuse religious dissenters from offensive parts of the curriculum." John H. Garvey, "Cover Your Ears," *Case Western Reserve Law Review* 761 (1993). But religious dissenters have been much more successful in preventing religious expression in public venues than religious believers have been in curriculum cases when they attempt to assert a free-exercise right to be excused from instruction that contravenes their religious beliefs. *Mozert v. Hawkins County Board of Education,* 827 F.2d 1058 (6th Cir. 1987), *cert. denied,* 484 U.S. 1066 (1988).

73. Stanley Ingber, "Religious Children and the Inevitable Compulsion of Public Schools," 43 *Case Western Reserve Law Review* 777 (1993).

74. *Mozert v. Hawkins County Board of Education,* 827 F.2d 1058, 1070 (6th Cir. 1987).

75. *West Virginia State Board of Education v. Barnette,* 319 U.S. 624 (1943) (invalidating West Virginia law requiring that schoolchildren recite Pledge of Allegiance).

76. Ibid., 642. The court ruled that if there "is any fixed star in our constitutional constellation, it is that no official, high or petty, can prescribe what shall be orthodox in politics, nationalism religion, or other matters of opinion or force citizens to confess by word or act their faith therein."

77. *Altman v. Bedford Central School District,* 245 F.3d 49 (2001).

78. Douglas Laycock, "Freedom of Speech That Is Both Religious and Political," 29 *University of California Davis Law Review* 793, 801 (1996).

79. *Illinois ex rel. McCollum v. Board of Education* 333 U.S. 203, 226–31 (1948).

80. *United States v. Associated Press,* 52 F.Supp. 362, 372 (D.C.N.Y. 1943).

81. *Playboy,* 529 U.S. 803, 818 (stating that "[w]ere we to give the Government the benefit of the doubt when it attempted to restrict speech, we would risk leaving regulations in place that sought to . . . silence dissenting ideas").

82. Rodney A. Smolla, *Free Speech in an Open Society* (New York: Knopf, 1992), 48–51.

83. *NAACP v. Claiborne Hardware Co.,* 458 U.S. 886, 927–28 (1982).

84. *Brandenburg v. Ohio,* 395 U.S. 444 (1969).

85. *Gitlow v. New York,* 268 U.S. 652 (1925).

86. *Tinker,* 393 U.S. 503, 509.

87. *Burch v. Barker,* 861 F.2d 1149, 1153 (9th Cir. 1988).

88. *County of Allegheny v. Greater Pittsburgh ACLU,* 492 U.S. 573, 620 (1989).

89. Ibid., 597. Under the endorsement test, the courts must "ascertain whether the challenged governmental action is sufficiently likely to be perceived

by adherents of the controlling denominations as an endorsement, and by the nonadherents as a disapproval, of their individual religious choices." The Court stated that perception turns on "what viewers may fairly understand to be the purpose of the display" (595).

90. Paulsen, "Lemon Is Dead," 815 (arguing that the "problem with the endorsement test is that it is no test at all, but merely a label for the judge's largely subjective impressions"); Arnold H. Loewy, "The Positive Reality and Normative Virtues of a 'Neutral' Establishment Clause," 41 *Brandeis Law Journal* 535, 537 (2003) (stating that a critique of the test "is that it is incapable of achieving certainty because those who apply it do not always reach the same result"); Steven D. Smith, "Symbols, Perceptions, and Doctrinal Illusions: Establishment Neutrality and the 'No Endorsement' Test," 86 *Michigan Law Review* 266, 301 (1987) (arguing that the endorsement test is incapable of achieving certainty, because it calls for judges to make assumptions about the impressions that unknown people may have received from certain religious speech or symbols).

91. In the Court's opinion in *County of Allegheny*, Justice Blackmun examined the setting in which individuals viewed the crèche on the courthouse staircase. *Allegheny*, 492 U.S. 573, 597. He noted that the flowers on the fence of the grand-staircase display drew attention to and actually enhanced the crèche's religious message (599). Furthermore, the location of the display on the grand staircase of the courthouse suggested to viewers that the government must be endorsing the message inherent in this religious symbol (599–600).

92. *Illinois,* 333 U.S. 203, 205–6 (1948) (striking down a policy of allowing religious teachers to enter public schools and provide religious instruction to desiring students).

93. *Roberts,* 921 F.2d 1047, 1049, *cert. denied,* 112 S. Ct. 3025 (1992).

94. *Bishop v. Aronov,* 926 F.2d 1066, 1068–69 (11th Cir. 1991).

95. Stuart J. Lark, "Religious Expression, Government Funds, and the First Amendment," 105 *West Virginia Law Review* 317, 352 (2003).

96. *Board of Regents of University of Wisconsin System v. Southworth,* 529 U.S. 217, 233 (2000).

97. Ibid., 355.

98. Alberto B. Lopez, "Equal Access and the Public Forum: Pinette's Imbalance of Free Speech and Establishment," 55 *Baylor Law Review* 167, 209 (2003) (arguing that the free-speech strategy "has proven effective with judges across the ideological spectrum against opponents who rely on the First Amendment's clause against the establishment of religion"). Ralph D. Mawdsley, "Leveling the Field for Religious Clubs: The Interface of the Equal Access Act, Free Speech, and the Establishment Clause," 174 *Education Law Reporter* 809, 815 (2003) (arguing that when courts shifted in their decisions from the Equal Access Act to free speech theories, the protections for religious activities increased).

99. *Engel v. Vitale,* 370 U.S. 421 (1962).

100. *Abington School District v. Schempp,* 374 U.S. 203 (1963); *Wallace v. Jaffree,* 472 U.S. 38 (1985); *Edwards,* 482 U.S. 578 (1987); *Stone v. Graham,* 449 U.S. 39 (1980); and *Lee,* 505 U.S. 577, respectively.

101. One of the reasons for this is that the default standard of review is

higher in free-speech cases than in free-exercise cases. When a law discriminates based upon the content or viewpoint of a group's message, the restriction receives strict scrutiny regardless of the forum. *Widmar v. Vincent,* 454 U.S. 263, 270 (1981).

102. Ibid., 273, 276. The Court did not base its ruling on exercise clause grounds. The Court held that "religious worship and discussion" are "forms of speech and association protected by the First Amendment" (265–66, 269).

103. *Lamb's Chapel v. Center Moriches Union Free School District,* 508 U.S. 384, 387, 394 (1993).The group was denied access to the public school building because it wanted to show a film series and hold a lecture that were religious in nature.

104. *Rosenberger v. Rectors and Visitors of the University of Virginia,* 515 U.S. 819, 835 (1995).

105. Brownstein, "Protecting Religious Liberty," 143 (stating that "most of the protection provided religious activity occurred under the auspices of the Free Speech Clause, not the Free Exercise Clause").

106. *Clark v. Dallas Independent School District,* 806 F.Supp.116, 121–22 (N.D. Tex. 1992).

107. *Hsu v. Roslyn Union Free School District,* 85 F.3d 839, 849, 858 (2d Cir. 1996).

108. *Chandler v. James,* 180 F.3d 1254, 1261 (11th Cir. 1999). By classifying student-initiated religious speech as an issue of free speech, the court diverged from the traditional analysis followed by other federal courts, and thus found a new avenue by which to analyze the constitutionality of such speech.

109. Ibid. The court went on to state that the cleansing of all religious expression from our public schools ultimately "results in the establishment of disbelief-atheism," which violates the constitutional goal of neutrality. Moreover, the constitution "affirmatively mandates accommodation, not merely tolerance, of all religions, and forbids hostility toward any" (1262). The Eleventh Circuit's interpretation held that it was not religious speech that was forbidden in public schools, but state involvement in that speech. Thus the argument can be made that if the exercise clause requires accommodation, the establishment clause cannot be used to prohibit the speech (1261). *Lynch,* 465 U.S. 668, 672–78 (noting how governmental accommodation action respects rather than endorses religion).

110. *Adler v. Duval County School Board,* 250 F.3d 1330, 1333 (11th Cir. 2001), *cert. denied* 534 U.S. 1065 (2001).

111. *Good News Club v. Milford Central School,* 533 U.S. 98, 103, 120 (2001). The previous year, the Court had decided *Santa Fe,* which held that a high school policy that allowed a student to lead a prayer before each varsity football game violated the establishment clause. But *Santa Fe* was not a free-speech case and had not been decided by the lower court under free speech analysis. *Santa Fe,* 168 F.3d 806, 819–20.

112. *Hills v. Scottsdale Unified School District,* 329 F.3d 1044 (9th Cir. 2003).

113. Ibid., 1050, 1055.

114. *Westfield High School L.I.F.E. Club v. City of Westfield,* 249 F.Supp.2d

98 (D. Mass. 2003). As the court stated, "this case concerns the rights of public high school students to personally express themselves during non-instructional time on school grounds during the school day" (129).

115. *Donovan v. Punxsutawny Area School Board,* 336 F.3d 211 (3d Cir. 2003). As the court stated, the "Supreme Court has repeatedly rejected Establishment Clause defenses in free speech cases" (226).

116. *Nichol v. Arin Intermediate Unit 28,* 268 F.Supp.2d 536 (W.D. Pa. 2003). The garb statute prohibited "the wearing of religious dress, emblems and insignia, specifically including crosses and stars of David" (543). In its opinion, the court interpreted the *Good News Club* decision, in which the Supreme Court "explained that any danger that elementary school children would misperceive an endorsement of religion . . . would be no greater than the danger that they might perceive a hostility toward religion" (553). Such an interpretation puts religious expression more on the same plane as secular speech, in terms of the assumption of risks and dangers.

117. Frederick Mark Gedicks, "Toward a Defensible Free Exercise Doctrine," 68 *George Washington Law Review* 925, 927–28 (2000); Brownstein, "Protecting Religious Liberty," 123 (arguing that "the shift from a rigorously enforced free exercise and establishment clause paradigm to a free speech model has significant problems, some of which undermine religious liberty and equality in important ways"). See also Daniel O. Conkle, "The Free Exercise Clause, How Redundant and Why?" 33 *Loyola University Chicago Law Journal* 95, 115 (2001) (arguing that under current case law, the exercise clause has limited doctrinal significance); Mark Tushnet, "The Redundant Free Exercise Clause," 33 *Loyola University Chicago Law Journal* 71, 72 (2001) (claiming that the use of the speech clause is, to some extent, making the exercise clause redundant).

118. *Unitarian Universalist Church of Akron v. City of Fairlawn,* No. 5:00CV 3021 (N.D. Ohio filed Dec. 4, 2000) (settled out of court) (alleging that city zoning ordinance does not permit new churches or church expansions anywhere in the city, although nonreligious assembly uses are routinely permitted).

119. Picarello quoted in David L. Hudson, "Zoning Gets Religion," *ABA Journal* (March 2004): 20.

120. *Congregation of Jehovah's Witnesses, Inc. v. City of Lakewood,* 699 F.2d 303, 307 (6th Cir. 1983).

121. Robert W. Tuttle, "How Firm a Foundation? Protecting Religious Land Uses after Boerne," 68 *George Washington Law Review* 861, 871–80 (2000); Douglas Laycock, "State RFRAs and Land Use Regulation," 32 *University of California Davis Law Review* 755, 763–69 (1999).

122. Tuttle, "How Firm a Foundation," 871–75; Laycock, "State RFRAs," 765. Many courts hold that land-use laws, even if facially discriminating against places of worship, do not require rigorous review. *International Church of the Foursquare Gospel v. City of Chicago Heights,* 955 F.Supp. 878, 881 (N.D. Ill. 1996); *Messiah Baptist Church v. County of Jefferson,* 859 F.2d 820 (10th Cir. 1988).

123. Tuttle, "How Firm a Foundation," 894 (arguing that laws excluding religious uses while permitting similar secular ones appear on their face to be content-based discrimination).

124. *Tenafly Eruv Association, Inc. v. Borough of Tenafly,* 309 F.3d 144, 151–52 (3d Cir. 2002).

125. *Rader v. Johnston,* 924 F.Supp. 1540 (D. Neb. 1996).

126. *Montgomery v. Country of Clinton, Michigan,* 743 F.Supp. 1253, 1255, 1259 (W.D. Mich. 1990).

127. *Cole v. Oroville Union High School District,* 228 F.3d 1092 (9th Cir. 2000).

128. *Fleming v. Jefferson Country School Dist.,* 298 F.3d 918, 921, 933 (10th Cir. 2002). Among the messages on the tiles were "Jesus is Lord," "4/20/99 Jesus Wept," and "There is No Peace Says the Lord for the Wicked" (921).

129. *Tinker,* 393 U.S. 503, 508–9.

130. The free-speech clause also does not cover the case of an individual landlord leasing the half of a duplex in which he or she does not reside and who has religious objections to renting to a cohabiting unmarried couple. Enforcing an ordinance prohibiting discrimination on the basis of marital status might compromise the landlord's religious beliefs and exercise. *Thomas,* 165 F.3d 692, *withdrawn for reh'g,* 192 F.3d 1208 (9th Cir. 1999),_ vacated en banc,_ 220 F.3d 1134 (9th Cir. 2000).

131. *Widmar,* 454 U.S. 263, 284 (White, J., dissenting).

132. Joseph P. Viteritti, "Reading Zelman: The Triumph of Pluralism and Its Effects on Liberty, Equality, and Choice," 76 *Southern California Law Review* 1105, 1146.

Notes to Chapter 2

1. Stephen L. Carter, "Reflections on the Separation of Church and State," 44 *Arizona Law Review* 293, 299 (2002).

2. Daniel Gordon, "Reestablishment of Religious Freedom: Developing an Alternative Model Based on State Constitutional Privacy," 66 *Mississippi Law Journal* 127, 128 (1996).

3. Stephen L. Carter, *The Culture of Disbelief: How American Law and Politics Trivialize Religious Devotion* (New York: Basic Books, 1993), 115.

4. Frederick Mark Gedicks, "Public Life and Hostility to Religion," 78 *Virginia Law Review* 671, 682–93 (1992). Many view religious symbolism in public life as inherently coercive. See Richard S. Myers, "A Comment on the Death of Lemon," 43 *Case Western Reserve Law Review* 903, 908 (1993).

5. Thomas McCoy, "Quo Vadis: Is the Establishment Clause Undergoing Metamorphosis?" 41 *Brandeis Law Journal* 547, 547–49 (2003) (suggesting that the desire to keep religion out of the public sphere is responsible for what is perceived to be irreconcilable tension between the two clauses). Not surprisingly, it has become common for the Court "to trump free exercise claims with findings of religious establishment." Joseph P. Viteritti, "Reading Zelman: The Triumph of Pluralism, and Its Effects on Liberty, Equality, and Choice," 76 *Southern California Law Review* 1105, 1145 (2003).

6. Robert J. Lipkin, "Reconstructing the Public Square," 24 *Cardozo Law Review* 2025. "In a democratic society, public discussion should reflect the importance of religion, as well as other convictions, in its citizens' lives" (2034).

7. *Everson v. Board of Education,* 330 U.S. 1, 15–16 (1947).

8. *McCollum v. Board of Education,* 333 U.S. 203, 212 (1948).

9. Alberto B. Lopez, "Equal Access and the Public Forum: Pinette's Imbalance of Free Speech and Establishment," 55 *Baylor Law Review* 167, 183 (2003).

10. *Lemon v. Kurtzman,* 403 U.S. 602, 606, 613 (1971). The Pennsylvania statute provided money to nonpublic schools by reimbursing the schools for expenses associated with teachers' salaries and teaching materials, including textbooks. Under the Rhode Island statute, the state made a supplemental payment of 15 percent of a teacher's salary directly to teachers in nonpublic schools (606–7).

11. Viteritti, "Reading Zelman," 1116.

12. *Lynch v. Donnelly,* 465 U.S. 668, 673 (1984).

13. The programs were provided as a part of a breakout session during the school day. Public school instructors were assigned separate classrooms in the nonpublic school, and at various times during the day students were sent to that classroom for special instruction. However, the courses were not integrated into the nonpublic school.

14. *Aguilar v. Felton,* 473 U.S. 402, 424 (1985) (O'Connor, J., dissenting); ibid., 412–13.

15. *County of Allegheny v. Greater Pittsburgh ACLU,* 492 U.S. 573 (1989), 579–81 (although the crèche was owned by a Roman Catholic group, the city of Pittsburgh stored, placed, and removed it); 616–17 (noting that the Christmas tree was once a sectarian symbol but that it has lost its religious overtones).

16. Mark D. Rosen, "Establishment, Expressivism, and Federalism," 78 *Chicago-Kent Law Review* 669, 688 (2003).

17. Carter, "Separation of Church and State," 296.

18. Michael Paulsen, "Lemon Is Dead," 43 *Case Western Reserve Law Review* 795, 810 (1993).

19. *Van Orden v. Perry,* 351 F.3d 173, 178 (5th Cir. 2003).

20. *School District of Abington Township v. Schempp,* 374 U.S. 203, 306 (1963) (Goldberg, J., concurring).

21. *McCollum,* 333 U.S. 203, 247 (Reed, J., dissenting).

22. *Everson,* 330 U.S. 1, 16.

23. *Lynch,* 465 U.S. 668, 687 (O'Connor, J., concurring). Justice O'Connor's concurring opinion in *Lynch* was adopted by a majority of the Court in *County of Allegheny,* 492 U.S. 573.

24. *Lee v. Weisman,* 505 U.S. 577, 593 (1992).

25. Daniel L. Dreisbach, *Thomas Jefferson and the Wall of Separation between Church and State* (New York: New York University Press, 2002), 68 (emphasis added). For other works examining the historical origins of the wall of separation, see Philip Hamburger, *Separation of Church and State* (Cambridge: Harvard University Press, 2002); John Witte Jr., *Religion and the American Constitutional Experiment: Essential Rights and Liberties* (Boulder: Westview Press, 2000); Steven D. Smith, *Foreordained Failure: The Quest for a Constitutional Principle of Religious Freedom* (New York: Oxford University Press, 1995); John C. Jeffries Jr. and James E. Ryan, "A Political History of the Establishment

Clause," 100 *Michigan Law Review* 279 (2001); J. Clifford Wallace, "The Framers' Establishment Clause: How High the Wall?" 2001 *Brigham Young University Law Review* 755 (2001).

26. A number of commentators have concluded that the establishment clause was designed to be primarily a "jurisdictional provision." Michael J. Malbin, *Religion and Politics: The Intentions of the Authors of the First Amendment* (Washington, D.C.: American Enterprise Institute, 1978); Smith, *Foreordained Failure,* 17–18 (arguing that the "religion clauses were purely jurisdictional in nature; they did not adopt any substantive right or principle of religious freedom," and that "the religion clauses, as understood by those who drafted, proposed, and ratified them, were an exercise in federalism"). As Professor Kmiec explains, Jefferson's "wall of separation" concern was not addressed to impermissible public support of religion but "to reminding the Congress of the United States that it was deprived of all legislative power over mere religious opinion, and could regulate practice only when such practice undermined the public order." Douglas W. Kmiec, "Oh God! Can I Say That in Public?" 17 *Notre Dame Journal of Law, Ethics and Public Policy* 307, 314 (2003).

27. Dreisbach, *Thomas Jefferson and the Wall of Separation,* 3, 59–60, 125.

28. *Annals of Congress,* 6th Cong., 2d sess., 10:797 (1800) ; James Hutson, *Religion and the Founding of the American Republic* (Washington, D.C.: Library of Congress, 1998), 89, 84.

29. Hamburger, *Separation of Church and State,* 109, 162 (contending that when Jefferson expressed such views they were not "widely published or even noticed"). "The dissenters who campaigned for constitutional barriers to any government establishment of religion had no desire more generally to prevent contact between religion and government" (13). Michael Paulsen, "Religion, Equality, and the Constitution: An Equal Protection Approach to Establishment Clause Adjudication," 61 *Notre Dame Law Review* 311, 320 (1986). Steven Smith argues that the establishment clause was designed to protect the established state religions from federal interference, and, as such, that "the religion clauses were understood as a federalist measure, not as the enactment of any substantive principle of religious freedom." Smith, *Foreordained Failure,* 30. Paulsen, "Religion, Equality, and the Constitution," 317 ("The original intention behind the establishment clause . . . seems fairly clearly to have been to forbid establishment of a national religion and to prevent federal interference with a state's choice of whether or not to have an official state religion").

30. Chester J. Antieau et al., *Freedom from Federal Establishment: Formation and Early History of the First Amendment Religion Clauses* (Milwaukee: Bruce Publishing, 1964), 42 (demonstrating that the religion clauses of the First Amendment were designed to prohibit the use of religion as an instrument of national policy by forbidding exclusive privileges to any one sect).

31. Michael W. McConnell, "Accommodation of Religion: An Update and a Response to the Critics," 60 *George Washington Law Review* 685, 693 (1992).

32. The *Congressional Record* from June 8 to September 24, 1789, chronicle the months of discussions and debates of the ninety framers of the First Amendment. *Annals of Congress,* 1st Cong., 1st sess., 1:440–948 (1789).

33. *Wallace v. Jaffree,* 472 U.S. 38, 91–114 (1985) (Rehnquist, J., dissenting).

34. Richard John Neuhaus, "A New Order of Religious Freedom," 60 *George Washington Law Review* 620, 623 (1992).

35. *Schempp,* 374 U.S. 203, 306 (1963) (Goldberg, J., concurring).

36. Carter, "Separation of Church and State," 309.

37. According to Professor Conkle, "the Court's establishment clause doctrines can be viewed as a product of mistaken history." Conkle, "Toward a General Theory of the Establishment Clause," 1144. He argues that "the framers and ratifiers did not intend to ban any of the practices that the Court has invalidated in applying the establishment clause to the states" (1145).

38. *United States v. MacIntosh,* 283 U.S. 605, 625 (1931); *Schempp,* 374 U.S. 203, 225. Harold Berman, "Religion and Law: The First Amendment in Historical Perspective," 35 *Emory Law Journal* 777, 779 (1986) (suggesting that prior to the mid-twentieth century, Americans thought of the United States as a Christian county).

39. Conkle, "General Theory of the Establishment Clause," 1117.

40. *Sloan v. Lemon,* 413 U.S. 825, 830–32 (1973).

41. *Bowen v. Kendrick,* 487 U.S. 589, 610 (1988). In their dissents in *Good News,* Justices Stevens, Souter, and Ginsburg restated this suspicion of anything "pervasively religious." They argued that some religious groups who employ overtly religious speech could be excluded from access to public facilities, that speech amounting to "proselytizing" or "worship" did not warrant similar protection under the speech clause. *Good News Club v. Milford Central School,* 533 U.S. 98, 130–34 (2001).

42. *Hunt v. McNair,* 413 U.S. 734, 743 (1973).

43. This was a presumption that seemingly was abandoned in *Mitchell v. Holmes,* 530 U.S. 793, 851 (2000) (O'Connor, J., concurring in the judgment). But the future of the "pervasively sectarian inquiry" remains unclear.

44. *Freedom from Religion Foundation, Inc. v. Bugher,* 249 F.3d 606, 613 (7th Cir. 2001). The Court has shown an antireligious bias in the "pervasively sectarian" inquiry. Justice Souter's dissent in *Mitchell,* for instance, argued that government aid should not go to schools that were "pervasively sectarian," because there the risk of impermissible diversion of public funds for religious uses was the greatest. *Mitchell,* 530 U.S. 793, 904–6 (Souter, J., dissenting). Justice Thomas rejected this pervasively sectarian view, stating that the traditional exclusion of pervasively sectarian schools from neutral aid programs had been nothing more than a manifestation of hostility to Roman Catholicism. He concluded his response to the Souter dissent by declaring that "this doctrine, born of bigotry, should be buried now" (829).

45. *Settle v. Dickson County School Board,* 53 F.3d 152 (6th Cir. 1995).

46. *C.H. v. Oliva,* 990 F.Supp. 341, 353–54 (D.N.J. 1997).

47. *Doe v. Duncanville Independent School District,* 70 F.3d 402, 406–7 (5th Cir. 1995).

48. *Hills v. Scottsdale Unified School District,* 329 F.3d 1044 (9th Cir. 2003).

49. "County Bans Xmas Tress in Public Buildings," *FoxNews,* Dec. 17, 2004, at www.foxnews.com/printer_friendly_story/0,3566,141805,00.html, accessed December 20, 2004.

50. *American Civil Liberties Union v. Mercer County,* 240 F.Supp.2d 623 (E.D. Ky. 2003).

51. Conkle, "General Theory of the Establishment Clause," 1160. Another commentator stated that "as a result of the multitude of tests and opinions stemming from Supreme Court establishment clause cases, there have been numerous inconsistencies among the lower courts, as well as a general sense of confusion within society." Roxanne Houtman, "ACLU v. McCreary County: Rebuilding the Wall between Church and State," 55 *Syracuse Law Review* 395, 403–4 (2005). Houtman notes that over the past thirty years, "the Supreme Court's Establishment Clause jurisprudence has become increasingly ambiguous."

52. Carl Esbeck, "Dissent and Disestablishment: The Church-State Settlement in the Early American Republic," 2004 *Brigham Young University Law Review* 1385, 1577.

Notes to Chapter 3

1. Russell L. Weaver, "Like a Ghoul in a Late Night Horror Movie," 41 *Brandeis Law Journal* 587, 590 (2003). As Justice William Rehnquist explained in a dissenting opinion in *Wallace v. Jaffree,* the *Lemon* test "has simply not provided adequate standards for deciding Establishment Clause cases. . . . For example, a State may lend [geography] textbooks that contain [maps], but the State may not lend [maps] for use in geography class. A State may lend textbooks on American colonial history, but it may not lend a film on George Washington, or a film projector to show it. . . . A State may lend classroom workbooks, but may not lend workbooks in which the parochial school children write, thus rendering them nonreusable. A State may pay for bus transportation to religious schools but may not pay for bus transportation from the parochial school to the public zoo or natural history museum." *Wallace v. Jaffree,* 472 U.S. 38, 111 (1985) (Rehnquist, J., dissenting).

2. William P. Marshall, "What Is the Matter with Equality? An Assessment of the Equal Treatment of Religion and Nonreligion in First Amendment Jurisprudence," 75 *Indiana Law Journal* 193 (2000).

3. Kent Greenawalt, "Quo Vadis: The Status and Prospects of 'Tests' under the Religion Clauses," 1995 *Supreme Court Review* 323, 323 (1995). "The failure to adopt a single Establishment Clause test has resulted in the use of a multitude of tests by lower courts, which is causing a growing number of disputes among the circuits." Roxanne Houtman, "ACLU v. McCreary County: Rebuilding the Wall between Church and State," 55 *Syracuse Law Review* 395, 419 (2005).

4. *Committee for Public Education and Religious Liberty v. Nyquist,* 413 U.S. 756, 790–91, 773, 784–87 (1973). This was anything but a decision based on neutrality, unless one sees the baseline for equality as being strictly secular. If anything, equality means that private schools should get a break to make up for taxes they pay to support public schools.

5. Keith Werhan, "Navigating the New Neutrality: School Vouchers, the Pledge, and the Limits of a Purposive Establishment Clause," 41 *Brandeis Law Journal* 603, 610 (2003). From 1971 to 1992 the Supreme Court applied the *Lem-*

on test in thirty of the thirty-one establishment clause cases it decided. *Lee v. Weisman,* 505 U.S. 577, 603n4 (1992) (Blackmun, J., concurring).

6. *Board of Education v. Allen,* 392 U.S. 236 (1968).

7. *Lemon v. Kurtzman,* 403 U.S. 602, 617–21 (1971).

8. *Wolman v. Walter,* 433 U.S. 229, 248–51 (1977); *Meek v. Pittenger,* 421 U.S. 349, 362–66 (1975).

9. *Meek,* 421 U.S. 349, 367–72, and *Wolman,* 433 U.S. 229, 239–48 (1977), respectively.

10. *Committee for Public Education and Religious Liberty v. Regan,* 444 U.S. 646 (1980).

11. *Levitt v. Committee for Public Education,* 413 U.S. 472 (1973).

12. Mark D. Rosen, "Establishment, Expressivism, and Federalism," 78 *Chicago-Kent Law Review* 669, 685 (2003).

13. Aguilar v. Felton, 473 U.S. 402, 410–14 (1985), overruled by *Agostini v. Felton,* 521 U.S. 203 (1997).

14. Werhan, "Navigating the New Neutrality," 610.

15. *Regan,* 444 U.S. 646, 662.

16. *County of Allegheny v. Greater Pittsburgh ACLU,* 492 U.S. 573, 655–56 (1989) (Kennedy, J., concurring in part and dissenting in part); *Edwards v. Aguillard,* 482 U.S. 578, 636–40 (1987) (Scalia, J., dissenting); *Aguilar,* 473 U.S. 402, 426–30 (O'Connor, J., dissenting); *Wallace,* 472 U.S. 38, 108–12 (Rehnquist, J., dissenting); *Roemer v. Maryland Board of Public Works,* 426 U.S. 736, 768–69 (1976) (White, J., concurring in the judgment).

17. Michael Paulsen, "Lemon Is Dead," 43 *Case Western Reserve Law Review,* 795, 801. The result was frequently a reading of the establishment clause that required functional hostility to religion "by treating the promotion of religious freedom—as distinguished from the promotion of religion—as an improper government motivation."

18. *County of Allegheny,* 492 U.S. 573.

19. *Lee,* 505 U.S. 577.

20. *Zelman v. Simmons-Harris,* 536 U.S. 639 (2002).

21. However, according to one legal scholar, "none of these doctrinal approaches has received widespread support, and none appears up to the task of providing a satisfying analytical framework for addressing problems that arise under either the Establishment Clause or the Free Exercise Clause." Brett G. Scharffs, "The Autonomy of Church and State," 2004 *Brigham Young University Law Review* 1217, 1236–37 (2004).

22. *Texas Monthly, Inc. v. Bullock,* 489 U.S. 1 (1989); *Lynch v. Donnelly,* 465 U.S. 668 (1984).

23. Alberto B. Lopez, "Equal Access and the Public Forum: Pinette's Imbalance of Free Speech and Establishment," 55 *Baylor Law Review* 167, 195 (2003). Since *County of Allegheny,* which confirmed the endorsement test as the Court's preferred method of analysis, the Court has continued its reliance on the endorsement test for establishment clause cases. The Court recently applied the test in *Santa Fe Independent School District v. Doe,* 530 U.S. 290, 316 (2000). See also Rosen, "Establishment, Expressivism, and Federalism," 684.

24. *Lee,* 505 U.S. 577, 586.

25. Paulsen, "Lemon Is Dead," 832. Moreover, the Court's ruling actually undermines First Amendment values, since social pressure usually occurs in the form of speech (ibid., 834).

26. *Tanford v. Brand,* 104 F.3d 982, 986 (7th Cir. 1997).

27. *Mellen v. Bunting,* 327 F.3d 355 (4th Cir. 2003).

28. *Lynch,* 465 U.S. 668, 687 (O'Connor, J., concurring); *Estate of Thornton,* 472 U.S. 703, 711 (O'Connor, J., concurring in the judgment); *Wallace,* 472 U.S. 38, 67 (O'Connor, J., concurring in part and concurring in the judgment).

29. *County of Allegheny,* 492 U.S. 573, 593, 578–79, 620–21. In *Allegheny* the Court concluded that, as to the crèche, "no viewer could reasonably think that it occupied this location without the support and approval of the government" (599–600). The tree and menorah, on the other hand, did not present a "sufficiently likely" probability that observers would see them as endorsing a particular religion (620).

30. Steven D. Smith, "Symbols, Perceptions, and Doctrinal Illusions: Establishment Neutrality and the 'No Endorsement' Test," 86 *Michigan Law Review* 266, 301 (1987).

31. *American Jewish Congress v. City of Chicago,* 827 F.2d 120, 129 (7th Cir. 1987) (Easterbrook, J., dissenting).

32. *Doe v. County of Montgomery, Illinois,* 915 F.Supp. 32 (C.D. Ill. 1996).

33. *County of Allegheny,* 492 U.S. 573, 669, 674. The banning of the crèche, in Kennedy's opinion, reflected "an unjustified hostility toward religion" and a "callous indifference toward religious faith that our cases and traditions do not require" (655, 664).

34. *Walz ex. rel. Walz v. Egg Harbor Township Board of Education,* 187 F.Supp.2d 232 (D.N.J. 2002).

35. *Buono v. Norton,* 212 F.Supp.2d 1202, 1216 (C.D. Calif. 2002).

36. *Van Orden v. Perry,* 351 F.3d 173, 181–82 (5th Cir. 2003).

37. Under the endorsement test, impermissible government involvement with religion exists when the public perceives that government is endorsing a religion. *Lynch,* 465 U.S. 668, 690 (O'Connor, J., concurring).

38. *Roberts v. Madigan,* 921 F.2d 1047, 1049 (10th Cir. 1990).

39. *Bishop v. Aronov,* 926 F.2d 1066, 1068–69 (11th Cir. 1991). In *Bishop,* the professor prefaced his remarks by labeling them his "personal bias," thus denying any implication of institutional endorsement (1066, 1068).

40. *Peloza v. Capistrano Unified School District,* 37 F.3d 517, 519–20 (9th Cir. 1994).

41. *American Civil Liberties Union of Ohio Foundation, Inc. v. Ashbrook,* 211 F.Supp.2d 873 (N.D. Ohio 2002).

42. *Van Orden,* 351 F.3d 173, 180 (5th Cir. 2003). On appeal, the Supreme Court upheld the constitutionality of this monument. *Van Orden v. Perry,* U.S., No. 03-1500, June 27, 2005. In a companion case, however, the Court struck down a wall-hanging display of a framed copy of the Ten Commandments at a Kentucky courthouse. *McCreary County v. American Civil Liberties Union of Kentucky,* U.S., No. 03-1693, June 23, 2005.

43. *Doe v. City of Clawson,* 915 F.2d 244 (6th Cir. 1990).

44. *Jocham v. Tuscola County,* 239 F.Supp.2d 714, 719, 743 (E.D. Mich. 2003). The issue of context and whether any religious message is sufficiently diluted is an almost unanswerable question. For example, what if the Ten Commandments were displayed between the U.S. Constitution and the Gettysburg Address, as documents underlying the nation's history? Would the other two documents sufficiently mute any religious message of the Ten Commandments? What if there were a dozen other documents surrounding the Ten Commandments? Or two dozen? Or what if the Ten Commandments were the only non-U.S. document in the display? What message would that send? Or, if no other religious documents were displayed, what would that say about the U.S. attitude toward religions outside the Judeo-Christian tradition? Hence, when it comes down to it, any religious expression could be suspect, even if that religious expression relates to the secular history of the nation.

45. *Americans United for Separation of Church and State v. City of Grand Rapids,* 980 F.2d 1538, 1544–46 (6th Cir. 1992).

46. *Rusk v. Crestview Local Schools,* 220 F.Supp.2d. 854, 858 (N.D. Ohio 2002).

47. *Skarin v. Woodbine Community School District,* 204 F.Supp.2d 1195, 1197 (S.D. Iowa 2002).

48. *Barnes-Wallace v. Boy Scouts of America,* 275 F.Supp.2d 1259, 1270, 1276 (S.D. Calif. 2003).

49. *Freiler v. Tangipahoa Parish Board of Education,* 975 F.Supp. 819, 829 (E.D. La. 1997).

50. *Capitol Square Review and Advisory Board v. Pinette,* 515 U.S. 753 (1995), 774 (O'Connor, J., concurring in part and concurring in the judgment). This may occur "even if the governmental actor neither intends nor actively encourages [the endorsement]" (777).

51. *American Civil Liberties Union v. City of Florissant,* 17 F.Supp.2d 1068, 1071, 1075 (E.D. Mo. 1998).

52. *Mercier v. City of La Crosse,* 276 F.Supp.2d 961 (W.D. Wis. 2003).

53. *Lynch,* 465 U.S. 668, 692, 688 (O'Connor, J., concurring). To Justice O'Connor, the endorsement test functioned to prevent government from "making a citizen's religious affiliation a criterion for full membership in the political community" (690).

54. Edward B. Foley, "Political Liberalism and Establishment Clause Jurisprudence," 43 *Case Western Reserve Law Review* 963, 972 (1993).

55. Steven G. Gey, "When Is Religious Speech Not 'Free Speech'?" 2000 *University of Illinois Law Review* 379, 444 (2000). They also argue that religious speech can be socially and politically divisive and hence should be discouraged from entering the public sphere. See Douglas Laycock, "Freedom of Speech That Is Both Religious and Political," 29 *University of California Davis Law Review* 793, 801 (1996).

56. *Capital Square Review,* 515 U.S. 753, 777 (O'Connor, J., concurring in part and concurring in judgment).

57. Lopez, "Equal Access," 218–19 (citing examples of threats and harass-

ment against religious dissenters and those who take court action to oppose public displays of religion).

58. *Brown v. Board of Education of Topeka, Shawnee County, Kansas,* 347 U.S. 483, 494 (1954).

59. *Jewish War Veterans of U.S. v. United States,* 695 F.Supp. 3, 8 (D.C. 1988).

60. Lopez, "Equal Access," 224.

61. Moreover, the whole purpose of religious faith and exercise is to confront people and make them uncomfortable with the status quo of their lives.

62. Even though a number of justices "find irresistible the proposition that government should not make anyone feel like an outsider by endorsing religion," these same Justices seem disinclined to overturn free-exercise exemptions for religious objectors, or the use of the national motto "In God We Trust," or even the opening of Supreme Court sessions with the plea, "God save the United States of America and this Honorable Court." Steven D. Smith, "Nonestablishment under God," 50 *Villanova Law Review* 1, 13–14 (2005). There is also the example posed by Justice Stevens: what about the observer who thinks the exhibition of an "exotic cow" in the national zoo conveys the government's endorsement of the Hindu religion? Ibid., 15–16. And, as Douglas Laycock observes, are the names of cities like Los Angeles and Corpus Christi unconstitutional endorsements? Ibid., 16.

63. *Mercier,* 276 F.Supp.2d, at 966–67.

Notes to Chapter 4

1. Keith Werhan, "Navigating the New Neutrality: School Vouchers, the Pledge, and the Limits of a Purposive Establishment Clause," 41 *Brandeis Law Journal* 603, 617 (2003). In *Zelman v. Simmons-Harris,* for instance, the Court took a big step toward adopting formal neutrality as the preferred means of interpreting the establishment clause. *Zelman v. Simmons-Harris,* 536 U.S. 639 (2002) (upholding the Cleveland school-voucher system, even as those vouchers were used in parochial schools).

2. Daniel O. Conkle, "The Path of American Religious Liberty: From the Original Theology to Formal Neutrality and an Uncertain Future," 75 *Indiana Law Journal* 1, 2 (2000).

3. *Good News Club v. Milford Central School,* 533 U.S. 98 (2001). For a discussion of this case, see Douglas Kmiec, "Good News for Religion," 21 *California Law Review* 25 (May 2001).

4. *Rosenberger v. Rectors and Visitors of University of Virginia et al.,* 515 U.S. 819 (1995).

5. Cases such as *Good News* and *Rosenberger* are often described as antidiscrimination cases that forbid discriminatory treatment of religion. However, they can also be characterized as neutrality doctrine cases, insofar as their antidiscrimination commands are just another way of demanding that religion be treated on a neutral basis with nonreligion.

6. *Wolman v. Walter,* 433 U.S. 229 (1977); *Meek v. Pittenger,* 421 U.S. 349 (1975); *Committee for Public Education v. Nyquist,* 413 U.S. 756 (1973). Begin-

ning in 1986, "the Court progressively elevated the nondiscrimination principle and subordinated the no-aid principle." Douglas Laycock, "Theology Scholarships, the Pledge of Allegiance, and Religious Liberty: Avoiding the Extremes but Missing the Liberty," 118 *Harvard Law Review* 155, 166 (2004). As Professor Laycock argues, "the no-funding tradition is a misinterpretation of the Establishment Clause, deeply rooted in historic anti-Catholicism." He states that "there is no sustained national tradition of any kind that refuses to fund religious delivery of social services," and that "billions of government dollars have flowed through religious charities over the decades" (185).

7. Thomas R. McCoy, "Quo Vadis: Is the Establishment Clause Undergoing Metamorphosis?" 41 *Brandeis Law Journal* 547, 549 (2003).

8. *Zobrest v. Catalina Foothills School District,* 509 U.S. 1, 8 (1993).

9. *Zelman,* 536 U.S. 639, 662–63. In *Zelman,* the Court's finding that the Ohio program was one of true private choice was based upon the determination that the program is neutral toward religion, gives aid directly to a broad class of citizens without consideration of religion, and permits both religious and secular private schools to participate (648–54). See also Douglas Kmiec, "Finally—School Vouchers," 22 *California Law Review* 15 (March 2002).

10. *Mueller v. Allen,* 463 U.S. 388, 397 (1983) (approving of an aid program benefiting public and private school students).

11. In the lower court, it was found that 96 percent of the students participating in the voucher program were enrolled in religious schools. See *Simmons-Harris v. Zelman,* 234 F.3d 945, 949 (6th Cir. 2000), *rev'd,* 536 U.S. 639 (2002).

12. However, state constitutions can still be used to ban neutral voucher programs. In 2002 a Florida trial court held that Florida's version of the Blaine Amendment prohibits the state from including religious schools in a statewide voucher program. *Holmes v. Bush,* 2002 WL 1809079 (Fla. Cir. Ct. 2002). (This decision was later upheld by a Florida appeals court, which held that a voucher program for students in failing schools violated the state's constitution because it ended up sending public money to religious institutions. Greg Winter, "Florida Court Rules against Religious School Vouchers," *New York Times,* Aug. 17, 2004, A15.)

13. Again, these cases are sometimes referred to as antidiscrimination cases.

14. *Lamb's Chapel v. Center Moriches Union Free School District,* 508 U.S. 384, 394 (1993).

15. *Rosenberger,* 515 U.S. 819.

16. Alan Brownstein, "Protecting Religious Liberty: The False Messiahs of Free Speech Doctrine and Formal Neutrality," 18 *Journal of Law and Policy* 119, 129 (2002). Constitutional protections for religious practice have "abruptly changed from a substantive liberty, triggered by a burden on religious practice, to a form of nondiscrimination right, triggered by a burden that is not neutral." Laycock, "Theology Scholarships," 156.

17. *Employment Division, Department of Human Resources of Oregon, et al. v. Smith,* 494 U.S. 872, 875, 884 (1990). *Smith* involved an Oregon law that criminalized the use of peyote, a drug made from cactus plants. Two members of

the Native American Church, which uses peyote as a sacrament, were dismissed from their jobs as drug counselors because of their peyote use. When they applied for unemployment benefits, the state denied their claims on the ground that they were terminated for "work-related misconduct" (874). They sued, arguing that the Oregon law violated their right to the free exercise of religion. Thus *Smith* posed the question of whether religious believers could be exempted from neutral laws of general applicability that nonetheless burdened their religious exercise.

18. *Sherbert v. Verner*, 374 U.S. 398 (1963). In *Sherbert*, a Seventh-Day Adventist was denied unemployment compensation after being fired from her job for refusing to work on Saturday. The Court held that a state unemployment law that provided benefits only to those willing to work on Saturdays violated the exercise clause, because it could not be justified by a compelling state interest (410). The Court focused on the fact that the state law required some individuals to forego a central tenet of their religion in order to qualify for the state funding (406).

In *Wisconsin v. Yoder*, 406 U.S. 205 (1972). *Yoder* reaffirmed the *Sherbert* doctrine when it held that the exercise clause prevents states from enforcing compulsory school attendance laws (234). When the respondent, an Amish man, claimed that religious beliefs exempted his daughter from such laws, the Court required that the State of Wisconsin show a compelling interest behind those laws (207–9).

Under the *Sherbert* and *Yoder* line of cases, statutory burdens on religious practice presumptively violated the exercise clause. See *Bowen v. Roy*, 476 U.S. 693, 728 (1986); *Bob Jones University v. United States*, 461 U.S. 574, 603 (1983); *Thomas v. Review Board*, 450 U.S. 707, 718 (1981). *Smith*, however, provides lower protections for religion than does the *Sherbert-Yoder* rule, because prior to *Smith*, religious liberty claims did not require proof of discrimination—instead, burdens on religious exercise themselves constituted prima facie violations of the exercise clause.

19. *Employment Division v. Smith*, 494 U.S. 872, 876–90 (1990).

20. *Smith* is best known for its holding that facially neutral statutes do not ordinarily violate the exercise clause, but the Court in *Smith* also reiterated the flipside of neutrality: that laws imposing special disabilities on the basis of religion are presumptively unconstitutional and subject to strict scrutiny. *Smith*, 494 U.S. 872, 877. Essentially, *Smith*, as well as *Church of the Lukumi Babalu Aye, Inc. v. City of Hialeah*, 508 U.S. 520 (1993), have "converted the right to free exercise of religion into some kind of discrimination right." Laycock, "Theology Scholarships," 171.

21. Brian J. Serr, "A Not-so-Neutral 'Neutrality': An Essay on the State of the Religion Clauses on the Brink of the Third Millennium," 51 *Baylor Law Review* 319, 324 (1999).

22. *United States v. Ballard*, 322 U.S. 78, 87 (1944). Yet, the neutrality of *Smith* treats religious-inspired conduct as no more elevated than any other form of conduct when affected by so-called neutral laws of general applicability. *Smith*, 494 U.S. 872, 877–79.

23. Serr, "A Not-so-Neutral 'Neutrality,'" 324. Prior to *Smith*, the Court did place religious exercise on a higher plane. Before *Smith*, the government had to establish a compelling interest in order to justify applying a law of general applicability to a religious practice in a way that substantially inhibited that practice. *Sherbert*, 374 U.S. 398, 403.

24. *Clark v. Community for Creative Non-Violence*, 468 U.S. 288 (1984). In *Clark*, the Court required that the National Park Service justify the application of an anticamping regulation to protesters who wanted to sleep in tents in Lafayette Park in order to demonstrate the plight of the homeless (293–99). Contrary to the rule in *Smith*, the Park Service had to do more than to simply point to the neutral rule of general applicability. Instead, the Park Service had to show that it was a sufficiently important rule backed by sufficiently important reasons to justify applying it to prohibit even the politically expressive camping at issue.

In *Berne v. Flores*, 521 U.S. 507 (1997), the *Smith* neutrality doctrine was reaffirmed. There, a generally applicable zoning ordinance that required permission to make structural changes in a designated historical area was enforced against a Catholic church wanting to expand so as to accommodate its growing congregation (511–13). (After permission to modify the church building was denied, the church filed suit.) Prior to *Smith*, the First Amendment itself would have required the demonstration of a compelling government interest before a zoning ordinance could trump a church's efforts to accommodate the worship needs of its parishioners. But after *Smith*, the First Amendment provided no protection to the church, effectively giving the city council the absolute power to deny the church an exemption from the ordinance.

25. *Witters v. Washington Department of Services for the Blind*, 474 U.S. 481 (1986); *Mueller v. Allen*, 463 U.S. 388 (1983); *Witters*, 474 U.S. 481; *Zobrest*, 509 U.S. 1; and *Agostini v. Felton*, 521 U.S. 203 (1997), respectively.

26. *Bowen v. Kendrick*, 487 U.S. 589 (1988).

27. *Zelman*, 536 U.S. 639; *Witters*, 474 U.S. 481; *Mueller*, 463 U.S. 388.

28. As long as the government does not engage in religious discrimination in its aid programs, then it should not matter whether the aid is indirect or direct. *Mitchell v. Helms*, 530 U.S. 793, 830 (2000).

29. *Zelman*, 536 U.S. 639, 663 (O'Connor, J., concurring).

30. Anthony T. Kovalchick, "Educational Aid Programs under the Establishment Clause: The Need for the U.S. Supreme Court to Adopt the Rule Proposed by the Mitchell Plurality," 30 *Southern University Law Review* 117, 148 (2003).

31. *Agostini v. Felton*, 521 U.S. 203, 234. In *Agostini*, the Court designed a test for purposes of evaluating the validity of governmental programs that include some degree of interaction between the public school system and competing schools, many of which are sectarian. Under the *Agostini* test, which is a modification of the old *Lemon* test, all three factors relate to the larger rule that the statute's primary effect must be one that neither advances nor inhibits religion.

32. Indeed, indoctrination occurs in public schools everyday, when children whose families believe in creationism are taught only the theory of evolution, and when sex education courses completely ignore or ridicule certain religious beliefs.

33. *Agostini,* 521 U.S. 203, 225–26.

34. For a discussion of law governing public funding of educational materials supplied to religious schools, see Douglas Kmiec, "Does the Establishment Clause Require Exclusion or Nondiscrimination in the Public Provision of Instructional Materials to Religious Schools?" *Preview U.S. Supreme Court Cases,* Nov. 18, 1999, 158.

35. *Mitchell,* 530 U.S. 793, 818, 841–44. In *Agostini,* the Court had relied on the principle of neutrality, as well as on two indirect-aid cases, to uphold a provision for direct aid to religious schools. The two indirect aid cases were *Zobrest,* 509 U.S. 1 and *Witters,* 474 U.S. 481.

36. *Mitchell* involved chapter 2 of the Education Consolidation and Improvement Act of 1981, which provided funds to both public and private schools for the acquisition and use of instructional and educational materials (802). The funds were distributed to each school based on the number of children enrolled in that school. Ibid., 820, 795.

37. Ibid., 840.

38. In the aftermath of *Agostini v. Felton,* most courts were of the view that "the Establishment clause required nothing more than governmental neutrality towards religion." Kovalchick, "Educational Aid Programs," 120n313. But Justice O'Connor's concurring opinion in *Mitchell* rejected such a broad interpretation of *Agostini* and instead argued that the government cannot include sectarian institutions in generally available aid programs without running afoul of the establishment clause.

39. *Mitchell,* 530 U.S. 793, at 826.

40. *Steele v. Industrial Development Board,* 117 F.Supp.2d 693 (M.D. Tenn. 2000).

41. *Bowen,* 487 U.S. 589, 621, 613. But this approach calls for too much line drawing—e.g., a religion may not engage in sectarian instruction with government money solely to advance a particular sect, but it may engage in instruction on a government program topic from a religious perspective or with some religious content.

42. *DeStefano,* 247 F.3d 397, 417–19 (2d Cir. 2001).

43. *School District of City of Grand Rapids v. Ball,* 473 U.S. 373, 389 (1985), *overruled in part* by *Agostini,* 521 U.S. 203.

44. As stated above, "neutrality" is a descriptive term applied to the *Rosenberger* and *Good News* opinions. In the legal literature, those opinions are often categorized under a label of antidiscrimination.

45. *Brownfield v. Daniel Freeman Marina Hospital,* 256 Cal. Rptr. 240 (Ct. App. 1989).

46. Heather Rae Skeeles, "Patient Autonomy versus Religious Freedom: Should State Legislatures Require Catholic Hospitals to Provide Emergency Contraception to Rape Victims?" 60 *Washington and Lee Law Review* 1007, 1017 (2003).

47. *Catholic Charities of Sacramento, Inc. v. Superior Court,* 10 Cal. Rptr.3d 283 (2004).

48. Jesse H. Choper, *Securing Religious Liberty: Principles for Judicial In-*

terpretation of the Religion Clauses (Chicago: University of Chicago Press, 1995), 21. Neutrality prevents any special treatment from being given to religion, but it does not always prevent special disadvantage from being cast on religion. The National Endowment for the Arts could never sponsor an exhibit called "Glorify Christ," as it did Andre Serrano's "Piss Christ."

49. Philip Howard, "Charity Case," *Wall Street Journal,* March 17, 2005, A16.

50. Choper, *Securing Religious Liberty,* 148.

51. Brownstein, *Protecting Religious Liberty,* 147–51.

52. Dean M. Kelley, "Free Enterprise in Religion, or How the Constitution Protects Religion and Religious Freedom," in *How Does the Constitution Protect Religious Freedom?* ed. Robert Goldwin and Art Kaufman (Washington, D.C.: American Enterprise Institute for Public Policy Research, 1987), 129–30; *Ethical Culture v. Spatt,* 51 N.Y.2d 449 (1980).

53. *Grace United Methodist Church v. City of Cheyenne,* 235 F.Supp.2d 1186, 1201 (D. Wy. 2002).

54. For cases upholding zoning regulations that burden religious groups, see *Islamic Center of Mississippi v. City of Starkville,* 840 F.2d 293, 302 (5th Cir. 1988); *Christian Gospel Church v. City and County of San Francisco,* 896 F.2d 1221 (9th Cir. 1990). On the other hand, for a case that discusses the dangers that zoning ordinances pose to religious exercise, as well as their "nonneutrality," see *Cam v. Marion County,* 987 F.Supp. 854, 862 (D. Ore. 1997).

55. *Vineyard Christian Fellowship of Evanston v. City of Evanston,* 250 F.Supp.2d 961 (N.D. Ill. 2003).

56. *Locke v. Davey,* 540 U.S. 1307 (2004). According to Professor Laycock, "the Court had never before held that the state can discriminate against religion." Laycock, "Theology Scholarships," 171. Surprisingly, the Court held that "*Lukumi's* ban on discriminatory regulation did not apply to a discriminatory refusal to fund the training of the clergy" (173). Thus, the discriminatory refusal to fund was not presumptively unconstitutional. Although *Smith* and *Lukumi* prohibit facial discrimination against religion as the most basic requirement of neutrality, "*Davey* upholds facial discrimination against religion, without requiring a compelling justification" (ibid., 213). Consequently, *Davey* constitutes "an important exception to the remaining protection for religious practice" (213–14).

57. The *Davey* Court stated that failure to fund did not impose a significant burden.

58. As Professor Laycock speculates, *Davey* "is likely to lead to a more general principle that all religious programs and institutions can be excluded from funding programs." Laycock, "Theology Scholarships," 186. Yet, according to Professor Berg, "the exclusion of religious schools or social services from funding programs creates a disincentive for beneficiaries to use religious options as compared with subsidized secular options." Thomas Berg, "The Voluntary Principle and Church Autonomy, Then and Now," 2004 *Brigham Young University Law Review* 1593, 1605 (2004). In the welfare state, "the vitality and mission of religious organizations also face threats if these organizations are denied assistance while their secular competitors receive it" (1605).

59. *Bagley v. Raymond School Department,* 728 A.2d 127 (Me. 1999).

60. California Civil Procedure Code §340.1(c) (2003).

61. Patrick J. Schiltz, "The Impact of Clergy Sexual Misconduct Litigation on Religious Liberty," 44 *Boston College Law Review* 949, 959, 973 (2003).

62. *KDM ex rel. WJM v. Reedsport School District,* 196 F.3d 1046, 1050 (9th Cir. 1999).

63. Ibid., 1050. While this rationale obviously curtails the ability of courts to protect the free exercise of religion, it seems to contradict the applicable law, as laid down in *Smith* and then in *Lukumi,* 508 U.S. 520. *Lukumi* requires that nonneutral laws burdening religious practice must undergo strict scrutiny (546). Although a plaintiff challenging a facially nonneutral law must still demonstrate that it burdens free exercise, the court is supposed to examine the burden within the context of strict scrutiny.

64. Conkle, "Path of American Religious Liberty," 14.

65. *Brown v. Board of Education of Topeka, Shawnee County, Kansas,* 347 U.S. 483 (1954).

66. Choper, *Securing Religious Liberty,* 21.

67. Conkle, "Path of American Religious Liberty," 25.

68. Chester J. Antieau et al., *Freedom from Federal Establishment: Formation and Early History of the First Amendment Religion Clauses* (Milwaukee: Bruce Publishing, 1964), 187–88 (describing the framers' understanding of the presence of religious ideals in governmental institutions). Some critics claim that neutrality is a ploy by which religious influences, implicitly recognized by the First Amendment, are rejected in favor of an opposing establishment such as secularism. Daniel L. Dreisbach, *Real Threat and Mere Shadow: Religious Liberty and the First Amendment* (Westchester, Ill.: Crossway Books, 1987), 73. They see neutrality is a mythical construct meant to advance the court's "religious" bias of secularism (ibid., 106).

Notes to Chapter 5

1. Thomas J. Curry, *The First Freedoms: Church and State in America to the Passage of the First Amendment* (New York: Oxford University Press, 1986), 22, 51 (1986); Leonard W. Levy, *The Establishment Clause: Religion and the First Amendment,* 2d ed. (Chapel Hill: University of North Carolina Press, 1994), 1–11. See also Charles J. Reid Jr., "The Fundamental Freedom: Judge John T. Noonan Jr.'s Historiography of Religious Liberty," 83 *Marquette Law Review* 367 (1999).

2. Michael W. McConnell, "Accommodation of Religion: An Update and a Response to the Critics," 60 *George Washington Law Review* 685, 714 (1992). Generally, whenever conflicts occurred between civil law and religious belief, the latter was accommodated; and these accommodations were never seen as amounting to impermissible establishments (715).

3. Jonathan Van Patten, "In the End Is the Beginning: An Inquiry into the Meaning of the Religion Clauses," 27 *St. Louis University Law Journal* 76 (1983).

4. Michael W. McConnell, "Establishment and Disestablishment at the Founding, Part I: Establishment of Religion," 44 *William and Mary Law Review* 2105, 2186.

5. Edmund Morgan, *The Puritan Dilemma: The Story of John Winthrop* (New York: Harper Collins, 1958), 155.

6. *Engel v. Vitale,* 370 U.S. 421, 429–30 (1962); *McGowan v. Maryland,* 366 U.S. 420, 437–40 (1961).

7. McConnell, "Establishment and Disestablishment," 2108.

8. Tocqueville likewise observed that the early Americans considered religion "necessary to the maintenance of republican institutions." Alexis de Tocqueville, *Democracy in America,* ed. J. P. Mayer (Garden City, N.Y.: Anchor Books, 1969), 293. He came to agree with this position, arguing that religion was desperately needed in a democratic republic (294). Jefferson, in his *Notes on Virginia,* expressed the sentiment that belief in divine justice was essential to the liberties of the nation: "And can the liberties of a nation be thought secure when we have removed their only firm basis, a conviction in the minds of the people that these liberties are of the gift of God?" Thomas Jefferson, *The Life and Selected Writings of Thomas Jefferson,* ed. Adrienne Koch and William Peden (New York: Random House, 1944), 278–79.

9. For a discussion on the influence of republican thought on the writing of the Constitution, see Thomas L. Pangle, *The Spirit of Modern Republicanism: The Moral Vision of the American Founders and the Philosophy of Locke* (Chicago: University of Chicago Press, 1988).

10. John Adams, *The Works of John Adams,* ed. C. F. Adams (Boston: Little, Brown, 1850–56), 9:229.

11. *The Spur of Fame: Dialogues of John Adams and Benjamin Rush,* ed. John A. Schutz and Douglass Adair (San Marino, Calif.: Huntington Library, 1966), 192. According to Benjamin Rush, "The only foundation for a useful education in a republic is to be laid in religion. Without it there can be no virtue, and without virtue there can be no liberty, and liberty is the object and life of all republican governments." Quoted in Brian Anderson, "Secular Europe, Religious America," *Public Interest* (April 1, 2004): 143.

12. Anson Phelps Stokes, *Church and State in the United States* (New York: Harper, 1950), 515.

13. *The Complete Anti-Federalist,* ed. Herbert J. Storing (Chicago: University of Chicago Press, 1981), 4:242.

14. Joseph Viteritti, *Choosing Equality: School Choice, the Constitution, and Civil Society* (Washington, D.C.: Brookings Institute Press, 1999). According to the framers, only within a religious congregation would people develop the civic virtue necessary for self-government.

15. David Barton, "The Image and the Reality: Thomas Jefferson and the First Amendment," 17 *Notre Dame Journal of Law, Ethics and Public Policy* 399, 428 (2003). George Washington saw religion as an incubator for the kind of civic virtue on which democratic government had to rely. Viteritti, *Choosing Equality,* 127.

16. Viteritti, *Choosing Equality,* 127.

17. A. James Reichley, *Religion in American Public Life* (Washington, D.C.: Brookings Institute Press, 1985), 99.

18. James D. Richardson, ed., *A Compilation of the Messages and Papers of the Presidents* (New York: Bureau of National Literature, 1897), 212. The framers believed, as for instance did George Washington, that religion and morality were the "indispensable supports" for democratic government. President George Washington, "Washington's Farewell Address (Sept. 17, 1796)," in *Documents of American History*, ed. Henry S. Commager (New York: Appleton-Century-Crofts, 1973), 1:169, 173.

19. J. William Frost, "Pennsylvania Institutes Religious Liberty," in *All Imaginable Liberty: The Religious Liberty Clauses of the First Amendment*, ed. Francis Graham Lee (Lanham, Md.: University Press of America, 1995), 45–46. Blasphemy laws, for instance, were predicated on the widespread belief that to attack the basics of Christianity was to endanger the foundation of society. And "virtually no one opposed some kind of a sabbatarian law in either the colonial or early national period, and every state had such a law" (ibid., 48).

20. Michael W. McConnell, "Why Is Religious Liberty the 'First Freedom'?" 21 *Cardozo Law Review* 1243, 1253 (2000); John G. West, *The Politics of Revelation and Reason: Religion and Civic Life in the New Nation* (Lawrence: University of Kansas Press, 1996), 11–78. Through the middle of the nineteenth century, it was common practice for religious schools to be supported by state-generated revenue. Carl F. Kaestle, *Pillars of the Republic: Common Schools and American Society* (New York: Hill and Wang, 1983), 166–67.

21. Richard Vetterli and Gary C. Bryner, "Religion, Public Virtue, and the Founding of the American Republic," in *Toward a More Perfect Union: Six Essays on the Constitution*, ed. Neil L. York (Provo, Utah: Brigham Young University, 1988), 91–92.

22. Dreisbach, *Real Threat and Mere Shadow: Religious Liberty and the First Amendment* (Westchester, Ill.: Crossway Books, 1987), 22.

23. Curry, *First Freedoms,* 218.

24. McConnell, "Accommodation of Religion," 2197.

25. And no one seriously disputed the close relation between government and religion. McConnell, "Establishment and Disestablishment," 2193.

26. John Witte, *Religion and the American Constitutional Experiment: Essential Rights and Liberties* (Boulder: Westview Press, 2000), 53.

27. Akhil Reed Amar, *The Bill of Rights: Creation and Reconstruction* (New Haven: Yale University Press, 1998), 32–33.

28. Edwin S. Gaustad, "Religion and Ratification," in *The First Freedom: Religion and the Bill of Rights*, ed. James E. Wood Jr. (Waco: Baylor University Press, 1990), 53.

29. Statutes at Large of Pennsylvania (1779), 9:313; Pennsylvania Statutes (1794), printed in James Dunlop, *General Laws of Pennsylvania* (1847), 151–54.

30. *The Federal and State Constitutions*, ed. Francis Thorpe (Washington, D.C.: U.S. Government Printing Office, 1909), 3:1189, 1705.

31. Curry, *First Freedoms,* 186.

32. Viteritti, *Choosing Equality,* 16. And those who advocated government

support of religion saw it as "compatible with religious freedom"; they did not equate it with establishment. Curry, *First Freedoms,* 217.

33. Ellis Sandoz, *A Government of Laws: Political Theory, Religion, and the Founding* (Baton Rouge: Louisiana State University Press, 1990), 16; Patricia U. Bonomi, *Under the Cope of Heaven: Religion, Society and Politics in Colonial America* (New York: Oxford University Press, 1986).

34. The Northwest Ordinance is reprinted in a footnote to Act of Aug. 7, 1789, chapter 8, 1, statute 50. Gaustad, "Religion and Ratification," 41–59.

35. Anson Stokes and Leo Pfeffer, *Church and State in the United States* (New York: Harper and Row, 1964), 85.

36. Witte, *Religion and the American Constitutional Experiment,* 58; Rodney K. Smith, *Public Prayer and the Constitution: A Case Study in Constitutional Interpretation* (Wilmington, Del.: Scholarly Resources, 1987), 66.

37. Thomas Nathan Peters, "Religion, Establishment and the Northwest Ordinance: A Closer Look at an Accommodationist Argument," 89 *Kentucky Law Journal* 743, 772 (2000–2001) (The Northwest Ordinance was originally enacted by the Continental Congress in 1787, and then reenacted and adopted in 1789 by the First Congress).

38. David Tyack et al., *Law and the Shaping of Public Education, 1785–1954* (Madison: University of Wisconsin Press, 1987), 26–27.

39. Peters, "Religion, Establishment and the Northwest Ordinance," 772, 103.

40. Saul Padover, *The Complete Jefferson* (Freeport, N.Y.: Books for Libraries 1969), 1110.

41. *Annals of Congress,* 1st Cong., 1st sess., 451. Beginning with the first session of the Continental Congress in 1774, the legislature opened its sessions with prayer; and the First Congress in 1789 established the office of congressional chaplain. Kurt T. Lash, "Power and the Subject of Religion," 59 *Ohio State Law Journal* 1069 (1998). Moreover, during the Constitutional Convention itself, Benjamin Franklin had asked that the convention resort to prayer to overcome an impasse on certain divisive issues. Charles E. Rice, *The Supreme Court and Public Prayer* (New York: Fordham University Press, 1964), 36–37.

42. Stokes and Pfeffer, *Church and State,* 87–88. Public religious proclamations were common in the postconstitutional period, beginning with George Washington's first inaugural address, in which Washington referred to the role of divine providence in guiding the formation of the United States. See Washington's First Inaugural Address, reprinted in Richardson, *Compilation of the Messages and Papers of the Presidents,* 43. See Smith, *Public Prayer and the Constitution,* 103, on opening sessions of Congress with a prayer.

43. Dreisbach, *Real Threat and Mere Shadow,* 150–51. James Madison saw religious duties as higher than civil duties. As he argued in his *Memorial and Remonstrance against Religious Assessments* (reprinted in *The Founders Constitution,* ed. Philip B. Kurland and Ralph Lerner [Indianapolis: Liberty Fund, 1978], 5:82), an individual's duty to God "is precedent, both in order of time and in degree of obligation, to the claims of civil society. Before any man can be considered as a member of civil society, he must be considered a sub-

ject of the Governor of the Universe." See also Thomas Jefferson, *The Papers of Thomas Jefferson,* ed. Julian Boyd (Princeton: Princeton University Press, 1950), 2:556.

44. James M. O'Neill, "Nonpreferential Aid to Religion Is Not an Establishment of Religion," 2 *Buffalo Law Review* 242, 255 (1952).

45. Curry, *First Freedoms,* 146, 192.

46. *Walz v. Tax Commission of City of New York,* 397 U.S. 664, 668 (1970) (stating that "for the men who wrote the Religion Clauses of the First Amendment the 'establishment' of a religion connoted sponsorship, financial support, and active involvement of the sovereign in religious activity").

47. As Noah Feldman argues, the establishment clause was meant to protect religious liberty. Noah Feldman, "The Intellectual Origins of the Establishment Clause," 77 *New York University Law Review* 346, 403–5, 428 (2002). Similarly, Philip Hamburger interprets the establishment clause in terms of protecting religious liberty. He argues that the notion of separation of church and state arose from the desire to keep religion uncorrupted by worldly influences. Philip Hamburger, *Separation of Church and State* (Cambridge: Harvard University Press, 2002), 29, 38–39. Hamburger concludes from his historical study that the framers did not expect church and state to be kept apart from each other, but that the state would protect the church and would be the beneficiary of its moral influence (22, 24, 27).

48. Elisha Williams, *The Essential Rights and Liberties of Protestants* (Boston: S. Kneeland and T. Green, 1744), 46.

49. Witte, *Religion and the American Constitutional Experiment,* 51.

50. The Anglican Church required use of the King James version of the Bible, dictated the contents of the *Book of Common Prayer,* and demanded adherence to the Thirty-Nine Articles of Faith.

51. McConnell, "Establishment and Disestablishment," 2131.

52. Religious doctrines and liturgies were governed by Parliament, which also enacted legislation restricting public worship by Catholics, Puritans, and Quakers. Indeed, an array of penal laws punished Catholics, Puritans, and Quakers who attempted the open exercise of religious faith outside the official church. Ursula Henriques, *Religious Toleration in England, 1787–1833* (Toronto: University of Toronto Press, 1961), 6.

53. Frederick Mark Gedicks, "A Two-Track Theory of the Establishment Clause," 43 *Boston College Law Review* 1071, 1091 (2002).

54. McConnell, "Establishment and Disestablishment," 2133.

55. William Blackstone, *Commentaries on the Laws of England,* vol. 4 (Philadelphia: R. Welsh and Co., 1961), 51–52.

56. Sanford H. Cobb, *The Rise of Religious Liberty in America: A History* (New York: Macmillan, 1902), 49–51.

57. Curry, *First Freedoms,* 211.

58. Patrick W. Carey, "American Catholics and the First Amendment," in Lee, *All Imaginable Liberty,* 115. Even in Virginia, with the established Anglican Church, the growing sentiment in the late eighteenth century was that, while government could indeed give aid to religion, there should be equal treatment

in such aid. Smith, *Public Prayer and the Constitution,* 45. This view that no single religion should be aided to the exclusion of others existed side by side during the founding era with the view that Christianity should be exclusively aided, though in a nondenominational sense and with tolerance toward other beliefs (Smith, 56). As the French philosopher Jacques Maritain observed in *Reflections on America,* the phrase "separation of church and state" in eighteenth-century America meant "a refusal to grant any privilege to one religious denomination in preference to others." Quoted in Michael Novak, "The Faith of the Founding," *First Things* (April 2003): 27.

59. Curry, *First Freedoms,* 209. "The dominant image of establishment Americans carried with them from the colonial period on was that of an exclusive government preference for one religion" (210).

60. Mary Virginia Geiger, *Daniel Carroll: A Framer of the Constitution* (Washington, D.C.: Catholic University of America Press, 1943), 83–84. This nonpreferentialist tradition approves of government aid to religion generally, so long as that aid is not discriminatory among particular sects. Levy, *The Establishment Clause: Religion and the First Amendment* (New York: Macmillan, 1986), 91.

61. Thomas M. Cooley, *A Treatise on the Constitutional Limitations* (Boston: Little, Brown, 1883). The Reverend Jaspar Adams, cousin of John Quincy Adams, wrote in 1833 that the term "establishment of religion" meant "the preference and establishment given by law to one sect of Christians over every other." Quoted in Dreisbach, *Real Threat and Mere Shadow,* 70.

62. Adam Smith, *An Inquiry into the Nature and Causes of the Wealth of Nations,* book 5, chapter 1, part 2, article 3 (1776; Oxford: Clarendon Press, 1976), 309–10.

63. Madison, "Memorial and Remonstrance against Religious Assessments."

64. Elisha Williams, *The Essential Rights and Liberties of Protestants: A Seasonable Plea for the Liberty of Conscience and the Right of Private Judgment in Matters of Religion without Any Controul from Human Authority* (1744), 24.

65. Carl Esbeck, "Dissent and Disestablishment: The Church-State Settlement in the Early American Republic," 2004 *Brigham Young University Law Review* 1385, 1506. As some eighteenth-century writers argued, an "established religion is ultimately a religion controlled by irreligious persons" (1521). The drive for disestablishment was motivated in part by a desire to "stop the corruption of institutional religion that follows from too close an embrace by Caesar" (1580).

66. McConnell, "Why Is Religious Liberty the 'First Freedom'?" 1257.

67. Jonathan Elliot, ed., *The Debates in the Several State Conventions on the Adoption of the Federal Constitution* (Philadelphia: J. B. Lippincott, 1941), 4:198–99.

68. Ibid., 3:330; Levy, *Establishment Clause,* 125.

69. James Madison, *Papers,* ed. William T. Hutchinson et al. (Chicago: University of Chicago Press, 1962), 8:149.

70. James McClellan, *Joseph Story and the American Constitution* (Norman: University of Oklahoma Press, 1971), 134.

71. Chester J. Antieau et al., *Freedom from Federal Establishment: Formation and Early History of the First Amendment Religion Clauses* (Milwaukee: Bruce Publishing, 1964), 132.

72. Curry, *First Freedoms,* 151, 159.

73. Witte, *Religion and the American Constitutional Experiment,* 91; Constitution of Arkansas (1874), article 2, 24, 25.

74. Dreisbach, *Real Threat and Mere Shadow,* 54.

75. Michael S. Ariens and Robert A. Destro, *Religious Liberty in a Pluralistic Society* (Durham: Carolina Academic Press, 1996), 89. The clause was not a prohibition on favoritism toward religion in general. Dreisbach, *Real Threat and Mere Shadow,* 70.

76. *Annals of Congress,* 1st Cong., 1st sess., 758.

77. Quoted in William Gerald McLoughlin, *New England Dissent, 1630–1833* (Cambridge: Harvard University Press, 1971), 2:864.

78. Curry, *First Freedoms,* 191.

79. Theodore Sky, "The Establishment Clause, the Congress, and the Schools: An Historical Perspective," 52 *Virginia Law Review* 1395, 1427 (1966).

80. Smith, *Public Prayer and the Constitution,* 56. What Madison opposed was government promotion of religion in a manner that would compel individuals to worship contrary to their conscience (82). He feared that one sect might obtain a preeminence and establish a religion to which it would compel others to conform. Laurie Messerly, "Reviving Religious Liberty in America," 8 *Nexus* 151, 154 (2003). Long after adoption of the First Amendment, Madison quoted the establishment clause as if it outlawed "religious establishments," as in particular sects, rather than *an* establishment of religion.

81. Walter Berns, *The First Amendment and the Future of American Democracy* (New York: Basic Books, 1976), 9. During the 1789 debates, Madison recognized that some people feared the dominance of one sect or the possibility that two might combine to establish a religion to which others would have to conform. Levy, *Establishment Clause,* 132.

82. Elliot, *Debates,* 3:330, 204, 659.

83. Curry, *First Freedoms,* 198. Even Rhode Island, which never gave any financial support to religion, proposed during its ratifying convention that the First Amendment provide that "no particular sect or society ought to be favored or established by law." Theodore Foster, *Theodore Foster's Minutes of the Convention Held at South Kingston, Rhode Island, in March, 1790,* ed. Robert C. Cotner (Freeport, N.Y.: Ayer Company, 1929), 93.

84. James Madison agreed with Justice Story's articulation of the intent of the framers: that the right of free exercise was the preeminent right protected by the First Amendment. Smith, *Public Prayer and the Constitution,* 84, 79. Professor Tribe likewise agrees that the framers intended that the protection of free exercise be considered preeminent, with the establishment clause merely promoting that end by precluding the national government from establishing a religion. Laurence H. Tribe, *American Constitutional Law* (Mineda, N.Y.: Foundation Press, 1978), 819.

85. Smith, *Public Prayer and the Constitution,* 84.

86. Daniel Webster, *Works of Daniel Webster* (Boston: Little, Brown, 1851), 6:176.

87. Ibid., 108; Joseph Story, *Commentaries on the Constitution of the United*

States, 2d ed. (1851), 593–97. According to Story, the establishment clause mere-ly helped to effectuate the inalienable right of free exercise by preventing any particular sect from being established, at the national level. Strict separationists have ignored the historical data in their effort to build their case. They have se-lectively used snippets of history to justify an otherwise historically unsupport-able position. Smith, *Public Prayer and the Constitution,* 55–56.

88. McClellan, *Joseph Story and the American Constitution,* 136. On the other hand, the more separationist view espoused by Jefferson "was clearly not shared by a large majority of his contemporaries" (ibid.). Until the mid-twenti-eth century, American courts consistently endorsed the importance of religion in the nation's public life. Douglas W. Kmiec and Stephen B. Presser, *The American Constitutional Order: History, Cases, and Philosophy* (Cincinnati: Anderson Pub-lishing, 1998), 185–86.

89. Thomas Jefferson, "Reply to a Committee of the Danbury Baptist Asso-ciation" (Jan. 1, 1802), in *The Writings of Thomas Jefferson,* vol. 16, ed. Andrew A. Lipscomb and Albert Ellery Bergh (Washington, D.C.: Thomas Jefferson Me-morial Association, 1905), 281–82. The "wall of separation" phrase, however, did make its first appearance in a Supreme Court opinion on free exercise in *Reyn-olds v. United States,* 98 U.S. 145, 164 (1878). But since Jefferson was not even present at the convention preparing the Constitution or at the congressional de-bates over the Bill of Rights, he is not an appropriate authority for stating the intended meaning of the establishment clause. *Reynolds,* 163 (Jefferson was in France).

90. Hamburger, *Separation of Church and State,* 454–55, 458. As Profes-sor Hamburger points out, the majority of eighteenth-century Americans did not wish to disconnect religion from government, only to disestablish denominations that were financially supported by the government (11–12). But when separa-tion was adopted as a constitutional principle in the mid-twentieth century, it was done so by justices who had become oriented by the prevailing culture to think of religious freedom in terms of separation of church and state (458). Thus, by 1947, the separation ideal had become so entrenched in American cultural thought, and so mistakenly attributed to the framers' intent, that the Supreme Court was persuaded to endorse it in *Everson* (434–35, 446, 449, 454–63).

91. *Wallace v. Jaffree,* 472 U.S. 38, 107 (1985) (Rehnquist, J., dissenting).

92. Reba Carolyn Strickland, *Religion and the State in Georgia in the Eigh-teenth Century* (New York: Columbia University Press, 1939), 166.

93. State of Delaware, *The First Laws of the State of Delaware,* vol. 2, part 1, ed. John D. Cushing (1797; Wilmington, Del.: Michael Glazier, 1981), 878–79.

94. *Journal of the Proceedings of the Legislative Council of New Jersey,* Sept. 13 and Oct. 30, 1789.

95. McConnell, "Establishment and Disestablishment," 2158.

96. Jacob Marcellus Kirk, *Church and State* (New York: Thomas Nelson and Sons, 1963), 116. Moreover, the words "church" and "state" refer to institutions, whereas "religion" refers more generally to the beliefs and practices of society. As Michael Novak notes, "the sphere of society is much larger than that of state." Novak, "Faith of the Founding," 28.

97. As Professor Esbeck argues, a "separation of religion-based values from government and public affairs would have been received with wide disapprobation in the new nation." Esbeck, "Dissent and Disestablishment," 1580.

98. Stephen L. Carter, "Reflections on the Separation of Church and State," 44 *Arizona Law Review* 293, 297 (2002).

99. Bernard Bailyn, *The Ideological Origins of the American Revolution,* enl. ed. (Cambridge: Belknap Press of Harvard University Press, 1992), 315. Ellis Sandoz, ed., *Political Sermons of the American Founding Era, 1730–1805* (Indianapolis: Liberty Fund, 1991), 139, 165, 713, 738.

100. Story, *Commentaries on the Constitution,* 3d ed. (1858), 2:663 (stating that "at the time of the adoption of the Constitution, and of the [first] amendment to it . . . , the general, if not the universal sentiment in America was, that Christianity ought to receive encouragement from the state, so far as was not incompatible with the private rights of conscience, and the freedom of religious worship"). Thomas M. Cooley, *The General Principles of Constitutional Law* (Boston: Little, Brown, 1880), 205–6 (stating that it "was never intended that by the Constitution the government should be prohibited from recognizing religion, or that religious worship should never be provided for in cases where a proper recognition of Divine Providence in the working of government might seem to require it, and where it might be done without drawing any invidious distinctions between different religious beliefs, organizations, or sects"). Moreover, the political debates of the framers made frequent use of biblical references. One scholar surveyed 3,154 citations made by the founders and discovered that more than one-third of them were to the Bible. Anderson, "Secular Europe, Religious America," 143.

101. Mark DeWolfe Howe, *The Garden and the Wilderness* (Chicago: University of Chicago Press, 1965), 31. Leonard W. Levy, *Constitutional Opinions: Aspects of the Bill of Rights* (New York: Oxford University Press, 1986), 142 (observing that "[m]any contemporaries [of the Constitutional Convention] . . . believed that governments could and should foster religion"). During the constitutional period, civic republicans believed that "the existence of healthy religious institutions was essential to the health of the state, and that the existence of healthy religious institutions depended on the support and protection of the state." Esbeck, "Dissent and Disestablishment," 1574.

102. Dreisbach, *Real Threat and Mere Shadow,* 84. Robert Allen Rutland, *The Birth of the Bill of Rights* (Chapel Hill: University of North Carolina Press, 1955), 127, 166–67, 184, 209.

103. Witte, *Religion and the American Constitutional Experiment,* 47; Antieau et al., *Freedom from Federal Establishment,* 187–88 (describing the framers' understanding of the presence of religious ideals in governmental institutions); Curry, *First Freedoms,* 190. This affirmative public support of religion was exemplified in the immediate postrevolutionary era, when the new state legislatures enacted assessments to be paid to the church or denomination designated by each taxpayer. Esbeck, "Dissent and Disestablishment," 1489.

104. McConnell, "Establishment and Disestablishment," 2194.

105. Thomas E. Buckley, *Church and State in Revolutionary Virginia* (Charlottesville: University Press of Virginia, 1977), 73–74, 81–82.

106. McConnell, "Establishment and Disestablishment," 2196.

107. Alexis de Tocqueville, *Democracy in America,* ed. J. P. Meyer and Max Lerner (1835; New York: Harper and Row, 1966), 294.

108. *Annals of Congress,* 1st Cong., 1st sess., 1759, cols. 18–19, 233.

109. *The Debates and Proceedings in the Congress of the United States, Compiled from Authentic Materials,* ed. Joseph Gales and W. W. Seaton, 42 vols. (Washington, D.C., 1834–56), 1:448–59.

110. McConnell, "Establishment and Disestablishment," 2205.

111. Curry, *First Freedoms,* 183.

112. Witte, *Religion and the American Constitutional Experiment,* 91.

113. Charles J. Russo, "Prayer at Public School Graduation Ceremonies: An Exercise in Futility or a Teachable Moment?" 1999 *Brigham Young University Education and Law Journal* 1, 2 (1999). For a review of the status of state-established churches at the time of the Revolutionary War, see Richard Hoskins, "The Original Separation of Church and State in America," 2 *Journal of Law and Religion* 221 (1984); Kent Greenwalt, "Religious Convictions and Lawmaking," 84 *Michigan Law Review* 352 (1985).

114. *Engel v. Vitale,* 370 U.S. 421, 445 (1962). This is evidence that "some forms of public prayer were not believed to constitute an establishment of religion." Jonathan Van Patten, "In the End Is the Beginning: An Inquiry into the Meaning of the Religion Clauses," 27 *Saint Louis University Law Journal* 1, 23 (1983). Even though article 6 of the Constitution barred religious tests from being a qualification for federal office, religious tests for office were commonplace at the state level. Gerard V. Bradley, "The No Religious Test Clause and the Constitution of Religious Liberty: A Machine That Has Gone of Itself," 37 *Case Western Reserve Law Review* 674 (1987). Indeed, they survived decades longer than any other aspect of religious establishment. This shows how much the framers intended to exert a religious influence on government and public affairs.

115. And late into the twentieth century, a congressional law still required the president "to set aside and proclaim a suitable day each year, other than a Sunday, as a National Day of Prayer." 36 U.S.C. §169(h) (1976).

116. Elton Trueblood, *Abraham Lincoln: Theologian of American Anguish* (New York: Harper and Row, 1973), 135–36.

117. Entitled "Let Our Hearts Be Stout: A Prayer by the President of the United States," it read in part: "Almighty God—Our sons, pride of our nation, this day have set upon a mighty endeavor, a struggle to preserve our Republic, our religion and our civilization, and to set free a suffering humanity."

118. *People v. Ruggles,* 8 Johns. 290, 295 (N.Y. Sup. Ct. 1811).

119. *Barnes v. First Parish in Falmouth,* 6 Mass. 401, 404 (1810).

120. *Vidal v. Girard's Executors,* 43 U.S. (2 How.) 127, 198 (1844).

121. Witte, *Religion and the American Constitutional Experiment,* 94, 96.

122. John T. Norman, Jr., *The Lustre of Our Country: The American Experience of Religious Freedom* (Berkeley and Los Angeles: University of California Press, 1998), 218.

123. Cobb, *Rise of Religious Liberty in America,* 516.

124. Bernard Bailyn, *Education and the Forming of American Society* (New York: Vintage Books, 1960).

125. Diane Ravitch, *The Great School Wars, New York City, 1805–1973: A History of the New York City Public Schools as a Battlefield of Social Change* (New York: Basic Books, 1974), 6–7.

126. Alexis de Tocqueville, *Democracy in America*, ed. Philips Bradley (New York: Knopf, 1945), 320n4.

127. Carl F. Kaestle, *Pillars of the Republic: Common Schools and American Society, 1780–1860* (New York: Hill and Wang, 1983), 166–67.

128. Tyack et al., *Law and the Shaping of Public Education*, 90–91.

129. Richard J. Gabel, *Public Funds for Church and Private Schools* (Washington, D.C.: Catholic University of America Press, 1937), 173–79.

130. Philip R. Popple and Leslie Leighninger, *Social Work, Social Welfare, and American Society* (Boston: Allyn and Bacon, 1990), 103–7. It was religious organizations that performed most social services, including education. William C. Bower, *Church and State in Education* (Chicago: University of Chicago Press, 1944), 23–24 (stating that "the earliest education in America was predominantly religious").

131. Mark E. Chopko, "Religious Access to Public Programs and Governmental Funding," 60 *George Washington Law Review* 645, 647 (1992).

132. *Bradfield v. Roberts,* 175 U.S. 291, 296–97 (1899).

133. Witte, *Religion and the American Constitutional Experiment*, 97.

134. *Abington School District v. Schempp,* 374 U.S. 203, 237 (1963) (Brennan, J., concurring).

Notes to Chapter 6

1. John C. Jeffries Jr. and James E. Ryan, "A Political History of the Establishment Clause," 100 *Michigan Law Review* 279, 280–82 (2001).

2. Alan E. Garfield, "A Positive Rights Interpretation of the Establishment Clause," 76 *Temple Law Review* 281, 285 (2003).

3. Note, "Neutral Rules of General Applicability: Incidental Burdens on Religion, Speech and Property," 115 *Harvard Law Review* 1713, 1718 (2002).

4. Alan Schwarz, "No Imposition of Religion: The Establishment Clause Value," 77 *Yale Law Journal* 692, 711 (1968).

5. *Sechler v. State College Area School District,* 121 F.Supp.2d 439, 444 (M.D. Pa. 2000).

6. Ira C. Lupu, "Reconstructing the Establishment Clause: The Case against Discretionary Accommodation of Religion," 140 *University of Pennsylvania Law Review* 555, 597–98 (1991); Steven Gey, "Why Is Religion Special? Reconsidering the Accommodation of Religion under the Religion Clauses of the First Amendment," 52 *University of Pittsburgh Law Review* 75, 174 (1990).

7. Stephen L. Carter, *The Culture of Disbelief: How American Law and Politics Trivialize Religious Devotion* (New York: Basic Books, 1993), 37 (arguing that the "power of resistance is part of what religions are for").

8. Amy Gutman, *Democratic Education* (Princeton: Princeton University Press, 1987), 121; John C. Goodlad, "Education and Community," in *Democracy, Education, and the Schools,* ed. Roger Stone (San Francisco: Jossey-Bass, 1996), 92.

9. Richard Rorty, *Philosophy and Social Hope* (New York: Penguin Books, 1999), 168. Also, secularists use such things as the mass suicide in Jonestown and the suicidal fanaticism of the Branch Dividians in Waco, Texas, to paint a negative picture of all religions as prone to extremist and violent tendencies.

10. Macedo argues that certain religious believers (notably Catholics) should be banned from certain public positions or functions, such as judgeships. James Hitchcock, "The Enemies of Religious Liberty," *First Things* (Feb. 2004): 26. In *Please Don't Wish Me a Merry Christmas,* Steven Feldman takes the position that none of the major Christian denominations should be allowed to proselytize among non-Christians. Kathleen Sullivan argues that religion should be tolerated only if it supports the establishment of a secular moral order. In *Religious Schools vs. Children's Rights,* James Dwyer states that religious education inculcates reactionary values in children, and that government does not violate the establishment clause so long as its actions inhibit rather than benefit religion. But in response to these claims, Stephen Carter, in *Dissent of the Governed,* notes that religious faith is both incomprehensible and threatening to the liberal order, which in turn defines religion as irrational and divisive.

11. Frederick Mark Gedicks, *The Rhetoric of Church and State: A Critical Analysis of Religion Clause Jurisprudence* (Durham: Duke University Press, 1995), 119, 38, 34. Gedicks also criticizes the Court for "suggesting that evolution is a matter of objective fact, whereas creationism is a matter of subjective belief" (33). He sees an unfair "privileging of secular knowledge as objective and a marginalizing of religious belief as subjective" (32).

12. An antireligious secularism was revealed in the wake of the September 11 terrorist attacks. A call went out for intellectuals to adopt a "secular consciousness" that would mute the religious fanaticism producing such terrorism. To many secularists, it was religion—"religious or moral fundamentalists"—that had prompted the attacks. Edward W. Said, "Islam and the West Are Inadequate Banners," *London Observer,* Sept. 16, 2001, 27.

13. Indeed, many Americans are suspicious of "high-intensity faiths" and of churches that are considered "conservative" or "evangelical." In 1993, "forty-five percent of Americans admitted to 'mostly unfavorable' or 'very unfavorable' opinions of 'religious fundamentalists.'" Douglas Laycock, "State RFRAs and Land Use Regulation," 32 *University of California Davis Law Review* 755, 760 (1999).

14. Michael W. McConnell, "Why Is Religious Liberty the 'First Freedom'?" 21 *Cardozo Law Review* 1243, 1260 (2000); Walter Williams, "Attacking Western Values," *Washington Times,* Jan. 2, 2005; Joseph P. Viteritti, *Choosing Equality: School Choice, The Constitution, and Civil Society* (Washington, D.C.: Brookings Institute Press, 1999), 120.

15. It makes a big difference whether the government is deliberately forcing people to be alienated, or whether individuals are just feeling alienated because of private religious differences with the majority culture.

16. David Brooks, "One Nation, Slightly Divisible," *Atlantic Monthly,* Dec. 2001, 53, 59.

17. Stephen J. Stein, "Religion/Religions in the United States: Changing Perspectives and Prospects," 75 *Indiana Law Journal* 37, 41 (2000).

18. Alan Wolfe, *One Nation, After All* (New York: Viking, 1998), 56, 39–87, 275–322.

19. *Searcey v. Harris,* 888 F.2d 1314, 1319 (11th Cir. 1989).

20. Daniel O. Conkle, "The Path of American Religious Liberty: From the Original Theology to Formal Neutrality and an Uncertain Future," 75 *Indiana Law Journal* 1, 15 (2000).

21. Francis J. Beckwith, *Law, Darwinism, and Public Education: The Establishment Clause and the Challenge of Intelligent Design* (Lanham, Md.: Rowman and Littlefield, 2003), 146.

22. *U.S. v. Seeger,* 380 U.S. 163, 166, 180 (1965).

23. But this definition blurs the distinction between religion and nonreligion in a way that sees religious beliefs as simply one form of "internally derived" beliefs. *Seeger,* 380 U.S. 163, 186. Stein, "Religion/Religions in the United States," 58 (arguing that "religion has become whatever a person declares to be the object of regard or pursuit"). The Court appears to believe that the line between religion and nonreligion is increasingly thin in contemporary America. Conkle, "Path of American Religious Liberty," 31.

24. *Welsh v. United States,* 398 U.S. 333 (1970).

25. John T. Noonan, *The Lustre of Our Country: The American Experience of Religious Freedom* (Berkeley and Los Angeles: University of California Press, 1998), 230; Rebecca French, "Shopping for Religion: The Change in Everyday Religious Practice and Its Importance to the Law," 51 *Buffalo Law Review* 127, 140 (2003).

26. *Alliance for Bio-Integrity v. Shalala,* 116 F.Supp.2d 166, 181 (D.D.C. 2000).

27. *Yusov v. Martinez,* 2000 WL 1593387 (S.D.N.Y. 2000). Judicial hostility toward religion has shown itself in cases where religious beliefs run counter to modern medical practices. In those cases, courts often impose criminal liability on parents whose religious practices prevent them from seeking medical treatment for their children's sickness. For instance, in *Commonwealth v. Barnhart,* 497 A.2d 616 (Pa. Sup. Ct. 1985) (holding that punishment for parents' failure to seek medical treatment for their child does not violate the parents' right to freedom of religion), the court upheld the involuntary manslaughter convictions of parents who because of their religious beliefs did not obtain medical treatment of their two-year-old son's cancerous tumor. Similarly, in *Hall v. State,* 493 N.E.2d 433, 434 (Ind. 1986), the court upheld the reckless homicide conviction of parents who relied solely on spiritual healing to cure their son's pneumonia, which resulted in his death. And in *Walker v. Superior Court,* 763 P.2d 852 (Cal. 1988), a manslaughter conviction was imposed on a mother who sought spiritual treatment for her daughter's acute meningitis.

28. *United States Catholic Conference and National Conference of Catholic Bishops v. Abortion Rights Mobilization,* 487 U.S. 72 (1988).

29. Thomas Byrne Edsall, "Blue Movie: The Morality Gap is Becoming the Key Variable in American Politics," *Atlantic Monthly,* Jan./Feb. 2003, 36.

30. One recent book details the way in which the *New York Times* incorporates an antireligion stance not only on its editorial pages but in its news report-

ing as well; and this bias then spills over into all the other media outlets that rely on the *Times* for those news stories. See Bob Kohn, *Journalistic Fraud: How the New York Times Distorts the News and Why It Can No Longer Be Trusted* (Nashville: WND Books, 2003).

31. Gal Beckerman, "Across the Great Divide Faith," *Columbia Journalism Review* (May 1, 2004): 26. "Religion writers remain a tiny minority" in the nation's newsrooms, according to Beckerman. Consequently, the media can often convey an indifferent or suspicious attitude toward religion, as indicated by the fact that news reports frequently single out religion with the prefatory phrase, e.g., "her opponent, a born-again Christian."

32. The dates of the study were April 5–7, 2002. It was reported by the Roper Center at the University of Connecticut, Public Opinion Online, Accession Number 0402247. It was a *Wall Street Journal*–NBC News poll.

33. Pam Belluck, "Boston Sexual Abuse Report Breaks Down Accusations," *New York Times,* Feb., 27 2004, A13. And one diocese reported that of the thirty-seven accusations that had been made against its priests since 1950, more than half had been levied against just one priest. "Diocese Reports 37 Allegations of Child Sexual Abuse since 1950," *Fairmont (Minn.) Daily Sentinel,* Jan. 9, 2004, 2.

34. "Scandals in the Church," *New York Times,* Feb. 28, 2004, A1.

35. Bob von Sternberg, "Insurance Falls Short in Church Abuse Cases; Catholic Dioceses Are Forced to Find Other Sources to Pay Settlements," *Minneapolis Star Tribune,* July 27, 2002, 1A.

36. Douglas Montero, "Secret Shame of Our Schools: Sexual Abuse of Students Runs Rampant," *New York Post,* July 30, 2001, 1.

37. Charol Shakeshaft and Audray Cohan, "In Loco Parentis: Sexual Abuse of Students in Schools," *Report to the U.S. Department of Education, Field Initiated Grants* (New York: Routledge, 1997).

38. Berta Delgado and Sarah Talalay, "Sex Cases Increase in Schools; Many Acts of Teacher Misconduct Not Being Reported," *South Florida Sun-Sentinel,* June 4, 1995, 1A.

39. Sharon Waxman, "New Film May Harm Gibson's Career," *New York Times,* Feb. 26, 2004, B1.

40. Julia Duin, "Passion Critics Retract Reviews," *Washington Times,* Feb. 27, 2004.

41. Frank Rich, "Mel Gibson Forgives Us for His Sins," *New York Times,* March 7, 2004, Arts and Entertainment sec., 1.

42. Waxman, "New Film May Harm Gibson's Career."

43. Ibid.

44. "Review and Outlook: What Would Jefferson Do?" *Wall Street Journal,* March 9, 2001, W15.

45. Daniel Henninger, "Gibson's 'Passion' Is the Story of the Week," *Wall Street Journal,* April 9, 2004.

46. Scott Savage, "Amish TV Show May Deliver Reality of Christian Bias," *Chicago Tribune,* July 25, 2004, B3. Each episode followed "the young people as they are tempted to behave in ways that erase their purity." Essentially, the show aimed to use "Christians for the purpose of amusement."

47. David Brooks, "People Like Us," *Atlantic Monthly*, Sept. 2003, 29, 32.

48. Paul Starobin, "The Angry American," *Atlantic Monthly*, Jan./Feb. 2004, 132, 134.

49. Carter, *Culture of Disbelief*, 57.

50. Eugene Volokh, "Diversity, Race as Proxy, and Religion as Proxy," 43 *University of California Los Angeles Law Review* 2059, 2072–73 (1996).

51. Scott Smallwood, "A Weblog Starts a Fire," *Chronicle of Higher Education*, Nov. 7, 2003, A10.

52. Another aspect of this double standard can be seen in the New York City school system's allowing the Muslim star and crescent but not the Christian nativity scene. Williams, "Attacking Western Values."

53. Paul C. Vitz, *Censorship: Evidence of Bias in Our Children's Textbooks* (Ann Arbor: Servant Books 1986), 16–18.

54. George W. Dent Jr., "Of God and Caesar: The Free Exercise Rights of Public School Students," 43 *Case Western Reserve Law Review* 707, 708 (1993).

55. A student who brought candy canes with a religious message attached was prohibited from passing them out as gifts to his fellow students. Kim Breen, "Plano ISD Again Threatened with Suit," *Dallas Morning News*, Dec. 18, 2003, B4. An evangelical Christian fifth-grade teacher was required to submit all class handouts to his principal, so that she could screen them for "inappropriate" religious content. Dean Murphy, "God, American History and a Fifth-Grade Class," *New York Times*, Dec. 5, 2004, Week in Review sec., 4. According to the teacher, he had been singled out because of his Christian beliefs.

56. Williams, "Attacking Western Values."

57. *Hansen v. Ann Arbor Public Schools*, 293 F.Supp.2d 780, 800 (E.D. Mich. 2003).

58. Peter Schneider, "Across a Great Divide," *New York Times*, March 13, 2004, A13. And more than a third reported that they attended a religious service once a month or more.

59. Beckerman, "Across the Great Divide," 26. The same poll found that 87 percent said they never doubted God's existence.

60. Diane Cole, "Hooked on the Book," *U.S. News and World Report*, March 15, 2004, 78.

61. J. Michael Parker, "Presidential Voting Also Will Be Test of Faith," *San Antonio Express-News*, June 27, 2004, A1.

62. Jim Wallis, "Putting God Back in Politics," *New York Times*, Dec. 28, 2003. Twentieth-century liberals have "sought to purge civil government of any distinct religion, including all Christian sects." Veronica Abreu, "Muddled Original Understandings of the Establishment Clause," 23 *Quinnipiac Law Review* 615, 624 (2004). This hostility or indifference toward religion could be seen in the case of Howard Dean, a 2004 Democratic presidential candidate, who proudly proclaimed that he had left his church over a dispute about a bike path.

63. Ramesh Ponnuru, "Secularism and Its Discontents," *National Review*, Dec. 27, 2004, 32–35. Not only Bush but his religious supporters were denounced as backward, intolerant, and ignorant. The campaign, in fact, revealed "liberalism's general tendency to identify reason with irreligion."

64. David Kirkpatrick, "Citing Falwell's Endorsement of Bush, Group Challenges His Tax-Exempt Status," *New York Times,* July 16, 2004, A16. These complaints were also in response "to the Bush campaign's effort to enlist thousands of pastors and churchgoers to help get members of conservative congregations to the polls." This opposition mirrored the early opposition to President Bush's faith-based initiative, aimed at eliminating obstacles to the participation of faith-based organizations in the provision of federally funded social services. Jean-Paul Jassy and Tiffany Zwicker, "First Things First: President Bush and Senator Kerry on the First Amendment," 22 *Communications Lawyer* 10, 12 (summer 2004).

65. Although the ACLU does not represent the majority viewpoint in America, it does exert a disproportionately strong influence on religion law, which is primarily formed in the courts—and the ACLU is a litigation organization.

66. The ACLU has waged a campaign against any public display of the Ten Commandments, even though a court has found that the Ten Commandments have influenced American civil law. *Mercer County,* 219 F.Supp.2d, at 784. Furthermore, this campaign is being waged even as more displays are being put up. As of 2003 there were 141 Ten Commandments monuments placed on public property across the nation. Roxanne Houtman, "ACLU v. McCreary County," 55 *Syracuse Law Review* 395, 422 (2005).

67. William A. Donohue, *The Politics of the American Civil Liberties Union* (New Brunswick, N.J.: Transaction Publishers, 1990), 308.

68. Michael Knight, "Constitution and Crowds," *New York Times,* Sept. 17, 1979, A18.

69. William A. Donohue, *Twilight of Liberty: The Legacy of the ACLU* (New Brunswick, N.J.: Transaction Publishers, 1990), 120, 97. Whenever local governmental bodies acquiesce in the display of any religious symbol or message, the ACLU rushes to file suit. Tarik Abdel-Monem, "Posting the Ten Commandments as a Historical Document in Public Schools," 87 *Iowa Law Review* 1023, 1045 (2002).

70. Leonard W. Levy, *The Establishment Clause: Religion and the First Amendment* (New York: Macmillan, 1986), 176–77.

71. Donohue, *Politics of the American Civil Liberties Union,* 228.

72. Nicholas Kristof, "Hug an Evangelist," *New York Times,* April 24, 2004, A25.

73. Carter, *Culture of Disbelief,* 57.

Notes to Chapter 7

1. *Thomas v. Anchorage Equal Rights Commission,* 165 F.3d 692, 717 (9th Cir. 1999).

2. Kathleen Sullivan, "Religion and Liberal Democracy," 59 *University of Chicago Law Review* 195 (1992).

3. Stephen L. Carter, "Reflections on the Separation of Church and State," 44 *Arizona Law Review* 293, 299 (2002).

4. Those who see a tension between the two clauses generally hold to the

privatization thesis: that religion is a private affair and should not play a role in public life. Frederick Mark Gedicks, "Public Life and Hostility to Religion," 78 *Virginia Law Review* 671, 682–93 (1992). Many view religious symbolism in public life as inherently coercive. Richard S. Myers, "A Comment on the Death of Lemon," 43 *Case Western Reserve Law Review* 903, 908 (1993). But the broad reading of the establishment clause comes more from a desire to limit the public role of religion than from any constitutional logic. But following this approach to its logical end would mean that the exercise clause could not really protect the practice of religious beliefs, since the establishment clause could be used to strike down instances of religious expression on public property. Thomas McCoy, "Quo Vadis: Is the Establishment Clause Undergoing Metamorphosis?" 41 *Brandeis Law Journal* 547, 547–49 (2003) (suggesting that the desire to keep religion out of the public sphere is responsible for what is perceived to be irreconcilable tension between the two clauses).

5. Mary Ann Glendon, "Law, Communities, and the Religious Freedom Language of the Constitution," 60 *George Washington Law Review* 672, 679 (1992).

6. *People of the State of Illinois ex rel. McCollum v. Board of Education,* 333 U.S. 203, 237.

7. *Bowen v. Kendrick,* 487 U.S. 589 (1988); *Texas Monthly, Inc. v. Bullock,* 489 U.S. 1 (1991).

8. *Corporation of the Presiding Bishop of the Church of Jesus Christ of the Latter-Day Saints v. Amos,* 483 U.S. 327 (1987); *Estate of Thornton v. Caldor,* 472 U.S. 703 (1985).

9. *Marsh v. Chambers* 463 U.S. 783 (1983); *County of Allegheny v. Greater Pittsburgh ACLU,* 492 U.S. 573 (1989).

10. Richard John Neuhaus, "A New Order of Religious Freedom," 60 *George Washington Law Review* 620, 630 (1992). Up until the late 1990s, the establishment and exercise clauses tended to conflict, especially when states sought to accommodate the right of religious speech in the public school systems. Lynne Rafalowski, "Can Public Schools Really Permit Religious Speech without Promoting Religion?" 45 *Villanova Law Review* 547, 548 (2000).

11. Neuhaus, "New Order of Religious Freedom," 630. George W. Dent Jr., "Of God and Caesar: The Free Exercise Rights of Public School Students," 43 *Case Western Reserve Law Review* 707, 723 (1993). Dent states that the "Free Exercise Clause should be viewed as embracing two complementary principles. First, government should be as neutral as possible about religion in the sense of neither promoting nor hindering any particular religion or religion in general. Second, government should aim to maximize religious freedom" (723). Mary Ann Glendon and Raul F. Yanes, "Structural Free Exercise," 90 *Michigan Law Review* 477, 541 (1991) (arguing that "if the two religion provisions are read together in the light of an overarching purpose to protect freedom of religion, most of the tension between them disappears").

12. Furthermore, the Constitution's commands regarding religion are both direct and repetitive. Michael W. McConnell, "The Problem of Singling Out Religion," 50 *DePaul Law Review* 1 (2000). The free-speech clause protects religious expression. The exercise clause protects religious practice and conduct and be-

liefs. And freedom of association, like the establishment clause, protects the integrity and autonomy of religious groups and organizations. *Boy Scouts of America v. Dale,* 530 U.S. 640, 648 (2000) held that the right of expressive association is impaired if the government "affects in a significant way the group's ability to advocate public or private viewpoints."

13. *Zorach v. Clauson,* 343 U.S. 306, 315 (1952) (stating that we "cannot read into the Bill of Rights such a philosophy of hostility to religion"). *Lynch v. Donnelly,* 465 U.S. 668, 673 (1983) (noting that when courts attempt to adhere to strict separation of church and state, they wage a war on religious exercise).

14. Neuhaus, "New Order of Religious Freedom," 627. Neuhaus further argues that "once we forget that the establishment provision is a means and instrument in support of free exercise, it is a short step to talk about the supposed conflict or tension between the two provisions. From there it is a short step to the claim that the two parts of the Religion Clause are pitted against one another and must somehow be balanced . . . [and t]hus establishment becomes the master of the free exercise that it was designed to serve . . . [and so,] in the name of avoiding establishment, religio[us exercise] must retreat wherever government advances" (628).

15. Michael W. McConnell, "Accommodation of Religion: An Update and a Response to the Critics," 60 *George Washington Law Review* 685, 690 (1992) (stating that "the concern of the Religion Clauses is with the preservation of the autonomy of religious life"). Stephen Carter argues that "despite what courts and commentators say, the First Amendment contains only one religion clause, not two, and the text will not admit of an interpretation that tries to assign two different meanings to the word *religion,* which appears only once." Stephen L. Carter, "Reflections on the Separation of Church and State," 44 *Arizona Law Review* 311. See also Michael Paulsen, "Lemon Is Dead," 43 *Case Western Reserve Law Review* 795, 798 (1993). Paulsen argues that if "nonestablishment and free exercise are understood as correlative rather than contradictory principles, it is logical to read the clauses as mirror-image prohibitions on government prescription and proscription, respectively, of the same thing—religious exercise" (808).

16. McConnell, "Accommodation of Religion," 718. "Anti-accommodationists object to singling out religion for special protection under the Free Exercise Clause, but they typically have no qualms about singling out religion for special prohibitions under the Establishment Clause. . . . The anti-accommodationists seemingly take the position that the government must never advance religion, but may inhibit, penalize, and punish it" (718–19). Although the anti-accommodationists view their position as neutral, it is neutral only for those "who believe that full religious practice can occur in the 'private' realm." Mark D. Rosen, "Establishment, Expressivism, and Federalism," 78 *Chicago-Kent Law Review* 669, 676 (2003). But there are many who believe that a full religious life is possible only if religious beliefs infuse every aspect of their life, both private and public. Justice Scalia, in his dissent in *Lee v. Weisman,* reflects such an integrationist perspective. *Lee v. Weisman,* 505 U.S. 577, 645 (1992).

17. And in the scheme of the Declaration of Independence, it was fundamental rights like religious freedom that the colonists were espousing, not the eradication of a state-established religious institution.

18. Any establishment of religion ultimately affects religious exercise, because it forces people into supporting a religion they don't espouse, or because it causes government to intrude into the religion they do espouse. And establishments of particular religions are distinctly repugnant to those who espouse other religions. To the irreligious, however, the injury caused by religion is no worse than the injury caused by governmental adoption of a nonreligious doctrine that they reject. Dent, "Of God and Caesar," 720.

19. Ibid., 720.

20. Carter, "Separation of Church and State," 309.

21. Laurence Tribe, *American Constitutional Law* (Mineola, N.Y.: Foundation Press, 1988), 1201.

22. Dent, "Of God and Caesar," 719.

23. Glendon, "Law, Communities, and the Religious Freedom Language," 678 (highlighting the claim being made that, for the sake of avoiding the establishment of religion, Americans must surrender some of their rights regarding the free exercise of religion). It has become common for the Court "to trump free exercise claims with findings of religious establishment." Joseph P. Viteritti, "Reading Zelman: The Triumph of Pluralism, and Its Effects on Liberty, Equality, and Choice," 76 *Southern California Law Review* 1105, 1145 (2003). As applied by the Court, "the Establishment Clause did not expand the legitimate claims of religious people; it worked to diminish them" (1146).

24. Neuhaus, "New Order of Religious Freedom," 629.

25. Associated Press, "Couple Claims City Unfairly Barred Jesus Brick from Playground," First Amendment Center Online, July 24, 2003, http://www.fac.org/news.aspx?id=11741, accessed July 26, 2003.

26. Associated Press, "Ministers Sue N.Y. School District over Religious Bricks," September 11, 2000, ibid., http://www.fac.org/news.aspx?id=5788, accessed October 19, 2004.

27. Associated Press, "School District Sued after Walkway Crosses Removed," ibid., March 28, 2003, http://www.fac.org/news.aspx?id=6569, accessed October 19, 2004.

28. Carter, "Separation of Church and State," 300.

29. As one justice noted about the words "under God" in the Pledge of Allegiance, they are simply not a "formal religious exercise." *Newdow v. United States Congress,* 321 F.3d 772, 778, 782 (O'Scanlan, J., dissenting).

30. Carl H. Esbeck, "The Establishment Clause as a Structural Restraint on Governmental Power," 84 *Iowa Law Review* 1 (1998). Nearly every member of the Court over the course of the development of the Court's establishment clause jurisprudence has subscribed to some form of the principle that even without any material aid to religion, government endorsement of religion will at some point constitute a violation of the establishment clause. McCoy, "Quo Vadis," 553. But there are some who are unwilling to see government encouragement of religion as a violation of the establishment clause until it reaches the level of designating an official state church. *Lee,* 505 U.S. 577, 640–42 (Scalia, J., dissenting) (joined by Rehnquist, C.J., White, J., and Thomas, J.); *Wallace v. Jaffree,* 472 U.S. 38, 84–90 (1985) (Burger, C.J., dissenting) (joined by White, J. and Rehnquist, J.).

31. Richard S. Myers, "The Supreme Court and the Privatization of Religion," 41 *Catholic University Law Review* 19, 22 (1991) (discussing the privatization thesis in the context of the establishment clause and substantive due process).

32. Glendon and Yanes, "Structural Free Exercise," 495–96 (asserting that the Court has ignored the exercise clause as it applies to groups).

33. *Abington School District v. Schempp*, 374 U.S. 203 (1963); *Stone v. Graham*, 449 U.S. 39 (1980); *Wallace*, 472 U.S. 38, respectively.

34. Preservation of religious institutional autonomy is one way of insuring separation of church and state. Mark E. Chopko, "Religious Access to Public Programs and Governmental Funding," 60 *George Washington Law Review* 645, 662 (1992). The essential themes that run through the pre-enactment debates, text, and postenactment history of the religion clauses are the preservation of individual liberty and the preservation of institutional autonomy. Chester J. Antieau et al., *Freedom from Federal Establishment: Formation and Early History of the First Amendment Religion Clauses* (Milwaukee: Bruce Publishing, 1964) (demonstrating that the religion clauses of the First Amendment were designed to prohibit the use of religion as an instrument of national policy by forbidding exclusive privileges to any one sect). In *Wisconsin v. Yoder*, 406 U.S. 205 (1972), noting that the clauses work together as complementary protections for religious liberty, the Court wrote that "[t]he Religion Clauses had specifically and firmly fixed the right to free exercise of religious beliefs, and buttressing this fundamental right was an equally firm, even if less explicit, prohibition against the establishment of any religion by government" (214).

35. *Elrod v. Burns*, 427 U.S. 347, 373 (1976).

36. *Lee v. Weisman*, 505 U.S. 577, 594 (1992).

37. *Santa Fe Independent School District v. Doe*, 530 U.S. 290, 294, 320, 311 (2000). The Court found that the practice created "the perception of encouraging the delivery of prayer at a series of important school events" (320).

38. But government should be free to accommodate the private exercise of religious beliefs, even if such exercise does occur in a public arena such as school football games. Some justices and scholars have theorized that the exercise clause is the constitutional provision concerned with the protection of the minority, in contradistinction to the provision on establishments. These arguments have often been raised in the context of the debate over free-exercise exemptions from generally applicable norms. For a revealing example of such arguments, see Charles J. Reid Jr., "The Religious Conscience and the State in U.S. Constitutional Law, 1789–2001," in *Religion Returns to the Public Square*, ed. Hugh Heclo and Wifred McClay (Baltimore: Johns Hopkins University Press, 2003).

39. *Engel v. Vitale*, 370 U.S. 421 (1962). But the holding in *Engel* is narrower than what is commonly thought. Jonathan Van Patten, "In the End is the Beginning," 27 *Saint Louis University Law Review* 1, 25 (1983). *Engel* did not outlaw prayer in the public schools; it simply forbade the state requirement of involuntary religious activity. Again, the basic rule is that of the exercise clause: government may not coerce.

40. *Schempp*, 374 U.S. 203, 207.

41. Charles J. Russo, "Prayer at Public School Graduation Ceremonies: An Exercise in Futility or a Teachable Moment?" 1999 *Brigham Young University Education and Law Journal* 1, 23 (1999). And yet, in cases where students were permitted to pray but the school participated in the student-initiated prayer in some way, it was considered unconstitutional state action in violation of establishment clause. *Doe v. Duncanville Independent School District,* 70 F.3d 402, 406–7 (5th Cir. 1995) (holding that coaches' and other school employees' participation in student prayer is unconstitutional state endorsement of religion); *Bishop v. Aronov,* 926 F.2d 1066, 1073 (11th Cir. 1991) (stating teacher's religious speech is representative of school action and unconstitutional endorsement of religion); *Jager v. Douglas County School District,* 862 F.2d 824, 826 (11th Cir. 1989) (finding pregame invocations given by clergymen at public school football game over which school exercises supervision unconstitutional); *Collins v. Chandler Unified School District,* 644 F.2d 759, 762–63 (9th Cir. 1981) (finding school policy on student prayer at school supervised and planned assemblies unconstitutional).

In *Capitol Square Review v. Pinette,* 515 U.S. 753 (1995), the Court used the establishment clause to analyze the propriety of a private group erecting a cross on public property. But again, this should not have been decided under the establishment clause. The establishment clause doesn't act against religious expression, it acts as a protector of institutional autonomy of religious organizations. And to be a violation, the government has to enter into some institutional intrusion; and that intrusion has to have some type of permanent characteristic, not just a holiday display of a crèche. This was also at issue in *Lynch v. Donnelly,* 465 U.S. 668 (1984), in which the court used the establishment clause to determine the constitutionality of a nativity scene on public grounds during the Christmas season.

42. *Westfield High School L.I.F.E. Club v. City of Westfield,* 249 F.Supp.2d 98 (D. Mass. 2003), 117.

43. *Donovan ex rel. Donovan v. Punxatawney Area School Bd.,* 336 F.3d 211, 227 (3d Cir. 2003) (holding that the club meetings would not carry with them "the imprimatur of a government's endorsement of religion").

44. Carter, "Separation of Church and State," 302.

45. The establishment clause is a protection given to religious institutions, a guard against the government granting preferential treatment to one sect over another. The big problem, and perhaps the only problem that the framers sought to address by the establishment clause, was that posed by the Church of England. This view comports with Justice Rehnquist's argument in *Wallace v. Jaffree* for a more simple and narrow establishment test that would primarily look to whether government was preferring one particular sect over others. *Wallace,* 472 U.S. 38, 106 (Rehnquist, J., dissenting). Or, as Justice Blackmun's concurrence in *Lee v. Weisman* stated: "Government may neither promote nor affiliate itself with any religious doctrine or organization, nor may it obtrude itself in the internal affairs of any religious institution." *Lee,* 505 U.S. 577, 599 (Blackmun, J., concurring).

46. Patrick M. Garry, *Scrambling for Protection: The New Media and the*

First Amendment (Pittsburgh: University of Pittsburgh Press, 1994), 118 (stating that "we can interpret some First Amendment clauses [free religious exercise and free speech] as focused on individual liberty and others [the religious establishment and press clauses] as focused on principles that apply to the relation between government and specific institutions existing in society").

47. *Lee,* 505 U.S. 577, 591–92.

48. Michael W. McConnell, "Establishment and Disestablishment at the Founding, Part I: Establishment of Religion," 40 *William and Mary Law Review* 2105, 2183–84 (2003).

49. But this use of the establishment clause exerts a restrictive effect on free exercise. These decisions often confuse establishment with exercise. But in Justice Rehnquist's words, "governmental assistance which does not have the effect of inducing religious belief, but instead merely accommodates or implements an independent religious choice does not impermissibly involve the government in religious choices and therefore does not violate the Establishment Clause." *Thomas v. Review Board,* 450 U.S. 707, 727 (1981) (Rehnquist, J., dissenting). The "inducing" of religious choices, however, would be governed by the exercise clause. One of the few areas in which the establishment clause should exert independent force is in the situation posed by *Corporation of the Presiding Bishop of the Church of Jesus Christ of Latter-day Saints v. Amos,* which involved the issue of whether secular laws could infringe on the institutional integrity of religious organizations, and whether religious organizations could employ religious criteria for hiring persons whose duties are closely connected to the religious mission of the church. *Amos,* 483 U.S. 327, 336 (1987). In his concurrence, Justice Brennan wrote that interference with the religious organization's hiring for religious activities "involves what we normally regard as infringement on free exercise rights" (342–43) (Brennan, J., concurring). But such interference is really a violation of the establishment clause.

50. Government does not threaten institutional autonomy with accommodation. In fact, the exercise clause may often mandate accommodation. The first stage of inquiry must be on the demands of the exercise clause.

51. Rodney K. Smith, "Conscience, Coercion and the Establishment of Religion: The Beginning of an End to the Wandering of a Wayward Judiciary?" 43 *Case Western Reserve Law Review* 917, 920 (1993). As one scholar has noted, it can "hardly be argued that the government establishes religion by the simple act of making public funding available on a formally neutral basis to all organizations, religious and non-religious, willing to provide an identifiably secular service." Paul E. Salamanca, "Quo Vadis: The Continuing Metamorphosis of the Establishment Clause toward Realistic Substantive Neutrality," 41 *Brandeis Law Journal* 575, 579 (2003). If the case were otherwise, religious organizations would then become essentially second-class citizens regarding their right to participate in governmental programs.

52. Such facilitation occurred in *St. Martin Evangelical Lutheran Church v. South Dakota,* 451 U.S. 772 (1981), where the Court ruled that a religious school was exempt from paying the unemployment compensation tax required by federal law. But the Court has also allowed public funds to go to religious institutions

to help them operate. In *Tilton v. Richardson,* 403 U.S. 672 (1971), the Court consented to federal construction funds flowing to church-affiliated colleges for buildings used for secular educational purposes. The Court also upheld, in *Hunt v. McNair,* 413 U.S. 734 (1973), a state-funded bonding program that allowed religious colleges to obtain construction loans at low interest. In addition, the Court allowed a blind student to receive public vocational rehabilitation aid that paid the student's tuition at a religious college. *Witters v. Washington Department of Services,* 474 U.S. 481 (1986).

53. Chopko, "Religious Access to Public Programs," 662.

54. Daniel O. Conkle, "Toward a General Theory of the Establishment Clause," 82 *Northwestern University Law Review* 1113, 1157 (1988).

55. Joseph Raz, *The Morality of Freedom,* 369–71 (New York: Oxford University Press, 1986).

56. Carl Esbeck, "Dissent and Disestablishment: The Church-State Settlement in the Early American Republic," 2004 *Brigham Young University Law Review* 1385, 1396 (2004).

57. Thomas Berg, "The Voluntary Principle and Church Autonomy, Then and Now," 2004 *Brigham Young University Law Review* 1593, 1597 (2004). The eighteenth-century notion of separation designed "primarily to protect the vitality and independence of religious groups" stood in "marked contrast to a separationism founded on a suspicion of religion."

58. This is contrary to existing law. In *Wallace v. Jaffree,* which invalidated an Alabama statute permitting public school teachers to announce a moment of silence for meditation or voluntary prayer, the Court proclaimed the principle that government may not prefer religion over irreligion. *Wallace,* 472 U.S. at 52–53. This same principle was at work in *Grand Rapids School District v. Ball* 473 U.S. 373 (1985), where the Court invalidated a government program under which publicly funded teachers taught secular subjects in religious schools.

59. *Texas Monthly,* 489 U.S. 1, 5, 15.

60. Ibid. at 18n8.

61. Ibid., 10–17. One of the most firmly ingrained principles of the religion clauses is that all religious faiths must enjoy equality of rights. James Madison, *Memorial and Remonstrance against Religious Assessments,* reprinted in *Everson v. Board of Education,* 330 U.S. 1, 66 (1947) (quoting the Virginia Declaration of Rights, articles 1, 16).

62. Neuhaus, "New Order of Religious Freedom," 629. As Professor Smith argues, "a principle that forbids governmental invocation of religion may have the effect of rendering us tongue-tied when it comes to explaining our most basic political commitments," and this muffling on "the most basic matters is not a promising foundation for enduring political community," Steven Smith, "Nonestablishment under God?" 50 *Villanova Law Review* 1, 11 (2005). The endorsement test of Justice O'Connor actually results in a constriction of the political process, since it inhibits the workings and expressions of those political groups (religious believers) that may somehow cause other political groups or individuals (the nonreligious) to feel like social outsiders.

63. *Thomas v. Anchorage Equal Rights Commission,* 165 F.3d 692, 717 (9th Cir. 1999).

64. William A. Donohue, *The Twilight of Liberty: The Legacy of the ACLU* (New Brunswick, N.J.: Transaction Publishers, 1994), 95.

65. The establishment clause addresses a specific kind of threat to religious liberty—the threat that exists when government entangles itself within one or more specific religious denominations through its taxing, regulatory, or law enforcement functions.

66. *Estate of Thornton*, 472 U.S. 703.

67. James E. Curry, *Public Regulation of the Religious Use of Land* (Charlottesville, Va.: Michie, 1964), 3.

68. Anson Phelps Stokes, *Church and State in the United States* (New York: Harper, 1950), 369, 419.

69. *Larkin v. Grendel's Den, Inc.*, 459 U.S. 116, 127 (1982). The Court's decision rested on the grounds that the relationship between church and state generated by the statute amounted to impermissible entanglement.

70. *Wallace*, 472 U.S. 38, 59 (noting that despite the state's argument that it was merely accommodating voluntary prayer in schools, the state's true intentions were to characterize prayer as a favored practice).

Notes to Chapter 8

1. There is some contention on this point, however. Scholars like Douglas Laycock argue that the founders (notably Madison and Jefferson) were as offended by compelled financial support for religion in general as they were for specific support of the Anglican Church.

2. Separationists, in fact, can oppose this nonpreferential aid model so much that they go to the other extreme—selectively discriminating against certain religions that receive widespread public support. For instance, in 2003 the ACLU demanded that the National Park Service remove plaques inscribed with Bible verses from three overlooks at the Grand Canyon but did not protest the names of park buttes—Brahma Temple, Vishnu Temple, Shiva Temple, Osiris Temple, and others—that commemorated Hindu and Egyptian deities. Julia Duin, "Religion under a Secular Assault," *Washington Times*, April 13, 2005.

3. *County of Allegheny v. Greater Pittsburgh ACLU*, 492 U.S. 573, 590 (1989); *Wallace v. Jaffree*, 472 U.S. 38 (1985); *Everson v. Board of Education*, 67 S.Ct. 504, 513 (1947).

4. *Roemer v. Board of Public Works of Maryland*, 426 U.S. 736, 746 (1977).

5. *Mueller v. Allen*, 463 U.S. 388, 393 (1983).

6. *Walz v. Tax Commission of City of New York*, 397 U.S. 664, 675 (1970).

7. *Larson v. Valente*, 456 U.S. 228, 244 (1982).

8. *Barnes-Wallace v. Boy Scouts of America*, 275 F.Supp.2d 1259, 1270, 1278 (S.D. Calif. 2003).

9. See *Roberts v. United States Jaycees*, 468 U.S. 609, 619 (1984).

10. See Frederick Mark Gedicks, "Towards a Constitutional Jurisprudence of Religious Group Rights," 1989 *Wisconsin Law Review* 99, 116 (1989).

11. Daniel O. Conkle, "Toward a General Theory of the Establishment Clause," 82 *Northwestern University Law Review* 1113, 1171 (1988). Religion

also encourages private altruism, and it serves as "the source of both present-day similarity and historical heritage, thereby performing a symbolic, unifying function." Since religion is one of the oldest institutions and traditions in society, it provides a "sense of common heritage" (1184). Thus the symbolic support of religion by government, if it involves no coercion, "should be upheld if the action is traditional" (1185). Consequently, the traditional references to God and religion "in our national motto and in Presidential proclamations should not be declared unconstitutional" (1185).

12. Jonathan Van Patten, "In the End Is the Beginning: An Inquiry into the Meaning of Religion Clauses," 27 *St. Louis University Law Journal* 80 (1983). Mary Ann Glendon notes that religious believers find individual dignity to be "grounded in the fact that human beings are made in the image and likeness of God." Mary Ann Glendon, "Foundations of Human Rights: The Unfinished Business," 44 *American Journal of Jurisprudence* 1, 13 (1999). Likewise, Michael Perry argues that the whole notion of human rights is "intertwined with religion." Michael Perry, *The Idea of Human Rights: Four Inquiries* (New York: Oxford University Press, 1998), 11–41. Even Thomas Jefferson stated that the "only firm basis" for liberties is "a conviction in the minds of the people that these liberties are of the gift of God." Thomas Jefferson, "Notes on the State of Virginia," in *The Portable Thomas Jefferson*, ed. Merrill D. Peterson (New York: Penguin Books, 1975), 215. In *The Universal Hunger for Liberty: Why the Clash of Civilizations Is Not Inevitable* (New York: Basic Books, 2004), Michael Novak argues that the essential American beliefs in human dignity, equality, and liberty would not have taken shape without prior belief in the religion of the Hebrew and Christian Bible.

13. For a discussion of the army's program, see Anne C. Loveland, "Character Education in the U.S. Army, 1947–1977," *Journal of Military History* 64 (July 2000): 795–818.

14. Regarding a fundamental foundation of social life, a majority of Americans consider marriage largely a religious matter. See Katharine Q. Seelye, "Strong Support Is Found for Ban on Gay Marriage," *New York Times,* Dec. 21, 2003, A1. For additional reference, see Charles J. Reid Jr., "The Unavoidable Influence of Religion upon the Law of Marriage," 23 *Quinnipiac Law Review* 493 (2004).

15. The harm done to American culture through the obsession with the self was outlined by Christopher Lasch in *The Culture of Narcissism: American Life in an Age of Diminishing Expectations* (New York: W. W. Norton, 1979).

16. Laurie Messerly, "Reviving Religious Liberty in America," 8 *Nexus* 151, 164 (2003). Sixty-nine percent of Americans polled said, "[m]ore religion is the best way to strengthen family values and moral behavior." Additionally, 85 percent believed that parents would do a better job raising their kids if more Americans were to become deeply religious; 79 percent felt that crime would decrease; and 69 percent felt that greed and materialism would decrease.

17. Douglas W. Kmiec and Stephen B. Presser, *The American Constitutional Order: History, Cases, and Philosophy* (Cincinnati: Anderson Publishing, 1998), 196.

18. Because the institution of religion mediates between the state and the people, it helps limit the authoritarian tendencies of the state. Religion can also limit the state by providing a free and independent criticism of the state. And a vibrant religion "can help temper selfish passions and oppressive tendencies and thus protect against harmful swings in popular sentiment to which republics are vulnerable." Carl Esbeck, "Dissent and Disestablishment: The Church-State Settlement in the Early American Republic," 2004 *Brigham Young University Law Review* 1385, 1581. A Pew Research Center report found that 71 percent of Americans believe strongly in God; and other polls have found that 95 percent attest to a belief in God. Rebecca French, "Shopping for Religion: The Change in Everyday Religious Practice and Its Importance to the Law," 51 *Buffalo Law Review* 127, 160 (2003).

19. John T. Noonan Jr., *The Lustre of Our Country: The American Experience of Religious Freedom* (Berkeley and Los Angeles: University of California Press, 1998), 256.

20. In February 1956 the Catholic archbishop of New Orleans issued a pastoral letter condemning racial segregation as a sin. The archbishop later forbade Catholic legislators to support a bill that would have required segregation in all of Louisiana's private schools, warning that to do so would be to risk excommunication. See also David L. Chappell's *A Stone of Hope: Prophetic Religion and the Death of Jim Crow* (Chapel Hill: University of North Carolina Press, 2004), which traces the intellectual roots of the civil rights movement and argues that the movement was not a "liberal" movement at all—far from it—but succeeded precisely because of its religious character. Chappell argues that, although southern segregationists outvoted and outgunned black integrationists, they lost, largely because they did not have a religious commitment to their cause and could not muster the support of their white southern denominations.

21. Van Patten, "In the End Is the Beginning," 83.

22. *Catholic Charities of Sacramento, Inc. v. Superior Court*, 10 Cal. Rptr.3d 283 (Cal. 2004).

23. Joseph P. Viteritti, *Choosing Equality: School Choice, the Constitution, and Civil Society* (Washington, D.C.: Brookings Institute Press, 1999) (arguing that religion is able to serve some social welfare goals or functions better than secular institutions).

24. *Zelman v. Simmons-Harris*, 536 U.S. 639, 644 (2002).

25. Joseph P. Viteritti, "Reading Zelman: The Triumph of Pluralism and Its Effects on Liberty, Equality, and Choice," 76 *Southern California Law Review* 1105, 1173 (2003) (arguing that almost a half-century after *Brown v. Board of Education* was handed down, most black students are still not getting a decent education, and so vouchers are a necessary next step beyond *Brown*).

26. Viteritti, *Choosing Equality*, 7. The most recent survey found that 66 percent of blacks and 67 percent of Hispanics favor vouchers. Ellis Cose, "A Dream Deferred," *Newsweek,* May 17, 2004, 59.

27. Viteritti, *Choosing Equality*, 80, 83, 84.

28. *Zelman,* 536 U.S. 639, 681–83.

29. Viteritti, "Reading Zelman," 1163–64.

30. In 1997, at the request of the Texas state legislature, PFM was given control over a wing at the state prison in Richmond. After assuming control, PFM implemented a regimen of prayer meetings, classes, and rehabilitation programs.

31. Daniel Brook, "When God Goes to Prison," *Legislative Affairs* 22 (June 2003): 24–25, 27. To avoid constitutional problems, taxpayer money pays for only those aspects of prison life that exists at state-run prisons. All the religious programs, which are completely voluntary, are paid for by private donations. And, as *Time* magazine asserted, "there is growing evidence that inmates who participate in religious programs while incarcerated are less likely to return once they get out." Tim Padgett, "When God Is the Warden," *Time* magazine, June 7, 2004, 50. Religious programs also drastically reduce the fights and tensions between inmates while they are in prison. John Leland, "Offering Ministry, and Early Release, to Prisoners," *New York Times,* June 10, 2004, A1.

32. *The Federalist* No. 10, 56–65 (James Madison).

33. *The Federalist* No. 51, 347, 351–52 (James Madison).

34. Van Patten, "In the End Is the Beginning," 28.

35. *Trustees of the First Methodist Episcopal Church v. City of Atlanta,* 76 Ga. 181, 193 (1886); *Murray v. Comptroller of Treasury,* 241 Md. 383 (1966).

36. Nicholas D. Kristof, "Hug an Evangelical," *New York Times,* April 24, 2004, A25.

37. *Ward v. New Hampshire,* 56 N.H. 508 (1876).

38. Religion also provides benefits in a much different respect. Studies have shown that religious people are "less depressed, less anxious and less suicidal than nonreligious people." Religious people are also "better able to cope with such crises as illness, divorce and bereavement." Furthermore, religion's contribution to individual well-being occurs across faith and ethnic boundaries. Moreover, a 2003 study found that "teens who attend services, read the Bible and pray feel less sad or depressed, less alone, less misunderstood" than their nonreligious peers. Pamela Paul, "The Power to Uplift," *Time* magazine, Jan. 17, 2005, A46.

39. Steven D. Smith, "The Rise and Fall of Religious Freedom in Constitutional Discourse," 140 *University of Pennsylvania Law Review* 149, 154–66 (1991).

40. The primacy of conscience is reflected throughout the constitutional documents. Michael W. McConnell, "Why Is Religious Liberty the First Freedom?" 21 *Cardozo Law Review* 1243, 1251 (2000).

41. For a reference to the views of James Madison and Joseph Story regarding the founders' belief that religious duties were more important than secular duties, see Reid, "Religious Conscience and the State."

42. Blaise Pascal, *Pascal's Pensees* § 233.

43. *Zelman,* 536 U.S. 639, 668, 663 (O'Connor, J., concurring), 648.

44. *American Civil Liberties Union of Louisiana v. Foster,* No. 02-1440, 2002 WL 1733651 (E.D. La. 2002). The court ruled against the involvement of these religious institutions in the federally funded program. It held that "disbursing government funds to pervasively sectarian institutions runs afoul of the Establishment Clause" (7).

45. *Warner v. Orange County Deptartment of Probation,* 870 F.Supp. 69 (S.D.N.Y. 1994).

46. *Freedom from Religion Foundation, Inc. v. McCallum,* 179 F.Supp.2d 950, 970–71 (W.D. Wis. 2002).

47. *Zorach* 343 U.S. at 313–14.

48. *Stark v. Independent School District, No. 640,* 123 F.3d 1068 (8th Cir. 1997).

49. *Children's Healthcare Is a Legal Duty, Inc. v. Min de Parle,* 212 F.3d 1084 (8th Cir. 2000).

50. Noonan, *Lustre of Our Country,* 220.

51. John Witte, *Religion and the American Constitutional Experiment: Essential Rights and Liberties* (Boulder: Westview Press, 2000), 156.

52. *Barense v. Town of Barrington,* 955 F.Supp. 151 (D.N.H. 1996).

53. Antiaccommodationists object to singling out religion for special protection under the exercise clause, but have no qualms about singling out religion for special prohibitions under the establishment clause. But far from enacting into law the religious preferences of the political majority, or bringing about an alliance between church and state, accommodations often reflect a decision to tolerate dissent from the policies adopted by the political majority. Michael W. McConnell, "Accommodation of Religion: An Update and a Response to the Critics," 60 *George Washington Law Review* 685 (1992).

54. *Thomas v. Review Board,* 450 U.S. 707, 727 (1981) (Rehnquist, J., dissenting).

55. *Texas Monthly, Inc. v. Bullock,* 489 U.S. 1, 18 (1989). Brennan's assertion supports one of the basic tenets of the nonpreferential model.

56. McConnell, "Accommodation of Religion," 709.

57. Ibid., 710–17.

58. McConnell, "Why Is Religious Liberty the 'First Freedom'?" 1261. Gedicks claims that "[i]n the modern welfare state that the contemporary United States has become, government aid to both individuals and organizations is widespread and pervasive. Since in the United States most persons and entities are entitled to some kind of government aid, religious neutrality would generally seem to require that this aid not be denied to otherwise qualified recipients simply because they are religious." Frederick Mark Gedicks, *The Rhetoric of Church and State: A Critical Analysis of Religion Clause Jurisprudence* (Durham: Duke University Press, 1995), 57. Thus, contrary to the separationist claim, the no-aid baseline is implausible in the late twentieth century.

59. In *Brown v. Gilmore,* the court outlined mandatory accommodation: "Not only is the government permitted to accommodate religion without violating the Establishment Clause, at times it is *required* to do so." 258 F.3d 265, 274 (4th Cir. 2001). In *Brown,* the Fourth Circuit held that Virginia's moment-of-silence statute, requiring that each school establish the daily observance of one minute of silence in each classroom, was constitutional as a minor and nonintrusive accommodation of religion (271, 278).

60. Witte, *Religion and the American Constitutional Experiment,* 188.

61. *Leebaert ex rel. Leebaert v. Harrington,* 193 F.Supp.2d 491 (D. Conn. 2002).

62. *Smith v. Fair Employment and Housing Com.,* 913 P.2d 909, 928 (Cal. 1996).

Notes to Conclusion

1. Robert F. Nagel, *Judicial Power and American Character* (New York: Oxford University Press, 1994), 51.

2. Robert H. Bork, *The Tempting of America: The Political Seduction of the Law* (New York: Free Press, 1990), 353.

3. Nagel, *Judicial Power,* 65.

INDEX